FAITH- AND COMMUNITY-BASED ORGANIZATIONS

SELECT RESEARCH ON THEIR ROLES IN JOB CLUBS AND HURRICANE RELIEF

RELIGION AND SPIRITUALITY

Additional books in this series can be found on Nova's website
under the Series tab.

Additional e-books in this series can be found on Nova's website
under the e-book tab.

RELIGION AND SPIRITUALITY

FAITH- AND COMMUNITY-BASED ORGANIZATIONS

SELECT RESEARCH ON THEIR ROLES IN JOB CLUBS AND HURRICANE RELIEF

GLENN P. BAGLEY

EDITOR

nova publishers

New York

NOTICE TO THE READER

The Publisher has taken reasonable care in the preparation of this book, but makes no expressed or implied warranty of any kind and assumes no responsibility for any errors or omissions. No liability is assumed for incidental or consequential damages in connection with or arising out of information contained in this book. The Publisher shall not be liable for any special, consequential, or exemplary damages resulting, in whole or in part, from the readers' use of, or reliance upon, this material. Any parts of this book based on government reports are so indicated and copyright is claimed for those parts to the extent applicable to compilations of such works.

Independent verification should be sought for any data, advice or recommendations contained in this book. In addition, no responsibility is assumed by the publisher for any injury and/or damage to persons or property arising from any methods, products, instructions, ideas or otherwise contained in this publication.

This publication is designed to provide accurate and authoritative information with regard to the subject matter covered herein. It is sold with the clear understanding that the Publisher is not engaged in rendering legal or any other professional services. If legal or any other expert assistance is required, the services of a competent person should be sought. FROM A DECLARATION OF PARTICIPANTS JOINTLY ADOPTED BY A COMMITTEE OF THE AMERICAN BAR ASSOCIATION AND A COMMITTEE OF PUBLISHERS.

Additional color graphics may be available in the e-book version of this book.

Library of Congress Cataloging-in-Publication Data

ISBN: 978-1-63321-578-8

Published by Nova Science Publishers, Inc. † New York

CONTENTS

PREFACE

Chapter 1 – Over the past several decades, job search support groups, commonly referred to as "job clubs," have evolved into one of several important activities used by the public workforce system and faith- and community-based organizations to enhance worker readiness and employability, as well as to provide ongoing support to unemployed and underemployed individuals as they search for jobs. The U.S. Department of Labor's (DOL) Chief Evaluation Office (CEO) contracted in September 2012 with Capital Research Corporation, Inc. and George Washington University to conduct an assessment of job clubs sponsored by faith-based and community-based organizations (FBOs/CBOs). The overall purpose of this evaluation effort was to systematically describe the key characteristics of job clubs being offered by a range of faith- and community- based organizations, document how they differ from and are similar to the job clubs operated by publicly-funded workforce agencies (such as at American Job Centers [AJCs]), and identify potential approaches that might be used for more rigorous formal evaluation of impacts and effectiveness.

Findings from the telephone interviews with stakeholders and in-person interviews with facilitators during the site visits indicate that job clubs operated by FBOs, CBOs and public workforce agencies are alike in many ways, with all of them emphasizing the critical importance of: (1) networking during the job search; (2) offering ongoing peer support and sharing of similar experiences among participants; and (3) providing instruction and guidance on the basics of the job search process (e.g., elevator pitches, resume development, job interview practice). Noteworthy differences between the FBO/CBO job clubs and those operated by public workforce agencies are related to staffing patterns and available resources for program operations and services. While public workforce agency job clubs are led by paid professional staff, supported by the full complement of workshops, activities, and other services typically available through AJCs/One-Stop Centers, FBO/CBO job clubs, in most cases, operate with limited budgets or no funding whatsoever. Additionally, compared with public sector agencies, FBOs/CBOs typically collect little in the way of participant-level data, such as participant identifiers, demographic characteristics, service receipt, or outcomes. Finally, although this report suggests several approaches to future rigorous experimental/non-experimental and process/implementation evaluation of FBO/CBO-sponsored job clubs, there are likely to be formidable challenges to implementation of rigorous evaluation methods because these job clubs rarely collect identifying information on participants, such as Social Security numbers, and are generally opposed to random assignment for their programs.

Chapter 2 – By almost any measure—geographic reach of the storm, population displaced, destruction of property, costs of disaster relief, and prospective costs of rebuilding—the effects of hurricanes Katrina and Rita represent the largest single natural disaster on U.S. soil in the past 100 years. The events also produced one of the largest disaster response efforts by nongovernmental, charitable organizations, including both faith-based and community organizations (FBCOs).

In: Faith- and Community-Based Organizations
Editor: Glenn P. Bagley

ISBN: 978-1-63321-578-8
© 2014 Nova Science Publishers, Inc.

Chapter 1

FORMATIVE EVALUATION OF JOB CLUBS OPERATED BY FAITH- AND COMMUNITY-BASED ORGANIZATIONS: FINDINGS FROM SITE VISITS AND OPTIONS FOR FUTURE EVALUATION[*]

John Trutko, Carolyn O'Brien, Stephen Wandner and Burt Barnow

ABSTRACT

Over the past several decades, job search support groups, commonly referred to as "job clubs," have evolved into one of several important activities used by the public workforce system and faith- and community-based organizations to enhance worker readiness and employability, as well as to provide ongoing support to unemployed and underemployed individuals as they search for jobs. The U.S. Department of Labor's (DOL) Chief Evaluation Office (CEO) contracted in September 2012 with Capital Research Corporation, Inc. and George Washington University to conduct an assessment of job clubs sponsored by faith-based and community-based organizations (FBOs/CBOs). The overall purpose of this evaluation effort was to systematically describe the key characteristics of job clubs being offered by a range of faith- and community- based organizations, document how they differ from and are similar to the job clubs operated by publicly-funded workforce agencies (such as at American Job Centers [AJCs]), and identify potential approaches that might be used for more rigorous formal evaluation of impacts and effectiveness.

Findings from the telephone interviews with stakeholders and in-person interviews with facilitators during the site visits indicate that job clubs operated by FBOs, CBOs and public workforce agencies are alike in many ways, with all of them emphasizing the critical importance of: (1) networking during the job search; (2) offering ongoing peer support and sharing of similar experiences among participants; and (3) providing instruction and guidance on the basics of the job search process (e.g., elevator pitches, resume development, job interview practice). Noteworthy differences between the FBO/CBO job clubs and those operated by public workforce agencies are related to

---

[*] This is an edited, reformatted and augmented version of a final report issued by the U.S. Department of Labor, May 2014. The report was prepared under contract.

staffing patterns and available resources for program operations and services. While public workforce agency job clubs are led by paid professional staff, supported by the full complement of workshops, activities, and other services typically available through AJCs/One-Stop Centers, FBO/CBO job clubs, in most cases, operate with limited budgets or no funding whatsoever. Additionally, compared with public sector agencies, FBOs/CBOs typically collect little in the way of participant-level data, such as participant identifiers, demographic characteristics, service receipt, or outcomes. Finally, although this report suggests several approaches to future rigorous experimental/non-experimental and process/implementation evaluation of FBO/CBO-sponsored job clubs, there are likely to be formidable challenges to implementation of rigorous evaluation methods because these job clubs rarely collect identifying information on participants, such as Social Security numbers, and are generally opposed to random assignment for their programs.

EXECUTIVE SUMMARY

Over the past several decades, job search support groups, commonly referred to as "job clubs," have evolved into one of several important activities used by the public workforce system and faith- and community-based organizations (FBOs/CBOs) to enhance worker readiness and employability, as well as to provide ongoing support to unemployed and underemployed individuals as they search for jobs. In 2011, the Department of Labor's Center for Faith-based and Neighborhood Partnerships launched the Job Clubs Initiative to reach out to FBO/CBO job clubs and better connect them and their job seeker members to the public workforce system. Activities in job clubs, which often meet weekly or bi-weekly, include sharing information, job leads, knowledge, networking possibilities, and other job search-related activities. While there have been past experimental evaluations of the impacts of participation in public sector-operated job clubs, there have been few formal evaluations or assessments of FBO/CBO-sponsored job clubs.

The U.S. Department of Labor's (DOL) Chief Evaluation Office (CEO) contracted in September 2012 with Capital Research Corporation, Inc. and George Washington University to conduct an assessment of job clubs sponsored by faith-based and community-based organizations. The overall purpose of this evaluation effort was to (1) systematically describe the key characteristics of job clubs being offered by a range of faith- and community-based organizations; (2) document how they differ from and are similar to the job clubs operated by publicly-funded workforce agencies (such as at American Job Centers); and (3) identify potential approaches that might be used in the future for more rigorous evaluation of the impacts and effectiveness of FBO/CBO-sponsored job clubs. This evaluation effort, conducted over a 20- month period, included three main research activities: (1) a literature review; (2) an "environmental scan," with a particular focus on conducting interviews with key stakeholders knowledgeable about job clubs and site visits to FBO/CBO organizations sponsoring job clubs in six localities; and (3) the identification and exploration of alternative evaluation designs for future rigorous study of FBO/CBO job clubs. Key study findings from each of these research activities are highlighted below.

Literature Review. The literature review was aimed at summarizing what is known about the job clubs operated by public sector agencies and FBOs/CBOs, including the results of available experimental and non-experimental research studies. The evaluations of public sector job clubs indicate that it is possible to apply experimental methods (involving random assignment of job club participants) to assess the impacts of various job club interventions. Such experimental studies of job clubs have demonstrated significant positive impacts on earlier return to work and job placement rates. For example, with funding from the U.S. Department of Labor, Azrin et al. (1980) conducted a large-scale experiment to determine whether job clubs were effective for welfare recipients participating in the Work Incentive (WIN) program (the national welfare-to-work program operating at the time). The study was carried out in five cities, and nearly 1,000 welfare recipients were randomly assigned to receive either group job search assistance through job clubs or the usual employment services provided to welfare recipients in their cities. The impact results were large and statistically significant -- at the 12-month follow-up point, 87 percent of the job club treatment group had obtained jobs compared to 59 percent of the control sample. There were statistically significant differences favoring the treatment group in all five sites and for every subgroup examined. In a follow-up to the 1980 WIN study, Azrin et al. (1983a) found that after six months about half the treatment group members were no longer receiving welfare, while only 22 percent of the control group had left welfare. The Azrin studies, as well as an MDRC replication of the Azrin work and other more recent experimental studies, have helped change the workforce community's perception about whether job seekers should be served individually or in groups. In part as a result of the positive impacts reported in these studies, group job search activities and job clubs are now widely used in the public sector workforce system, and, increasingly, faith-based and community-based organizations are offering such group-based work search assistance.

Unlike the experimental research studies that have been conducted since the 1970s on job search assistance and job clubs provided by the public sector, there appear to be no rigorous experimental studies (or even non-experimental studies) of the impacts of FBO/CBO-affiliated job clubs on employment outcomes for job seekers. The lack of experimental studies of FBO/CBO job clubs may be because there is little funding available to sponsor such evaluations, because there is a lack of expertise in setting up and implementing random assignment-type studies, or because FBOs/CBOs sponsoring such initiatives are unwilling or unable to subject their job clubs to more rigorous study.

Environmental Scan – Findings from the Stakeholder Interviews. As part of the environmental scan, the research team conducted telephone interviews with seven stakeholders knowledgeable about the operation of job clubs, including those sponsored by FBOs/CBOs. These interviews provided an opportunity to question each stakeholder on a range of topics related to job clubs operated by FBO/CBOs. Among the study findings that emerged from these interviews were the following:

- **According to several stakeholders, the steep downturn of the U.S. economy in 2007-08 and surging numbers of unemployed and underemployed workers created a strong demand for job search assistance, providing an impetus for FBOs/CBOs to form job clubs to meet urgent needs within their communities.** Stakeholders cited several other contributing factors for the apparent expansion of FBO/CBO-sponsored job clubs, including the desire of churches/congregations to help unemployed individuals within their own congregations as well as the surrounding communities and the relatively low costs for establishing and maintaining job clubs. However, despite an apparent surge in numbers of FBO/CBO-sponsored job clubs, stakeholders observed that there was little empirical data to support this apparent trend.

- **Stakeholders maintained that there is substantial diversity across FBOs and CBOs in the format, content, and operation of job clubs.** Several stakeholders noted that while some faith-based organizations might begin and end their job clubs with a prayer, the job club session itself might have little or no faith-based/religious content. Even those FBO-sponsored job clubs infused with religious/spiritual references tend to focus the bulk of their job club meetings on many of the same principles and instructional techniques as those covered in secular job clubs operated by CBOs and public sector organizations – e.g., the importance of networking, developing/practicing "elevator speeches," basics of developing an effective resume, job interviewing techniques, and effective job search approaches. Several stakeholders noted that compared to the public sector, faith-based job clubs often place more emphasis on personal encouragement, raising self-esteem, providing time for peer group discussions related to job search challenges, and generally responding to emotional needs of participants.

- **None of the stakeholders interviewed were able to identify past or ongoing evaluations of FBO/CBO job clubs.** According to stakeholders, many of the FBOs operate their programs with only volunteer staff and on a shoestring budget and, consequently, lack computer equipment and/or the technical knowledge or staffing to set-up and manage an automated participant-level data system. None of the stakeholders felt it would be feasible to apply a random assignment-type experimental design to explore FBO/CBO-sponsored job club impacts (in part, because of concerns over denial of services to control group members and data collection burden/ complexity associated with random assignment-type studies).

Environmental Scan – Findings from the Site Visits. The second component of the environmental scan focused on site visits conducted in Fall 2013 to six localities across the country where job clubs are operated by FBOs and CBOs: (1) Northern New Jersey; (2) Cleveland/Akron, OH; (3) Atlanta, GA; (4) Minneapolis/St. Paul, MN; (5) Washington, DC Metro (MD/VA); and (6) San Francisco/Bay Area (CA). Within these six areas selected for visits, the site visit team observed regularly-scheduled job clubs and conducted in-depth interviews with staff in 16 organizations – eight FBOs, four CBOs, and four public workforce agencies – selected purposively to represent the range of characteristics, formats, and activities of job clubs currently operated by FBOs, CBOs, and public workforce agencies. Key findings that emerged from the site visits included the following:

- **Most of the 16 organizations visited as part of this study had no eligibility criteria for attendance at their job club sessions, with an overall aim of serving any and all unemployed job seekers within their service area or community.** The group of workers most represented in the FBO/CBO job clubs visited was middle- and upper-aged, white collar technical/professional workers. Job clubs also sought to serve new entrants to the labor market (such as recent college graduates) and employed individuals looking to change careers, increase earnings, or move from part- to full-time work (though typically, these individuals made up a very small share of job seekers attending job clubs). Most often, FBOs/CBOs simply indicated in their brochures and outreach efforts that "all job seekers are welcome."

- **The job clubs operated by FBOs and CBOs were held at community locations made available free-of-charge by either the sponsoring organization or other neighborhood institutions, thereby eliminating any operating costs for meeting rooms but also making the sessions convenient for participants to attend.** All the FBO-sponsored job clubs held their main sessions in meeting/conference rooms or fellowship halls in the church or on the church's campus. Job clubs sponsored by CBOs met in a variety of rent-free locations; for example two of the CBO job clubs (Career Transition Group for Women and Neighbors-helping-Neighbors) held sessions in community meeting rooms in local public libraries.

- **Most typically, FBOs/CBOs visited as part of this study had between 10 and 30 attendees at job club sessions, though all the job clubs visited indicated that there was variability in the numbers of attendees from session to session.** Among the 12 FBO/CBO job clubs visited, there were three outliers in terms of attendance at job club sessions: (1) Roswell United Methodist Church's Job Networking typically had up to 300 participants at their regular bi-monthly meeting, although they often saw from 350 to 375 attendees when they included job fairs in the program; (2) the McLean Bible Church averaged 150 attendees each week at its Career Network Ministry job clubs (ranging from 125 to 160 each week); and (3) ProMatch, often had over 100 attendees (including around 45 first-time participants) at General Membership meetings.

- **Nearly all the 16 job clubs observed held group job club sessions either weekly or twice a month**. The majority (nine) of the job clubs observed held sessions that met for approximately two hours. Most of the FBO, CBO, and public workforce agency job clubs observed followed an "open entry, open exit" format for participation in their job club sessions. Because their job clubs were designed to be open-entry, open-exit sessions (rather than a set number of meetings covering a specific list of instructional topics and issues), most of the FBO/CBO job clubs (as well as those operated by the public workforce agencies) visited did not use a formal curriculum or facilitator's guide to structure the sequence or the content of the activities and/or the instructional material presented in their job club sessions. However, most of the job clubs observed followed a standard format, and, in some cases, a fixed agenda, to guide and structure their sessions.

- **One critical difference between the job clubs sponsored by FBOs and CBOs and those operated by public workforce agencies is the staffing arrangements.** Job clubs held at AJC/One-Stop Centers are led by paid professional staff, often with the help of support staff and an array of equipment and tools (e.g., computers, printers) to support the job search. Although a few of the FBO-sponsored job clubs received limited assistance from paid church staff, the vast majority of these clubs were organized, managed, and facilitated solely by unpaid volunteers. Most of the FBO/CBO job clubs rotated a small group of volunteer facilitators or used two or three facilitators to lead each meeting. Larger job clubs such as the McLean Bible Church's Career Network Ministry needed up to 30 volunteers to operate multiple sessions and breakout groups at a single meeting.

- **The FBO/CBO job clubs visited operated with little or no external funding, and most functioned with only a limited budget, particularly when compared to job clubs operated by professional staff in a public workforce center.** Because they were able to keep their expenses to a minimum, FBOs/CBOs did not require grants or major funders to initiate or maintain their job clubs – and most of the administrators/staff preferred structuring and operating their job clubs so that they would not require outside fund raising or solicitation of government/foundation grants.
- **FBO/CBO-sponsored job clubs rarely collect in-depth information on participants, activities, and outcomes; in addition, they have not participated in evaluations in the past and would likely have deep reservations about participation in future evaluation efforts.** While collecting name and other contact information, CBOs and FBOs do not typically collect other identifying information, such as Social Security numbers, that would enable an evaluator to link individual data to administrative data such as the Unemployment Insurance (UI) wage records. Many FBOs/CBOs (and all those visited as part of this study) do not maintain automated management information systems that provide information about participants' background characteristics, services received, and outcomes. Finally, FBOs and CBOs are generally opposed to participating in an evaluation that involves random assignment and typically do not have excess demand for their services – hence, for most FBOs/CBOs, random assignment would mean turning away job seekers who could have been served.

Future Evaluation of FBO/CBO-Sponsored Job Clubs. Based on the results of the environmental scan, the prospects for rigorous, particularly experimental, evaluation of FBO/CBO-sponsored job clubs appear to be bleak. It is a remote possibility that a select group of FBOs/CBOs could be enticed to be part of an enhancement type experimental study, though such a study would not be helpful in determining the net impact of enrollment versus non- enrollment in a job club, but rather only would explore the incremental effects of some added feature to an existing job club. Such a study would need to carefully select among CBO/FBOs serving sufficient numbers of job seekers (likely to be in the neighborhood of 400 to 500 job seekers, unless pooling of samples is possible across sites) and provide substantial levels of technical assistance to ensure that: (1) an appropriate point of randomization is established, (2) treatment group members receive the enhanced services in an appropriate dosage and there is no contamination of individuals assigned to the control group, (3) participating organizations collect data elements necessary to support the analysis component of the study (including necessary personal identifiers, services received, and, if appropriate, outcomes, all of which organizations may be reluctant to collect), and (4) a participant tracking system is designed and implemented to support random assignment and ensure maintenance of participant characteristics, services, and outcomes.

With respect to non-experimental study designs, while before/after, regression discontinuity, and interrupted time series research designs do not appear appropriate or feasible, there is some potential for using "randomized encouragement" and propensity score matching (PSM). Most promising of these two non-experimental methods is the random encouragement approach, though even this approach is likely to run into a host of implementation challenges. Under a randomized encouragement approach, potential

FBO/CBO job club users would be divided into a treatment and a control group using random assignment. The treatment group would then be encouraged to participate in a FBO/CBO-sponsored job club by providing them with information about the program and perhaps a small allowance to defray the costs of attending, while the control group would receive nothing. The evaluation would be conducted as follows. First, a pool of potential job club users must be identified and randomly assigned to encouragement treatment or control status. If a state unemployment insurance (UI) office were willing to participate, targeted claimants could be assigned to encouragement status at the time of their initial claim or at some other pre-designated time, e.g., after the sixth week of the claim. Those in the treatment group would receive an inducement to enroll in a FBO/CBO job club, while those in the control group would receive no inducement. The inducement would include, at a minimum, information on the job club(s) of interest, including the time and location of meetings. Stronger encouragement could include financial inducements such as a transportation allowance to attend the job club. There are, however, both practical and statistical issues that must be investigated before it can be determined if the approach is an appropriate choice for an evaluation. On the practical side, one key problem is that the strategy requires the FBO/CBO job clubs that are to be evaluated to provide the evaluator with the participation status of all claimants randomly assigned to treatment and control encouragement status. As noted previously, FBO/CBO job clubs are generally reluctant to collect Social Security numbers, but that would be the most accurate way to identify members of the treatment and control groups who participate in the job club. A second potential problem is that the state Unemployment Insurance agency may balk at providing any form of encouragement to attend a private sector job club, particularly at a faith-based institution.

Building on this exploratory study, perhaps the most promising (and feasible) next step from an evaluation perspective would be to conduct a more detailed process/implementation study of FBO/CBO job clubs, possibly in conjunction with AJC job clubs, to better define what the distinctions are across the different types of job clubs. A process/implementation study would be appropriate for periodic efforts to assess and track implementation of the job clubs over time, as well as to identify strengths and weaknesses/challenges of the job clubs from varying perspectives (e.g., job club attendees, job club facilitators, and other organizational administrators/other staff). The strength of such studies is in obtaining contextual information for understanding the environment in which interventions occur, as well as gaining rich qualitative perspectives on the intervention. Such information, particularly if collected over time, can help to identify ways in which job clubs are exceeding or falling short of expectations from various perspectives, and identify potential approaches to improving workshop content, facilitation, facilities, and participant outcomes.

SECTION 1. INTRODUCTION

A. Background

Over the past several decades, job clubs have evolved to become one of several important activities used by the public workforce system and faith and community-based organizations to enhance job search skills and work readiness, as well as to provide ongoing support to unemployed and underemployed individuals as they search for jobs. Job clubs, which typically meet on a weekly or bi-weekly basis, may be sponsored by the public workforce system – through the approximately 2,500 American Job Centers (AJCs) and over 500 local workforce investment areas (LWIAs) across the nation – or a considerable range of faith-based or community-based organizations (FBO/CBOs). The focus of this report is on better understanding the types of job clubs operated by FBOs/CBOs and determining the extent to which such job clubs could be more rigorously evaluated in the future (for employment and other impacts on job seekers attending such job clubs). Often such job clubs (whether operated by the public or non-profit entities) are open to any and all unemployed and underemployed individuals in a local workforce area or community in which they serve. However, some job clubs may be aimed at more narrowly-defined subpopulations of job seekers -- for example, recruiting and serving public assistance recipients (e.g., those subjected to work requirements under the Temporary Assistance for Needy Families (TANF) or Supplemental Nutrition Assistance Program (SNAP) programs), formerly incarcerated individuals, separating or retiring active duty military personnel, unemployed/underemployed veterans, older workers and other seniors, persons with disabilities, unemployed white-collar workers, and individuals dislocated from various manufacturing or service sectors.

The "club" dimension of group job search sessions, whether they are formally called job clubs or not, implies that participants share information, job leads, knowledge, networking possibilities, and other job search-related activities. In 2011, a U.S. Department of Labor Training and Employment Notice (TEN) catalogued key features of job clubs:

- **Facilitated meeting-based approach:** Job clubs are typically organized around regular meetings, which take place on a weekly, bi-weekly, or monthly basis, in most cases. Meetings often occur in the evenings or weekends and generally seem to provide coffee/tea and refreshments. Job club meetings are led and organized by a facilitator, often a volunteer or member of the church or community organization.
- **Small group and inclusive setting:** Most job clubs work in small group settings, with meetings of 5 to 30 participants for at least a three-month period. While job clubs often advertise to their congregation or community members, they tend to be open to the broad public.
- **Peer support:** A central tenet of most job clubs is to act as a support group for unemployed people. In many (though not all) cases, job clubs view their work as more closely aligned with a grieving process model or 12-step treatment model rather than a workforce development model, where there are various stages of unemployment (grief, anger, denial, acceptance, etc.). The facilitator's role is to help participants work through these various stages.
- **Network and education models:** In addition to peer support, job clubs also offer assistance in the areas of job search and career development. Often times, they take a networking approach where participants share their various networks to help each other identify job opportunities. Job clubs will also use an education model where they provide participants with information and skills in areas such as job search techniques, résumé building, and interview preparation.
- **Guest speakers:** A hallmark of job clubs is to invite outside guests and experts to speak to participants. Guest speakers could be human resources experts, small

business owners, employer representatives, and former, employed job club participants.

(Oates and Tom, 2011, TEN 42-10)

Job clubs, whether they are sponsored by the public workforce system or faith-based organizations and community-based organizations (FBO/CBOs), offer a variety of activities aimed at helping job seekers to better plan and execute their job search activities, answering questions or troubleshooting job search challenges that may emerge, and allowing job seekers to share their experiences and provide support for one another. Though there is much variability across job clubs, some typical activities include:

- classroom instruction on job readiness and effective job search strategies;
- information about labor market conditions, industry sectors, and job openings;
- planning job search activities for an upcoming period and identifying job leads (through discussion among job club members, searches of Internet job boards and employer websites, and other networking activities);
- resume and cover letter development/refinement;
- peer group discussion among job club participants about available job openings, job search challenges, and strategies for dealing with rejection and other job search challenges;
- employer recruitment sessions and presentations to share information about industry sectors and potential job openings; and
- mock or actual interviews for jobs.

An important accompanying goal of job clubs is to break the isolation that can often accompany lengthy periods of unemployment and counter the discouragement and anxiety that can set in during the job search process (e.g., as a result of unsuccessful job interviews, unanswered correspondences, and exhausting job leads or networking opportunities).

As is discussed in greater detail in Section 2, a substantial number of job clubs have sprung up across the country in recent years, often affiliated with community-based organizations, faith-based organizations, and congregations. These FBO/CBO-sponsored job clubs provide an opportunity for such organizations to serve their communities and bring much needed employment/job placement-related services to job seekers within their communities. Such clubs may also target and serve job seekers who may not be aware of or are reluctant to use similar services available at American Job Centers and or through other public sector agencies. FBO/CBO-sponsored job clubs may also be offered at times and venues that are more convenient than those provided by AJCs or other public employment agencies. Finally, some job seekers may be simply more comfortable and willing to attend job clubs held by a church or community- based organization conveniently located within their neighborhood.

While there have been some past evaluations of the impacts of participation in public sector-operated job clubs on job placement, there has been little assessment of FBO/CBO-sponsored job clubs. As discussed in greater detail in the literature review (in Section 2), during the 1980s, there was a great deal of interest in job clubs designed to help a wide variety of unemployed workers including older workers, welfare recipients, and reentrants from the criminal justice system. A number of evaluations found that job clubs operated by the public workforce system had a large impact on speeding up participants' return to work. [1] For example, older workers who were Employment Service customers were assigned to either a job club treatment or control group; after 12 weeks, 74 percent of the job club treatment group participants were employed, compared to 22 percent for the control group (Gray 1983). Work Incentive Program (WIN) welfare clients in five cities were randomly assigned to a job club program; of those assigned to the treatment group, 87 percent found jobs within 12 months compared to 58 percent in the control group (Azrin et al. 1980). A follow-up study found that after six months, about half of the treatment group members were no longer receiving welfare while only 22 percent of the control group had left welfare. Based on these earlier studies, job clubs offered by public employment and welfare agencies generally appear to connect job seekers to the labor market more quickly, though there is no evidence from these studies that attendance in such job clubs has any effect on earnings or job retention.[2] While it would seem likely that FBO/CBO-sponsored job clubs could have similar effects in terms of speeding the return to work for unemployed individuals, there have been few (if any) rigorous empirical studies completed on this subject. As discussed in the next section, an important focus of this report is exploring the possibilities for future rigorous experimental studies to gauge the employment and earnings impacts of participating in FBO/CBO-sponsored job clubs.

B. Study Objectives, Methodology, and Organization of Report

As stated in DOL's original statement of work (SOW), the purpose of this formative evaluation effort was to systematically describe the key characteristics of the job clubs being offered by a range of faith- and community-based organizations, document how they differ from and are similar to the job clubs operated by publicly-funded workforce agencies (such as the American Job Centers), and identify promising practices in FBO/CBO-based job clubs that might warrant more rigorous formal evaluation of individual impacts and effectiveness. Primary research questions that were the focus of this exploratory study were the following (based in part on questions provided in DOL's original Statement of Work for this study):

- What types of community-based and faith-based organizations sponsor job clubs? Why do they operate these clubs?
- What are the various program designs and key characteristics of these jobs clubs? For example, how often do the clubs meet and for how long? Do individuals start and end as a cohort or is there open entry/open exit? How are individual club sessions structured and what topics are covered? What role does agency staff play in coordinating and running job club sessions?
- What are the targeted subpopulations (if any) served by such clubs and how might the groups served differ from job clubs sponsored by public sector organizations?
- What resources are used by and for job clubs (e.g., staff, volunteers, cash and in-kind donations, technology, facilities/space, public funding)? What are the costs associated with developing and implementing job clubs? How much are the ongoing costs of job clubs for sponsoring organizations?

- How do the job clubs interact with the public workforce development system? For example, are there referrals to and from the workforce development system? Are job seekers attending FBO/CBO-sponsored job clubs encouraged to visit American Job Centers and make full and appropriate use public workforce development resources?
- What types of data are being collected on participant characteristics and outcomes by job clubs? For example, have FBOs/CBOs developed data systems to track participant characteristics, services received, and outcomes (in terms of job placement, earnings, and job retention)? Have these organizations conducted any evaluations of the results of the job clubs they have held?
- Are FBOs/CBOs interested in more rigorously evaluating their job clubs for impacts on participant employment and earnings outcomes, and if so, are there outcome/impact evaluation designs that could be practically applied to assess FBO/CBO-sponsored job clubs?

The data collection, analysis, and report preparation tasks under this effort, conducted over a 20- month period, included three main research activities: (1) a literature review (see Section 2); (2) an "environmental scan," with a particular focus on conducting interviews with key stakeholders knowledgeable about job clubs and site visits to FBO/CBO organizations sponsoring job clubs in six localities (see Section 3); and (3) the identification and exploration of alternative evaluation designs for future rigorous study of FBO/CBO job clubs (see Section 4).[3]

Section 2. Review of the Literature on Faith-Based and Community-Based Sponsored Job Clubs

The literature review for this project is aimed at summarizing what is known about the job clubs operated by public sector agencies and FBO/CBOs, including the results of available experimental/non-experimental research studies. This literature review begins with a brief discussion of job search theory and what is known from the research about job clubs provided by public sector organizations. A key focus of this initial section is on impacts on return to work, employment, and earnings of job club participation. This is followed by a review of available literature on FBO/CBO provision of job search assistance and other employment-related and support services. This section concludes with a discussion of the implications of literature review findings for future evaluation of FBO/CBO-sponsored job clubs.

A. Review of Literature on Job Search and Job Clubs Provided by the Public Workforce System

1. Job Search Theory

Neo-classical economists view labor markets as governed by the forces of supply (by workers) and demand (by employers), which determine wage rates and the quantity of labor the workers provide.[4] In conventional labor market theory, workers (seeking to maximize their well-being or "utility" function) make choices between income and leisure (i.e., they will work when working seems more attractive than not working). The advantage of working more hours for the individual is that he or she will have higher earnings. The trade-off in working more, however, is a loss of leisure time, potentially a loss of public benefits (such as unemployment insurance benefits or means-tested welfare payments), added costs (e.g., added expenses associated with traveling to and from work, child care, and work clothing and tools/equipment), and other physical and psychological costs of working. From an employer's perspective, the neo-classical model holds that a firm will hire additional workers as long as the additional product from the last hired worker exceeds total wages paid the worker (e.g., the value of the marginal product of labor exceeds the total marginal cost in terms of wages, fringe benefits, taxes, etc.).

Over the past several decades, research on job search behavior has substantially expanded and refined our understanding of the process by which unemployed workers search for, find, and retain jobs. Economists have tried to understand and explain the fact that at any time there are both unemployed workers and posted job vacancies. Job search theory said that the contemporaneous occurrence of both unemployed workers and posted vacancies does not necessarily mean a serious mismatch between workers and jobs or that wages are not set at a reasonable level. Rather, job search theory suggests that the search for work is a sequential process, involving obtaining information about available job openings, then contacting and interviewing with one or more firms. In the early 1960s, in a seminal work, Stiglitz (1961) examined the role of information in determining labor market behavior, for example, examining the role that imperfect, incomplete, and asymmetric information plays in labor markets and in producing inefficient market outcomes. Building on the work of Stiglitz (1961, 1962) and others, McCall (1970) examined the relationship between information and job search behavior and developed a dynamic model of job search behavior, proposing a "reservation wage" whereby the worker is willing to accept job offers with wages above a reservation wage and, at which time, job search activity is terminated. This dynamic model of job search has been further refined over the past couple of decades using "matching theory," culminating in the award of the 2010 Nobel prize in economics to Diamond (2010), Mortensen (1994), and Pissarides (2000). The job search process takes time, involves the gathering of information, and has costs for the job seeker, involving three critical steps: (1) identifying job openings, (2) converting job openings to job offers, and (3) deciding whether to accept job offers or continue searching (Klerman et al., 2012).

Job search theory, thus, suggests the possibility that job search assistance – for example, in the form of a job club – could provide instruction and support to improve labor market outcomes during each of the three critical steps identified above (e.g., generating more job offers with higher wages, encouraging more intensive job search, and better informing job seekers about whether to accept specific job offers). Typically, workers with better skills and with better job vacancy information are likely to have better search outcomes and shorter job search periods (Diamond 2010).

A more in-depth and practical understanding of the process by which workers search for and secure jobs has been derived in part from the job search questions administered by Bureau of Labor Statistics (BLS) as part of the Current Population Survey (CPS),[5] and other data sources such as the American Time Use Survey. For example, using data from the American Time Use Survey between 2003 and 2007, Krueger and Mueller (2010) reported that, on a given weekday, roughly one-quarter of the unemployed engage in job search activities. On average, the unemployed searched for about 41 minutes per day. Conditional on engaging in at least some search activity, the average increases to about 2¾ hours (167 minutes). Krueger and Mueller (2011) estimated that during a period of high unemployment (in late 2009 and early 2010), New Jersey UI recipients spent, on average, between 65 and 100 minutes a day on job searches. As a result, Klerman et al. (2012) concluded that job search intensity among unemployed job seekers is low – "standard advice is to treat job search like a job, but the reality is quite different." Hence, given such low levels of job search intensity among many unemployed job seekers, it is possible that job clubs and other types of job search assistance could play a role in increasing the intensity of job search activity among unemployed job seekers, as well as the quality and productivity of their job search approach and strategies utilized.

Analysis of the CPS data reveals the various methods that job seekers typically use during the job search process to identify job leads. The most commonly reported job search methods are direct employer contact and sending out a resume/filling out a job application. Contacting and working with an employment service/job placement agency, networking with friends or family to identify job openings, and looking at ads are also common job search methods. Some studies have emphasized the importance of informal job search methods, such as networking with family, relatives, and friends to obtain information about employers and job vacancies (Rosenfeld 1977, Bortnick and Ports 1992). Bishop, Barron, and Hollenbeck (1993) found large variations between the employment likelihoods resulting from different job search methods. They suggested that job search methods such as contact with employers directly and with friends or relatives are more likely to lead job seekers to employment. A considerable literature exists on networking (e.g., through family, friends, co-workers, and other contacts), and increasingly about use of social media to expand a job seeker's network and improve job search outcomes. Below are some highlights of the research that has been conducted on networking and using other job search methods:

- In a study of status attainment using social network analysis, Granovetter (1974) interviewed 282 professional and managerial men in Newton, Massachusetts. He found that individuals who used interpersonal channels found jobs that were more satisfactory to them and yielded higher incomes. This analysis of higher income men led to other studies to determine whether Granovetter's findings could be generalized, and especially what the implications were for low-wage workers.[6]

- A number of job search studies have found that race, ethnicity, income, and geographic location play a role in the extent of networking and the way individuals search for work. For example, Elliott and Sims (2001) found that race and income play important roles in the way unemployed workers search for and find new jobs, with Latinos being significantly more likely to use friends, relatives, and eventual coworkers than blacks. However, Elliott and Sims found that the difference in use of informal methods between Latinos and blacks declines as income decreases, particularly for individuals living in more segregated neighborhoods.

- A number of other studies also have found lower incidence of informal employment networks among minorities, and also that Latinos were much more likely to find jobs through friends, relatives and other personal contacts than blacks (Falcon and Melendez 1996; Green, Tigges, and Diaz 1999; Holzer 1987, 1988; Marx and Leicht 1992). Elliott (1999) came to a different conclusion. He found that among low-wage individuals with a high school education or less in urban areas of Atlanta, Boston, and Los Angeles, the highest paid jobs during the early 1990s were acquired through formal job search methods. Elliott suggests that the use of personal contacts as a search strategy is used as a last resort, rather than being a means to find a better job.

- On the other hand, in a study looking at unemployed youth in the Youth Cohort of the National Longitudinal Survey for the year 1981, Holzer (1988) found methods such as networking with friends and relatives, as well as direct employer applications, were the most frequently used search methods and also the most productive at generating job offers and acceptances. Rosenbaum et al. (1999) examined the long-term effects of search methods used when youth leave high school. They found that American high schools sometimes help students find work, and blacks and females were more likely to get their first job through school placements than white males. They found that placements made through relatives and friends had small effects on early earnings, but jobs found through relatives led to higher earnings nine years later.

The literature appears to confirm that low-wage workers and most minority workers have weaker employment networks than most white and high-wage workers. Studies of job search methods and variation in utilization by various subpopulations suggest that job clubs could play a pivotal role in assisting job seekers in learning about various job search methods and structuring job search activities to improve probabilities of earlier return to employment. The next section examines in more detail the role job clubs can play in helping job seekers to find and secure jobs, with a particular focus on the net impacts on employment outcomes of attending a job club, based on results from experimental research studies.

2. Research Findings on Job Clubs

Job search assistance (JSA) provided by public and non-profit organizations is typically characterized as relatively short-term, low-intensity, and low-cost assistance to help job seekers find and secure jobs. Klerman et al. (2012) have identified four main types of job search assistance, described below; job clubs fit into the second category, "facilitated group activities":

> ...we identify group specific program activities, or components, into four modes, or methods, of service provision: (i) *self-directed activities* (e.g., consulting with social networks, filling out job applications); (ii) facilitated *group activities* such as the group process in job club and classes in job search and soft skills; (iii) *one-on-one meetings*, including counseling related to job search strategies (e.g., assessment of skills and goals, help using computer search tools and completing job applications), conveying job leads (from past experience or from job developers), and monitoring of job search activities (checking job search logs and copies of job applications completed, contacting employers to verify claimed activities); and (iv) *job development*, in which a program staff person works with employers to identify (i.e., develop) job openings, without direct contact with the job seeker. (Klerman et al., 2012)

Although facilitated group job search activities, such as job clubs or job search workshops, are commonly used by public sector workforce and welfare programs today, they were rarely used prior to the 1970s. Over the past several decades, job clubs have evolved to be one of several important activities used by the public workforce system (and increasingly, community- and faith-based organizations) to enhance worker readiness, improve job search skills, coordinate and intensify job search activities, and provide ongoing support for job seekers. Such job clubs offer a variety of activities that are aimed at helping unemployed individuals to better plan and execute their job search activities, to answer questions or troubleshoot problems that may emerge during the active job search period, and to allow workers to share their experiences and provide emotional support to one another. There is a group dynamic involved in these job clubs, with guidance provided by a job coach or workforce development official (e.g., in American Job Centers it might be a Wagner-Peyser or Workforce Investment Act-funded staff person) and also substantial interaction among job club participants.

Beginning in the mid-1970s, there was a great deal of interest in public sector-sponsored job clubs to help a wide variety of unemployed workers, particularly welfare recipients, unemployment insurance (UI) claimants/exhaustees, and certain hard-to-employ subpopulations with special needs (e.g., older workers and reentrants from the criminal justice system). The structure and activities involved in job clubs has remained relatively unchanged since job clubs were established in the 1970s and 1980s.[7] Goldman (1989) provides a basic description of the structure and main activities involved in job clubs, which remain applicable today:

> ...Participants were told to treat job search as a full-time job and were encouraged to use friends and relatives to obtain leads. They were trained in interviewing and social skills and used standardized scripts on the telephone to uncover job openings and get interviews. The basic philosophy is that there are many jobs that become vacant and subsequently filled without going through an elaborate job referral network. Frequent telephone calls will locate these vacancies and provide participants with opportunities they would not have had had they relied on job developers or want ads. As part of the program, they were also given regular staff supervision and assistance and were involved in a peer support network. (Goldman, 1989)

Klerman et al. (2012) provide additional details about the job club process:

> ...We make several observations about this characterization of the job club process. First, the formal assistance component usually covers all three stages of our conceptualization of individual job search: identifying job openings, converting job openings into job offers, and deciding which job offers to accept. However, the focus has traditionally been on identifying job openings. There is also some attention to how to convert identified job openings into job offers (training in and help with filling out job applications; mock job interviews; guidance on appropriate dress and behavior). In most JSA programs for AFDC/TANF recipients (and only slightly less so for UI), there has been little focus on which job offers to accept; the guidance is to accept all job offers. Second, note that this description of a job club is that it is clearly a group process; it is neither exclusively one-on-one work with a counselor, nor self-directed job search. However, the mutual support group aspect is only part of the job club process. Note also the emphasis on hidden jobs.

With the increased emphasis on moving welfare recipients into jobs, particularly since the enactment of the Temporary Assistance for Needy Families (TANF) program in 1997, job clubs have been used both as an activity to assist welfare participants in improving their job search methods and effectiveness, as well as an enforcement mechanism to increase job search intensity and to meet work search requirements under TANF. Brown (1997) and Holcomb (1998) observe that job clubs operated by TANF tend to be relatively short in duration and to combine the group process and meetings with classroom activities or instruction focused on job readiness skills with active job search, as well as access to resource room materials such as computers, phone, banks, and a variety of job listings. Klerman et al. (2012) note that TANF- sponsored job clubs may include an assessment component to identify and resolve participants' barriers to employment, such as limited English proficiency, limited computer skills, lack of appropriate work clothing/tools, lack of childcare, and transportation-related issues. Additionally, TANF job clubs tend to meet daily and more closely approximate the idea of treating job search like a job (e.g., requiring regular attendance).

A number of evaluations of demonstration projects found that job clubs have a large impact on speeding up job club participants' return to work as well as other benefits for workers. In a series of social experiments conducted by Nathan Azrin and colleagues, group job search was tested against the more conventional (at the time) individual-oriented approach. In the first such study, a job-finding club was established in the early 1970s in a small college town. The main criterion for selecting participants was that individuals desired a permanent, full-time job and were not currently employed full-time. The participants also could not be currently collecting unemployment insurance. Individuals desiring to participate in the job-finding club were selected as matched pairs based on demographic and labor market characteristics. Matched pairs were dropped if the individuals in the treatment group did not attend at least five sessions. The result was 60 treatment and 60 control group members with similar characteristics. The treatment group showed significantly better employment outcomes than the control group. Although the analysis was not up to the standards commonly used today, the results were very strong—within two months, 90 percent of the treatment group members had a job, but only 55 percent of the control group was employed.[8] The treatment group also had a mean starting salary that was significantly greater than the control group. Additionally, the speed of finding a job was greater for clients who attended the job-finding club regularly than for those who attended irregularly. The researchers concluded that while the job-finding clubs worked for a general population, the results for more disadvantaged populations were uncertain (Azrin et al. 1975).

Azrin replicated his efforts with two specialized target groups. Azrin and Philip (1979) tested the job club approach against an individualized assistance approach for individuals with disabilities – individuals referred from a state hospital for the mentally ill and developmentally disabled – in Southern Illinois. Again using random assignment methods, the study included 154 job seekers who desired a full-time job, attended two or more sessions of the job club, and had job-finding problems or had been unsuccessfully looking for work for at least two months. Once again, the results were striking – 95 percent of the treatment group was employed at the six- month follow-up point compared to only 28 percent of the control group. The speed of obtaining jobs correlated with the consistency of session attendance and the number of interviews obtained. About 90 percent of clients received jobs after attending 15 sessions and conducting 15 interviews.

With funding from the U.S. Department of Labor, Azrin et al. (1980) conducted a much larger scale experiment to determine whether job clubs are effective for welfare recipients participating in the Work Incentive (WIN) program. This study was carried out in five cities, and nearly 1,000 welfare recipients were randomly assigned to receive either group job search through job clubs or the usual employment services provided to welfare recipients in their city. The impact results were large and statistically significant -- at the 12-month follow-up point, 87 percent of the job club treatment group had obtained jobs compared to 59 percent of the control sample. There were statistically significant differences favoring the treatment group in all five sites and for every subgroup examined. In a follow-up to the 1980 WIN study, Azrin et al. (1983a) found that after six months, about half the treatment group members were no longer receiving welfare, while only 22 percent of the control group had left welfare.

The Azrin group (1983b) also tested two different pedagogical approaches intended to help workers find jobs through job clubs presenting the same material. One approach, "informational counseling," consisted of explaining and discussing job search techniques; it was advisory rather than participatory. The second "supervision" approach involved practicing and performing job search techniques under direct supervision. A total of 346 clients participated in the project, with 196 clients in the supervision group and 150 in the advisory group. There was no control group. The results revealed that the supervision approach was more successful than the advisory group for a number of outcomes. After six months, 88 percent of the supervision group had found a job compared to 71 percent for the advisory group; the supervision group had worked 75 percent of all work days compared to 61 percent for the advisory group; the mean number of days to obtain a job was 32 days for the supervision group but 61 days for the advisory group; and the mean salary was $4.99 per hour for the supervision group but $3.93 for the advisory group.

The U.S. Department of Labor retained the Manpower Demonstration Research Corporation (now MDRC) to replicate a group job search assistance (or job club) demonstration on a large scale in Louisville, Kentucky, a site that had agreed to serve as a laboratory to test promising strategies for female welfare recipients registering for the WIN program. Welfare recipients who registered in Louisville between October 1980 and May 1981 were eligible to participate in the experiment.[9] Wolfhagen and Goldman (1983) found that a total of 750 individuals participated. Two calendar quarters after random assignment, 49 percent of the treatment group members who were ever employed compared to 34 percent of the control group; earnings for the treatment group over this period were $550 for the treatment group and $144 for the control group. There was, however, no significant decline in total average Aid to Families with Dependent Children (AFDC) payment for the treatment group.

Finally, Klerman et al. (2012) note that with respect to the Unemployment Insurance program, evidence on the separate effect of a job search workshop or job club is mixed, citing results from two demonstration efforts:

- The Maryland Unemployment Insurance Work Search Demonstration included a treatment arm that added a four-day job search workshop to the regular job search requirement. The evaluation found that doing so cut UI durations by 0.6 weeks (on a base of about 12 weeks). (Klepinger et al., 1998).
- In contrast, the Charleston Demonstration included a treatment arm that added a job search workshop in addition to other services—a strong work test and enhanced placement services. The differential effect of adding the job search workshop was to cut UI durations by only an additional 0.15 weeks (i.e., Treatment 2 had an impact of

-0.61 weeks while Treatment 3 which added the workshop had an impact of -0.76 weeks). A formal test of the incremental impact is not provided, but it seems unlikely that the incremental impact of the workshop was statistically significant.

The Azrin studies, the MDRC replication, and other more recent experimental studies have helped change the workforce community's perception about whether job seekers should be served individually or in groups, including in job clubs. In part as a result of the positive impacts reported in these studies, group job search activities and job clubs are now a widely used strategy within the public sector workforce system, and increasingly, faith-based and community-based organizations are offering such group-based work search assistance, which is the focus of the next section of this report.

B. Review of Literature on Job Search and Employment and Training-Related Assistance Provided by FBO/CBOS

1. Extent of FBO/CBO-Affiliated Job Clubs

There is some evidence suggesting that job clubs affiliated with community-based organizations, faith-based organizations, congregations, and other community groups have expanded substantially throughout the United States over the past decade, particularly in response to the deep recession of 2007-08. There are no precise counts of the number of job clubs currently in operation nor the number of clubs that have been formed only recently, although in a 2011 Training and Employment Notice (Oates and Tom, 2011), the U.S. Department of Labor estimated that there were over 3,000 nationwide at that time (though it is not clear what portion of these job clubs in this estimate are operated by FBO/CBOs):

> …Job Clubs grow in number during economic downturns. Through its own research, CFBNP (Center for Faith-based and Neighborhood Partnerships) estimates that there are at least as many Job Clubs in operation across the country as there are One-Stop Career Centers (approximately 3,000).

The Center for Faith-based and Neighborhood Partnerships launched the Job Clubs Initiative in 2011. The initiative has three primary purposes: (1) create a community of practice for job club leaders and volunteers to share practices, lessons learned, and resources; (2) facilitate partnerships among job clubs, the public workforce system, and other public and private programs; and (3) provide technical assistance and training to individuals interested in starting or expanding job clubs. The Center manages a community of practice web site at www.dol.gov/jobclubs that includes a web-based "State Job Club Directory," which invites FBOs/CBOs to register active job clubs on-line at the CFBNP website.[10] This website also provides FBOs/CBOs with resources and toolkits aimed at helping FBOs/CBOs establish and enhance job clubs in their communities, as well as a blog, discussion board, and a calendar board of job club-related events to spur sharing of information among FBO/CBO-affiliated job clubs. While not necessarily representative of the total number or distribution of job clubs across the country (i.e., organizations voluntarily list job clubs to this website and so many operating job clubs are likely not included), as of March 2014, the CFBNP directory included 679 job clubs spread across 31 states. (Note: A total of 20 states, mostly less populous states, had no listings on this directory.) Most (but not all) of the listings in this directory appear to be job clubs affiliated with FBO/CBOs, often operating out of churches, congregations, local libraries, and other community locations. Though far from complete or representative, the CFBNP listing shows the considerable reach of FBO/CBO-affiliated job clubs across the country. Among the states with the most listings of job clubs in this directory are: Minnesota (62 job clubs listed), Texas (53), Georgia (48), California (41), Ohio (40), Illinois (35), New Jersey (33), North Carolina (29), Missouri (28) and Florida (24).

These FBO/CBO-sponsored job clubs provide an opportunity to reach groups of unemployed workers who may not come to public employment agencies for a variety of reasons. Such job clubs may be offered at times and places that are more convenient than those offered at American Job Centers or other public employment agencies. Attendees may be more willing and comfortable attending job clubs held, for example, at a congregation or community-based organization with which they are already familiar. Job club attendees, for example, may be part of the congregation that is sponsoring the job club or may know a family or friend that is a member of the congregation who recommends that they attend the job club; they may also hear about the job club from acquaintances who have themselves participated in the job club. Additionally, it is possible that the more religiously/spiritually-infused job club environment offered by some FBOs/CBOs may resonate with some attendees more than the secular curriculum used by public sector organizations.

2. Background on Curriculum Used in FBOC-Affiliated Job Clubs

Much of the existing literature on FBO/CBO-affiliated job clubs is not evaluative, but rather advocates for establishment of job clubs by FBO/CBOs; provides step-by-step guidance on how to plan, initiate, and sustain a job club; and/or provides a curriculum to guide the structure, substantive content, and instructional methods used in job clubs. For example, there is an emerging body of material to guide instructors of job club sessions and workbooks that can be distributed to job club participants.[11] A review of several curriculum guides available on the CFBNP website suggests that the substantive topics covered and the step-by-step instructions provided in curriculum guides used in FBO/CBO-affiliated job clubs are similar to what would be included in curriculum used in job clubs held at American Job Centers and other public workforce agencies, with one important exception: to varying degrees, the faith-based curricula are often infused with spiritual and/or explicitly religious guidance. For example, one curriculum guide available on the CFBNP website, "Career Network Ministry (CNM) Handbook: A Guide to Discovering Your Gifts and Pursuing Your Professional Career Search" is infused quite substantially with spiritual and religious guidance, and provides a side-by-side comparison of what is termed to be a secular versus a Christian way of finding a job:

- **"Finding a Job the Secular Way.** Most of us have been taught to approach the professional job search in a secular way:
  - Get over anger, disappointment, and fear, and "get on with it"
  - Prepare a resume and job hunt materials
  - Research your options
  - Identify the job you want, where you want
  - Research companies/participate in informational interviews

- Target best options
- Go for it! Make the best deal for you!"
- **"Finding a Job the Christian Way.** At the CNM, we encourage you to discover your Gifts and find a job in the Christian Way:
    - Recognize that God knows what's going on. He has a place for you. *Jeremiah 1:5, Psalms 25:12, Psalms 27:11, Psalms 32:8, Psalms 37:5,23, Isaiah 30:21*
    - Pray over your anger, fear, and disappointment
    - Pray and invite others to pray
    - Relax, invite God to intercede for you
    - Identify the job/vocation to which you are led
    - Prepare a resume, job hunt materials
    - Research your options
    - Research companies/informational interviews
    - Target best options based on where God leads.
    - Wait! Expect a miracle!"
    (Career Network Ministry, 2009, p. 3)

Despite blending in references to daily prayer, spiritual encouragement, and specific references to proverbs from the Bible, the job search topics covered are quite similar in tone and content to those likely to be covered in a more secular setting and offer common sense strategies for effective job search. For example, this same *Career Network Ministry* guide that highlights differences for "Finding a Job the Christian Way" includes chapters on the following: (1) Marketing Strategy (including subsections on Research, Elevator Speech, Resume Creation, Business Cards, and Define Your Target Market/Industry/Companies); (2) Traditional and Non- Traditional Approach (Responding to Ads; Cover Letter Writing; Internet Usage; Using Recruiters; Associations; Networking; and Accountability); and Interviewing (Preparing for the Interview; Thank You Letters and Follow-up; and Rejection). When this guide narrows the focus to the specifics of how to search for a job, interview, and negotiate a salary, it dispassionately dispenses guidance and common sense approaches to job search that would similarly be covered in a job club held at a public agency. For example, none of the 13 tips provided in the CNM curriculum with regard to social networking are infused with spiritual references; several examples of these tips follow:

- "Ensure that your profile is complete and compelling. Conversely, "an incomplete profile makes you appear lazy and does not showcase all your accomplishments and abilities," cautions Christine Hassler of The Huffington Post.
- Let your network know through your status updates that you seek a job and what kind.
- If you blog, link your blog content to your profiles and status updates.
- Include links to your Website/portfolio/blog in your profiles.
- Ask and answer questions through LinkedIn Answers.
- Research employers through company pages on Facebook and LinkedIn.
- Recommend people on LinkedIn and ask your contacts to recommend you.
- Participate in discussion forums and boards in your career field.

- See if professional organizations in your field offer social-networking tools.
- Always offer help to those with whom you connect and thank your contacts for their assistance and advice."

(Career Network Ministry, 2009, p. 28)

Another guide available on the CFBNP website, *Empowering Job Seekers – A Ministry of the Hills* (2011), similarly devotes several pages of its curriculum to "Why God may not be answering your prayer for a new job, By Billy Graham," which is very much spiritually-focused. For example:

> "Q: How do I know God is listening to me when I pray? To be honest, I've about given up on prayer because it doesn't seem to make any difference. Has God turned His back on me?
>
> A: No! God has not turned His back on you. He loves you and wants you to bring your burdens and cares to Him in prayer. The Bible says, "Do not be anxious about anything, but in everything, by prayer and petition, with thanksgiving, present your requests to God." Philippians 4:6. Only two things can keep God from giving us what we ask for in our prayers. The first is sin - and the reason is because sin erects a barrier between us and God. Until that barrier is torn down, God can't answer our prayers. The Bible says, "The Lord is far from the wicked but he hears the prayer of the righteous." Proverbs 15:29. This is why the first step you need to take is to turn by faith to Jesus Christ and ask Him to forgive your sins and come into your life. When we do that, the barrier of sin is removed - and God hears our prayers."

(A Ministry of The Hills, p. 6)

The next section of this curriculum guide, however, provides very down-to-earth guidance on "20 things to take 10 to 15 years off your image and be perceived as more youthful in the interview or in the office," which includes, for example, the following four "rules" (from the list of 20 rules):

- **"Rule #1:** Crest Whitestrips. Yup, this is a shallow, cosmetic-based tip. But I get so many letters from people who just don't understand that having coffee-stained teeth doesn't do you any favors in the interview department. Stop rolling your eyes; go buy the strips (use the store brand for all I care – I'm not picky); and whiten those teeth. Then smile. Smiling makes you look and feel younger – not bitter, old and unemployed. I don't care if you really are bitter, old and unemployed. It's about perception, remember?
- **Rule #2:** If you are over 40, make sure you have an appropriate LinkedIn profile and Facebook page today. If you don't know how to join, let your kids show you, or even better, have a young person at work "reverse mentor" you on how it works. Let that same person help you choose your profile picture.
- **Rule #3:** Know about and frequently use Google and Wikipedia. Bookmark them on your computer, and set one as your homepage.
- **Rule #4:** Peruse your local Apple store. At least learn the difference between an iPod, an iPhone and an iPad. It's all about perception."

(A Ministry of The Hills, p. 9)

Findings from the site visits to FBOs/CBOs during this study, which are discussed in Section 3, suggest that there is considerable variability in the extent to which spirituality and religious content are infused into job clubs delivered by faith-based organizations.

3. Research Findings on Employment and Training Services Provided by FBO/CBOs

Unlike the steady stream of experimental research studies that have been conducted since the 1970s on job search assistance and job clubs in the public sector (discussed earlier), there appear to be no rigorous experimental studies (or even non-experimental studies) of the effects/impacts of FBO/CBO-affiliated job clubs on employment outcomes for job seekers. Despite the lack of empirical studies on the differences that FBO/CBO-affiliated job clubs might make in terms of improving job search methods, intensifying job search activities, and ultimately speeding the return to work for unemployed individuals, there have been some implementation studies of the role of community-based and faith-based organizations in providing employment/training services and other human services. For example, a study for DOL conducted early in the implementation of the George W. Bush Administration's faith-based initiatives documented and assessed the role of faith-based organizations in providing employment-related services, based on telephone interviews conducted in five cities with congregations and other faith-based organizations and local WIA officials (Kramer et al., 2003a). This study assessed the role of these organizations in delivering employment-related services broadly defined, which could include job postings, clothing or transportation assistance for job interviews or more programmatic or extensive services. At the time, only a few large congregations provided programmatic services, and none used government funds. Since that study, small grants issued under the Department of Health and Human Services (DHHS) Compassion Capital Fund (CCF) have provided mentoring, ministerial counseling, and other types of assistance to help with transitioning unemployed individuals into the workforce, but none of these grant-funded efforts have as yet been evaluated.

The limited literature on other employment programs operated by faith-based organizations suggests some specific attributes that might broadly apply to FBO/CBO-sponsored job clubs. Three assessments offer similar findings on differences in the nature of services provided by secular and faith-based programs, and a glimpse of the possible effects of the infusion of faith-based/spiritual content into job club curriculum:

- In a study of the comparative effectiveness of faith-based and secular (government, nonprofit, and for-profit) welfare-to-work programs, Monsma (2006) found that the secular programs studied emphasized vocational and hard skills training and had, particularly among for-profit providers, significantly higher completion and employment rates, and that overall, faith-based programs were not more effective.[12] However, the faith-based programs emphasized soft skills training, and, as expressed by client perceptions, were especially effective in providing a sympathetic understanding and emotional support.
- Kennedy and Bielefeld (2007) studied the Indiana Manpower Placement and Comprehensive Training (IMPACT) program, Indiana's welfare-to-work program. They developed dimensions of religiosity in contractors providing employment services under Charitable Choice and then assessed the characteristics of non-faith based (NFB), moderately faith-based (MFB), and strongly faith-based (SFB) programs in providing services. They found SFB providers reported more clients

participated in religious activity, but also reported more negative reactions to religious elements of programming. They also found SFB organizations were somewhat less connected to community networks than MFB organizations and provided fewer job-related services than MFB or NFB providers. Taken together with the Monsma findings above, strongly faith-based programs may have less emphasis on direct job services and weaker connections with community and workforce networks.

- An evaluation funded by the Department of Labor of Reclamando Nuestro Futuro (Reclaiming Our Future, or RNF), assessed outcomes for 28 programs (22 faith-based and 6 community-based) to assist at-risk and adjudicated Latino youth obtain education or training, find employment, and avoid involvement with the juvenile justice system. RNF was a three-year, $10 million effort administered by the Latino Coalition for Faith and Community Initiatives, and the programs operated in six cities under sub-grants from the Coalition, which functioned as an intermediary for the sub-grantees. Program participants engaged in job skills training (classes and other hard skills training), job readiness or job preparation (e.g., soft skills, resume writing, interviewing, anger management), and mentoring (with adult volunteers or program case managers). Monsma and Smidt (2009) assessed RNF program outcomes as well as the relationship between the small FBOs/CBOs and the intermediary organization, a typical model used to provide technical assistance to engage small and grassroots organizations in public programming. Although the target population in RNF was more challenging than in many adult employment programs, and only about one-fifth to one-quarter of the participants engaged in substantial hours of skills or job preparation training, the study found about 28 percent experienced positive employment outcomes (entered an occupational training course or full-time post-secondary education, or unsubsidized employment) and 91 percent did not recidivate. Time spent in the program was associated with the largest positive outcomes. An interesting finding from this study is that the standards, systems, and training provided by the Latino Coalition greatly increased subgrantees' level of professionalism, their ability to serve needy youths, and their ability to sustain their programs using a variety of funding sources. The authors also noted that the subgrantees whose funding was discontinued by the Coalition tended to have worse outcomes than those whose funding had continued.

The findings from these employment-related efforts suggest that FBOs/CBOs may be particularly effective at providing more personalized and supportive job club environments, which may be appealing to and more effective for certain subpopulations of job seekers. Additionally, they suggest the need to examine linkages between FBOs/CBOs and the public workforce system, in that some FBO/CBO job club participants may require more substantive remedial education and occupational training services before job search assistance provided by a FBO/CBO or public sector job club might be an effective intervention.

4. Research Findings about Other Human Services Provided by FBO/CBOs
Although there is a sparse literature on FBOs/CBOs providing job clubs and other employment-related services, the literature on FBO/CBO provision of human services is more plentiful and addresses several other issues applicable to the evaluation of FBO/CBO-

provided job clubs. The research is instructive regarding services in which grassroots organizations, including faith-based organizations, may have particular expertise, including the role of religion/spirituality in the content/provision of human services; as well as the capacity of FBOs/CBOs to deliver desired services and, in particular, to operate under public rules.

Researchers have noted that FBOs/CBOs with deep roots in the community and perceived legitimacy may have a particular advantage in engaging individuals who are not motivated to seek assistance from large programs that feel less familiar or more bureaucratic, or who are resistant to any intervention at all. Monsma (2006) found that participants in faith-based welfare-to-work programs reported a more supportive environment than welfare recipients participating in public or for-profit programs. For programs that serve hard-to-reach populations, such as runaway youth or substance abusers, establishing contact and building trust are the difficult but essential first steps to making connections to needed treatment, and FBOs/CBOs may be especially equipped to do so (Kramer et al., 2003a). Individuals already involved with a local congregation or other community groups may be more inclined to join a job club operated by such a congregation or community organization, compared to joining a job club at a public workforce agency with which they are unfamiliar.

FBOs/CBOs themselves represent a broad array of organizational types. FBOs/CBOs can have active religious connections or not. Organizations with reference to religion in their name may reflect long lost religious affiliations, or they may maintain a connection to religion in mission or governing structure but deliver primarily or only secular services.[13] Or they may be driven by faith issues and provide religious/spiritual-infused services. Religion can be a defining feature of the mission, structure, and administrative processes of an organization, which affects the style and content of services, or it can be an explicit component of the services themselves. Further, FBOs/CBOs can offer informal services or more programmatic and structured services. They can be small, locally-based and regarded as grassroots but have highly professional staff, or they can be large but still be locally-based and maintain an intimate connection to the community they serve. FBOs/CBOs tend to extensively use volunteers in the provision of services (e.g., volunteer job club instructors or case managers/mentors provided by a congregation).

Faith itself is sometimes touted as a potentially powerful tool in personal transformation and may be inferred to play a role in helping job seekers to emotionally cope with job loss and challenges (such as rejection) during the job search period. The role of faith may have particular relevance for jobs clubs in which faith and prayer may be used as part of job search skills training and motivational techniques to intensify job search efforts. The important role of faith and prayer in dealing with job loss and reconnecting to the job market is to varying degrees emphasized in the curriculum that guides job clubs (as illustrated earlier). For definitional and methodological reasons, identifying the "faith factor" has proven to be more problematic, and determining its effect on outcomes correspondingly difficult. Similar to faith-based organizations, it should be noted that "secular" job clubs operated by the public sector and community-based organizations rely on peer support, fellowship, and case management to provide participants with emotional/psychological support. It is possible that the fellowship and support that is part of job clubs (and in the case of faith-based job clubs, spiritual/faith content infused in job clubs) may help to mitigate the potentially deleterious psychological consequences of long-term spells of unemployment. For example, Diette et al.

(2012) have documented that long-term unemployment can be associated with psychological and emotional distress:

> ...The fundamental idea is that if involuntary joblessness leads to psychological distress, then persons moving from an employed to an unemployed state will exhibit a decline in mental health, and those switching over time from an unemployed to a working state will experience an improvement in psychological well-being. Numerous researchers report evidence consistent with this perspective. Their findings, although compelling, are not definitive evidence in favor of the hypothesis that unemployment causes deterioration in mental health. (Diette et.al, in Appelbaum, 2012).

Drawing on data from two large nationally-representative data sources – the National Comorbidity Survey Replication (NCS-R) and the National Latino and Asian American Study (NLAAS), Diette et al. (2012) estimate the impact of short- and long-term unemployment on a broad measure of emotional health. Diette et al. (2012) find that short- and long-term unemployment is associated with psychological distress among "vulnerable" individuals and that "buffers" can help to mitigate effects of unemployment for this group:

> Among these persons, exposure to either short- or long-term unemployment over the past year leads to a significant increase in their reporting to have experienced poor emotional health in the past year relative to similar persons who worked throughout the past year. For instance, vulnerable individuals who were subject to long-term unemployment were 58 percent more likely (Model 3) to experience psychological distress compared to those vulnerable persons in the labor force who worked the entire past year. Consistent with our theory, we find that a number of buffers—being married, having adult children, having friends with whom you are in regular contact, and being part of a religious community—significantly reduce the odds of experiencing psychological distress over the past year, regardless of exposure to unemployment, for vulnerable persons (see Appendix Table 4A.4). However, emotional health does not appear to be directly related to such buffers for resilient persons. (Diette et al., 2012)

In some recent work, researchers have attempted to develop dimensions of religiosity, including formal and informal religious affiliation or financial support, religious presence in mission, and governing structures and administrative processes (Green and Sherman 2002; Kennedy and Bielefeld 2003; Monsma 2004; Kramer et al. 2005; Noyes 2008; Gais 2008). A recent attempt to characterize the faith components in 20 substance abuse services delivered by Gospel Rescue Missions illustrates the complexities (De Jong and Horn 2008). Gais (2008) attempted to use random assignment to study the dimensions of program attributes, including faith, which might explain treatment outcomes of substance abusers in faith-infused and secular treatment programs. Randomization of study participants could not be completed, but reported findings illustrate the challenge of isolating the effects of religion on treatment outcomes, given the variation in the nature and intensity of religious elements and variation in client characteristics and subtle client/staff interactions (Gais and Arria 2010; Gais et al. 2010).

Noyes (2008) reviewed outcome studies of faith-based interventions and cites selection bias, lack of attention to intervening variables, challenges disentangling the effect of faith from other program characteristics, and imprecision around measuring the intensity of the treatment. In addition, reviewers have observed that faith-based and secular organizations have different perspectives on measures of success—religiously-based interventions tend to focus on personal transformation informed by religious teaching, while secular organizations focus on tangible outcomes such as job attainment or parenting skills (Noyes 2008 and Smith 2006).

Two major efforts considering a broad swath of research have attempted to assess the comparative effectiveness of faith-based and secular services. Boddie and Cnaan (2006) produced an edited volume that addressed methodological challenges in evaluating the effects of faith-infused services and the comparative effectiveness of social services delivered by faith- based and secular organizations. As in other research, specifying faith content, measuring the degree of faith integration in administration and service delivery, and specifying outcome measures across interventions were common challenges raised. In this volume, Grettenberger et al. cite small sample sizes, selection bias (a particular challenge when faith adherents may be predisposed to choose faith-infused programs), attrition and lack of long-term tracking, and receipt of multiple treatments all make it difficult to decipher the effects of faith-infused services on outcomes. Boddie and Cnaan conclude from the multiple papers that the research does not permit a clear understanding of the comparative effectiveness of faith-based interventions. The editors cite the need for more research to classify religious and spiritual content, to tease out the effects of organizational characteristics on the content and effectiveness of services, to better specify outcome variables in order to refine the measurement of effectiveness, and to address internal and external validity problems arising from high attrition rates. It is clear from the literature that there have been formidable challenges both to planning and executing rigorous studies of FBO/CBO-based human services.

C. Implications of the Literature Review for Evaluation of FBO/CBO-Sponsored Job Clubs

This literature review – and the lack of empirical impact findings on FBO/CBO-affiliated job clubs – underscore the importance and need for additional rigorous evaluations to better understand the interventions offered by FBO/CBO job clubs and the results for participants of such job clubs in comparison to job clubs offered by public employment agencies. The evaluations of public sector job clubs indicate that it is possible to apply experimental methods (involving random assignment of job club participants) to assess the impacts of various job club interventions. As discussed earlier in this report, such experimental studies of job clubs have demonstrated significant positive impacts on earlier return to work and job placement rates – and it is likely that such impacts would translate to FBO/CBO-affiliated job clubs. However, the fact that there have not been experimental studies of FBO/CBO job clubs may be because there is a lack of resources available to sponsor such evaluations, lack of expertise in setting up and implementing random assignment-type studies, or because FBO/CBO sponsoring such initiatives are unwilling or unable to subject their job clubs to more rigorous study. For example, there may be an unwillingness or inability for churches/congregations to randomly assign job seekers to treatment and control groups for ethical reasons (e.g., unwillingness to withhold much needed job search assistance to unemployed individuals). Further, such initiatives may not serve sufficient numbers of participants within a year or several-year period to generate minimal detectable effects under experimental research designs.

Based on the lack of systematic and empirical-based findings about FBO/CBO-sponsored job clubs, it is important for this study (and subsequent evaluations) to: (1) provide a more detailed understanding of the differences/similarities between FBO/CBO- and public sector-based job clubs, (2) gain input from FBO/CBO job club operators about the types of data collected on participants and perspectives on whether their organizations would be willing and capable of participating in experimental/non-experimental studies, and (3) examine the potential challenges for mounting future rigorous, experimental evaluations to assess the net impacts of FBO/CBO job clubs. Though not exhaustive, some of the evaluation-related issues not addressed by the existing literature that need to be further explored (and which were the subject of discussions with key stakeholders and program staff during site visits conducted under this study) include the following:

- Are there existing quantifiable measures of the extent to which job club curriculum and instruction are infused with religiosity/spirituality or secular forms of fellowship?
- In developing alternative evaluation designs for the future study of FBO/CBO job clubs, what is the best strategy for classifying faith-based job clubs for evaluation purposes? For example, should all faith-based clubs be studied as a group, or are there natural groupings that would permit an evaluation to explore the efficacy of alternative types of faith-based job clubs?
- Why have there been few studies of FBO/CBO job clubs and, in particular, why have experimental studies not been mounted to explore net impacts of FBO/CBO job clubs? Was it because it was not feasible to mount such rigorous studies or because the researchers have not been interested in impacts?
- Are there difficulties inherent in obtaining job club participant data and tracking participants over extended follow-up periods that are specific to FBO/CBO job clubs versus public sector operated job clubs (e.g., difficulty collecting intake/background data or establishing automated participant tracking systems, difficulties conducting follow-up surveys and obtaining satisfactory response rates, unavailability of earnings data similar to Unemployment Insurance (UI) wage record data and other programmatic/ administrative data that can sometimes be secured for evaluations of public sector initiatives (e.g., for UI claimants, TANF participants, etc.)?
- The literature indicates that it is likely that people who enroll in faith-based job clubs are different from those who participate in secular job clubs: is it feasible and/or ethical to use random assignment to determine which type of job club participants are offered?
- If random assignment is not feasible, what are the most promising nonexperimental strategies for evaluating FBO/CBO-based job clubs, noting the problems of selection bias, measuring key variables, and other factors that can lead to biased evaluations?

The next two sections of this report provide some exploratory findings with respect to FBO/CBO views on evaluation and data collection necessary to support more rigorous evaluation, as well as assesses the potential for implementing more rigorous experimental study of FBO/CBO- sponsored job clubs.

Section 3. Key Finding from the Environmental Scan

This section provides a synthesis of key findings from an "environmental scan" that included: (1) interviews with seven stakeholders knowledgeable about job clubs; and (2) site visits conducted in six localities, focusing on job clubs operated by FBOs/CBOs. This section first highlights results of the stakeholder interviews and then provides a more detailed and expansive synthesis of the key findings from the site visits. The final section of this section offers some final thoughts and conclusions based on the key findings from the stakeholder interviews and site visits, especially with regard to more rigorous study of the impacts on job seekers of participation in FBO/CBO-sponsored job clubs.

A. Key Findings from Interviews with Key Stakeholders

As part of the environmental scan, the research team conducted telephone interviews with seven stakeholders knowledgeable about the operation of job clubs, including those sponsored by FBOs/CBOs. Using a semi-structured discussion guide (see Appendix A for a copy of this guide), the evaluation team completed interviews with stakeholders lasting 60 to 90 minutes. These interviews provided an opportunity to question each stakeholder on a range of topics related to job clubs operated by FBO/CBOs, including types of individuals targeted and served by these job clubs (and whether there has been an increase/decrease in the numbers/types of individuals served and in the number of FBOs/CBOs sponsoring job clubs); differences in format/characteristics/strategies of FBO/CBO versus public sector (American Job Centers) operated job clubs; and the extent to which FBO/CBO-sponsored job clubs have been evaluated in the past and the prospects for evaluating such job clubs in the future. The stakeholders interviewed were: (1) Lisa Rice, Brevard (Florida) Workforce; (2) Brad Turner-Little, Goodwill Industries International; (3) Elizabeth Wilson, Church of God in Christ (COGIC); (4) Joy Maguire-Dooley, Lisle Township (Illinois), an operator of job clubs for over 20 years; (5) Peter Weddle of Weddles.com and the International Association of Employment Web Sites; (6) Stephen Monsma, Research Fellow, Paul B. Henry Institute for the Study of Christianity and Politics, Calvin College (formerly of Pepperdine University); and (7) Jennifer Noyes, Institute for Research on Poverty, University of Wisconsin–Madison. Stakeholders were identified through the literature review conducted as part of this study and based on input from DOL. Key findings from these stakeholder interviews are briefly highlighted below.

Stakeholders See General Increase in Number of Job Clubs Operated by FBOs/CBOs and Other Organizations in Recent Years. Several stakeholders indicated that they believe there has been growth in the number of job clubs in operation across the country, especially in response to the massive dislocations occurring as a result of the deep recession of 2007/08 and the continuing elevated levels of unemployment and underemployment that have persisted during the recovery. According to some stakeholders, increases in the number of job clubs and individuals attending job clubs have occurred for public sector-sponsored job clubs, as well as among those sponsored by faith-based and community-based organizations. For example, one stakeholder observed the following: *"Yes, there is an increase in the* *number of people participating as well as the number of Job Clubs...The faith-based community has done a great job with this, providing a space in their congregations as well as in the community at large for people who have lost jobs or [their] jobs have gone away. They've provided a good safe place for people to go – so you've seen growth. When the economy recovers, it may be that this type of service [job clubs] offered by CBOs and FBOs, and the need for it, may go away."*

Despite a Perceived Increase in the Number of Job Clubs (and the Number of Attendees), There Is a Lack of Systematic Data Available to Document This Change. Several stakeholders noted there is a lack of systematic data available to document just how much of a change has occurred in recent years in both the number of job clubs run by FBOs/CBOs and the number of attendees at FBO/CBO-sponsored job clubs. A number of stakeholders reported that they were unaware of any reliable registry or count of the number of FBO/CBO-sponsored job clubs held on a weekly/monthly basis, or the attendance at such job clubs. Overall, job clubs run by FBOs/CBOs are constantly in flux, with new job clubs coming into existence each month and others disbanding for a variety of reasons (e.g., lack of attendees, loss of volunteer facilitators, and changing priorities of congregations). Further, while many job clubs keep lists of attendees and contact information for each job club held, according to several stakeholders interviewed, it is very unusual for FBOs/CBOs to maintain participant-level automated data systems (similar to public sector organizations, such as American Job Centers, or what is maintained by some well-established CBOs, such as Goodwill). Consequently, there is no reliable way to systematically document the number or types of job seekers attending such job clubs during a given year or over time.

The Apparent Increase in the Number of FBO/CBO-Sponsored Job Clubs Is Due to Several Factors, Including the Deep Recession and Interest of FBOs/CBOs in Addressing Critical Needs of Community Members. According to several stakeholders, the steep downturn of the U.S. economy in 2007-08 and surging numbers of unemployed and underemployed workers created strong demand for job search assistance, providing an impetus for FBOs/CBOs to form job clubs to meet urgent needs within their communities. Stakeholders cited several other contributing factors for the apparent expansion of FBO/CBO-sponsored job clubs, including the desire of churches/congregations to help unemployed individuals within their own congregations as well as the surrounding communities and the relatively low costs for establishing and maintaining job clubs (i.e., with volunteers and a donated church meeting room, initial start-up costs of a job club are quite low for a congregation). Further, the formation of a job club conforms well to the mission of many FBOs/CBOs to serve their communities and, particularly in the case of churches, may provide meaningful, ongoing volunteer service opportunities for members of the congregation.

FBO/CBO Job Clubs Tend to Draw Job Seekers Reflective of the Area Served and Sometimes Attract a Somewhat Different Group of Job Seekers Compared to Public Sector Sponsored Job Clubs. One stakeholder observed that FBO/CBO job clubs may offer an attractive alternative to similar clubs operated by the public sector: *"Job Clubs sponsored by FBOs/CBOs provide a sense of community and connectedness; it is safe place. That's been an important tactic that their job clubs are based on – it appeals to this population. These are people who had been in the middle class and are teetering on moving down; they are the long- term unemployed, including white-collar professionals. The job club strategy is not threatening; it is welcoming. It doesn't have the look and feel of the traditional public workforce system with a case management component."* Job clubs offered by FBOs/CBOs may be held in locations (e.g., at a nearby church meeting room) and at times (e.g., in the evening) that are more convenient than those operated by the public sector. The lack of paperwork burden may also appeal to some job seekers (versus intake forms and other documentation that might be required by public sector agencies operating job clubs).

There is Significant Diversity in the Structure and Content of FBO/CBO-Sponsored Job Clubs, with Varying Degrees of Emphasis on Spirituality/Religious Content. Stakeholders maintained there is substantial diversity across FBOs and CBOs in the format, content, and operation of job clubs. Several stakeholders noted that while some faith-based organizations might begin and end their job clubs with a prayer, the job club session itself might have little or no faith-based/religious content. Even those FBO-sponsored job clubs infused with religious/spiritual references tend to focus the bulk of their 60- to 90-minute job club meetings on many of the same principles and instructional techniques as those covered in secular job clubs operated by CBOs and public sector organizations – e.g., the importance of networking, developing/practicing "elevator speeches," basics of developing an effective resume, job interviewing techniques, and effective job search approaches. According to some stakeholders, one important difference in job clubs operated by FBOs/CBOs is that they may provide more opportunity than those operated by public-sector organizations for peer group discussions, including discussion of the emotional stress involved in job loss and the frustrations accompanying job search, as well as the role that faith and prayer (particularly in FBOs) can play in helping job seekers cope with stress and feelings of despair and hopelessness. Several of the stakeholders highlighted what they perceived as potential differences in the format and content of job clubs, while emphasizing that there is a lot of variability across FBOs/CBOs. Some of the stakeholder observations about possible structural/operational differences between job clubs sponsored by FBOs/CBOs and public sector organizations are highlighted below:

- **Size/numbers attending job club sessions/operation of sessions.** One stakeholder observed that FBO/CBO-sponsored job clubs can be quite small in terms of attendance compared with those held at American Job Centers. For example, one or two FBO/CBO volunteers may operate a job club, which serves no more than 10 participants each week. Another stakeholder reported that attendance at the job clubs operated by the FBOs/CBOs in her area averages from 10-15 participants, with no more than 30 attendees in the largest. Attendance at the job club at the local public workforce agency ranges from 10 to 30. Another stakeholder noted that a FBO job club may operate on a shoestring budget out of a church basement; in comparison, public sector-sponsored job clubs tend to be held in larger government-operated facilities and run by larger/more professional paid staff (capable of serving larger numbers of job seekers).

- **Curriculum used and topics covered during job clubs.** According to several stakeholders interviewed, facilitators for FBO/CBO-sponsored job clubs may or may not be guided by a curriculum, although they will typically follow a basic structure and format during each meeting. Several stakeholders noted that compared to the public sector, faith-based job clubs often place more emphasis on personal encouragement, raising self-esteem, providing time for peer group discussions related to job search challenges, and generally responding to emotional needs of participants. One stakeholder noted that some, but not all, FBOs infuse religion and spiritual content as a support for job club attendees – for example, emphasizing: *"God loves you and has a plan for you – and we are here to help you discover that plan."* Another stakeholder noted the important focus FBOs often place on motivation and positive re-enforcement for job club attendees (in comparison to public sector organizations): *"More emphasis is placed on the positive, helping people stay motivated, encouraging them through positive affirmations. FBOs are more likely to provide touchy support as opposed to dealing only with the facts and figures of resumes. That is the juice that keeps people coming back to FBO job clubs. It feels good. The door is open, welcoming. Individuals don't have to stand in line or take a number to get services...It is totally different in FBOs – they are open, welcoming, they provide food, are encouraging, they look beyond fault lines and help in a much more positive manner. They are more engaging, faith-friendly and much less regimented about providing services. Document requirements are important for public sector workforce organizations – less stringent with FBOs. There is no turn away because you don't have the paper requirements. These are the things that make being unemployed unpleasant – you are already unemployed and then you have to feel bad about it. FBOs do a better job at acknowledging the pain people are in."*

- **Kinds of instructional methods used during job clubs.** FBO/CBO-sponsored job clubs typically emphasize peer group and small group discussions, often in direct response to the immediate challenges that attendees are experiencing as they search for a job. Often such sessions offer ample time for participants to share experiences and pose questions – and often attendees will have the opportunity to address questions and share feedback with others attending the job club. For example, one stakeholder observed: *"FBOs are more interactive – they are sharing a lot more, the hurt and grief over the loss of the job. The FBO is trying to move them through all of that with a more holistic approach."* Another stakeholder added: *"FBO job clubs are more likely to be in small groups – more feedback, open dialogue, more sharing as opposed to lecture style in the public workforce development system...[There is] more interaction in FBOs where there is not as much restriction to get through a discussion within a quick framework. Web-based instruction is more likely in the public sector – they have more access to that. FBOs do not have as many resources."*

- **Types of instructors/facilitators used.** Several stakeholders noted faith-based organizations are more likely to rely on volunteers to lead their job clubs, whereas public sector organizations and larger CBOs typically rely upon paid professional staff. They felt that facilitators leading job clubs at FBOs may have little formal training or past experience in providing workforce services (e.g., and may even come to their facilitation roles from being a former participant of the job club): *"Sometimes job club facilitators have struggled with joblessness themselves and may draw on their personal experiences...job club participants may be linked up with a volunteer from the church...Often there are discussions in FBO job clubs to talk through issues faced by participants."* A second stakeholder noted: *"...FBOs are volunteer-based. CBOs also have volunteers to help out as well, but CBOs have people who are trained in workforce development strategies. Local congregations have a minister or lay person who is responsible for job clubs but they are volunteer-based."* Other stakeholders noted that FBOs often identify and recruit speakers to make presentations on their area of expertise (e.g., a corporate hiring manager) for periodic job club sessions.

- **Job development/placement assistance provided.** According to one stakeholder, public sector-operated job clubs tend to make more systematic efforts in terms of identifying job openings in their localities and providing job leads, including making available automated job bank databases. In comparison, FBO/CBO-sponsored job clubs are likely to provide more informal job placement assistance: *"...[FBO-operated] job clubs may provide some job leads; support is important in FBO job club – participants may get a hug and told maybe tomorrow will be better even if they do not find a job."* One stakeholder noted that FBOs typically have fewer links with employers and less comprehensive listings of job vacancies in their locality: *"FBOs don't have as many connections with employers who are hiring. They refer back to the public workforce system. Some FBOs scan the Internet for [job] openings. But if the job club is only meeting monthly or quarterly, they might not be as accurate, up-to-date [as listings available through the public workforce system] – so there is not as much referral to employers."* However, stakeholders reported that as part of job club discussions at FBOs/CBOs as well as in the public sector, job seekers are often encouraged to share job openings that they identify in the course of their searches that might be appropriate for other attendees.

- **Availability of training, support services and case management.** According to several stakeholders, compared to what is available via the public workforce system and larger CBOs, there are typically fewer resources available in faith-based organizations to provide ongoing case management, training, childcare, transportation, housing, and other assistance/support services needed by job seekers. When training is needed, FBOs are likely to refer participants to an American Job Center, community college, or other education/training provider for help (and rarely have resources available to support short- or longer-term training). Sometimes churches and congregations will have clothing closets on-site or will stock emergency food supplies that can be made available for job club participants; they may also be able to offer participants bus passes or gas reimbursement on a limited basis. However, for longer-term and more sustained types of assistance to overcome barriers to finding or retaining a job (such as housing, childcare, education, training, and health care assistance), churches and congregations typically refer job club participants to more deeply-funded partners within the public sector or to larger and better funded CBOs within their communities.

- **Nature of religious and spiritual content in FBO job clubs.** Stakeholders observed that the extent to which FBOs infuse religious or spiritual content in their job clubs varies substantially and provided several examples of the ways in which faith-based organizations included such content. One stakeholder observed: *"Some FBOs offer a bible study class, but typically as a separate activity from the job club – bible study class may precede the job club and job club members may want to attend prior to the job club. FBOs may stress during job clubs that 'God has a plan for your life; He loves you; you may have made a mistake in the past, but He forgives you; informal references may be made to a loving God...FBO job clubs tend to be aimed at building confidence and self- esteem and sense of self-worth and may use religious references to achieve this."* A second stakeholder commented on the differences in content of job clubs run by CBOs versus some FBOs: *"One of the critical differences between CBOs and FBOs is that FBOs [sometimes] ground the job club experience from the 'place of call' – you are on this Earth for a reason and that reason is connected to a divine purpose or objective. You have that element of spirituality that gets woven into FBO job clubs. We don't do that at [our CBO]. We try to help people to understand what their interests are but the language of call is a filter that the FBO community applies to the job club strategy – 'God loves you, He is part of this process.' The public workforce system does not talk about that and most CBOs don't get into that component. Our organization looks at the sense of self-discovery/re-discovery and purpose but that lens of spirituality/religious- connectivity is not there."*

Stakeholders Indicate There Is a Paucity of Past Evaluations of FBO/CBO Job Clubs and Are Not Optimistic About the Feasibility of Implementing Experimental or Quasi-Experimental Evaluation Designs to Explore Impacts of FBO/CBO Job Clubs. None of the stakeholders interviewed were able to identify past or ongoing evaluations of FBO/CBO job clubs, including non-experimental or experimental studies. Several of the stakeholders indicated that FBOs and smaller CBOs generally collect very little participant-level data, usually limited to the job club attendee's name, date(s) of job club attendance, contact information (usually a telephone and email contact), and, in some cases, occupation/type of job the individual is seeking. Virtually no outcome data are collected, although some FBOs/CBOs maintain anecdotal information about job club attendees who find jobs (in part, to be able to share "success stories" with other job club attendees). FBOs and smaller CBOs do not typically maintain, and appear not likely to be interested in maintaining, a participant-level data system, though some do maintain rudimentary registries of attendees (for example, a listing of attendees in an Excel spreadsheet). One stakeholder reported that she keeps a handwritten log of all job club attendees and the number who have found jobs after participating in her job club. According to several of the stakeholders interviewed, one of the most attractive aspects of FBO/CBO-sponsored job clubs for attendees (and the FBOs/CBOs sponsoring such clubs) is the lack of paperwork/bureaucracy associated with such programs. Further, many of the FBOs operate their programs with only volunteer staff and on a shoestring budget and, consequently, lack computer equipment and/or the technical knowledge or staffing to set-up and manage an automated participant-level data system. Further, few (if any), FBO-sponsored job clubs collect identifying information (such as Social Security number) that could be used to match to administrative data maintained by the government (such as the Unemployment Insurance wage record data). It should, however, be noted that one stakeholder interviewed (from a large, nationwide CBO) indicated that his organization maintained a fairly sophisticated participant- level data system, which included participant characteristics, services received, and some tracking of participant outcomes over a limited period (in part, in response to requests for such data from major funders). Overall, none of the stakeholders were optimistic about the prospects for faith-based organizations (and most CBOs, except for the largest and most well-funded) to collect additional and systematic participant characteristics data at the time of job seeker entry into job clubs, nor to be able to collect employment outcomes over time in a systematic manner for job club attendees. Additionally, when asked, none of the stakeholders felt it would be feasible to apply a random assignment-type experimental design to explore FBO/CBO-sponsored job club impacts (in part, because of concerns over denial of services to control group members and data collection burden/complexity associated with random assignment-type studies). None of the stakeholders had suggestions for how to apply either experimental or a range of non- experimental methods to evaluate FBO/CBO-sponsored job clubs in the future.

B. Key Findings from Site Visits to Job Clubs in Six Local Areas

The second component of the environmental scan focused on site visits conducted in Fall 2013 to six localities across the country where job clubs are operated by FBOs and CBOs. Two- person research teams spent two to three days in each selected local area, observing at least one (and, in some sites, two) job club(s) sponsored by an FBO, one job club operated by a CBO (in most sites) and, if possible, one job club operated by a local public workforce agency. In addition to the observations, team members also met with job club facilitators/leaders either before or after the job club session and, using a semi-structured discussion guide, conducted a 1.5 to 2 hour interview that covered various topics and issues related to the job club's organizational structure, program objectives, services and activities provided, and data collection efforts (see Appendices B and C for copies of site visit discussion guides). If the local public workforce agency/AJC did not sponsor a job club at the time of the visit, team members still met with agency staff and completed an interview to learn about any experiences operating job clubs in the past, reasons for not offering a job club currently, and any linkages with FBOs/CBOs sponsoring job clubs.[14] This section summarizes key findings from the observations and interviews conducted during these site visits.

1. Overview of Job Clubs Visited

In selecting the locations for the six site visits, the research team relied on a number of resources, including recommendations from the key stakeholders who participated in the telephone interviews conducted earlier, a review of the Center for Faith-Based and Neighborhood Partnerships (CFBNP) website's state-by-state directory of job clubs, and input from DOL's CFBNP staff. Criteria considered for site selection included: geographic diversity (e.g., region of the country, urban/ suburban/rural service area); targeted populations for the job clubs; extent of religious influence in the job clubs (i.e., use of strongly faith-based curriculum vs. more secular instructional material); length of time job clubs have been in operation (i.e., newly-formed vs. more established); size of job clubs (i.e., under 20 versus over 100 attendees per job club); job clubs' use of innovative strategies for serving job seekers; and presence of job clubs operated by and/or linked with the public workforce agencies. A purposive site selection process was used to select the following six localities for visits:

- Northern New Jersey
- Cleveland/Akron, OH
- Atlanta, GA
- Minneapolis/St. Paul, MN
- Washington, DC Metro (MD/VA)
- San Francisco/Bay Area (CA)

Within these six areas selected for site visits, the research team identified 21 local organizations (ten FBOs, four CBOs, and seven local public workforce agencies/WIBs) for site visits. As shown in Table 3-1, the team ultimately observed regularly-scheduled job clubs and conducted in-depth interviews with staff in 16 of these organizations – eight FBOs, four CBOs, and four public workforce agencies – selected to represent the range of characteristics, formats, and activities of job clubs currently operated by FBOs, CBOs, and public workforce agencies.

Table 3-1. Overview of Job Club Sites Visited

Name of Job Club	Organization Sponsoring Job Club	Site Visit Location
FBO-SPONSORED JOB CLUBS		
Job Seekers	Trinity Church of Princeton, NJ	Northern New Jersey
Job Partnership of Cleveland (JPC)	Mt. Zion Congregational Church	Cleveland/Akron, OH
Crossroads Career Network	Snellville United Methodist Church	Atlanta, GA
Roswell United Methodist Church(RUMC) Job Networking	Roswell United Methodist Church	Atlanta, GA
SOAR 4 Jobs	St. Odilia Catholic Community	Minneapolis/St. Paul, MN
Career Network Ministry (CNM)	McLean Bible Church	Washington, DC Metro(MD/VA)
Severna Park United Methodist Church Employment Network Group	Severna Park United Methodist Church	Washington, DC Metro(MD/VA)
Christ the King (CTK) Parish Job Networking Ministry	Christ The King Parish in Pleasant Hill, CA	San Francisco/Bay Area (CA)
CBO-SPONSORED JOB CLUBS		
Neighbors-helping-Neighbors (NhN)	Neighbors-helping-Neighbors USA, Inc.	Northern New Jersey
Community Job Club of Stow	Community Job Club, Inc.	Cleveland/Akron, OH
Career Transition Group for Women	None – the job club is organized and operated by one volunteer	Minneapolis/St. Paul, MN
The Job Forum	San Francisco Chamber of Commerce	San Francisco/Bay Area (CA)
PUBLIC SECTOR-SPONSORED JOB CLUBS		
Jersey Job Club	New Jersey Department of Labor and Workforce Development	Northern New Jersey
Veterans Networking Group	Hennepin South Workforce Center	Minneapolis/St. Paul, MN
Arnold Station Job Club	Arnold Career Center/Anne Arundel Workforce Development Corporation	Washington, DC Metro(MD/VA)
ProMatch (a Chapter of Experience Unlimited)	NOVA WIB and California Employment Development Department (EDD)	San Francisco/Bay Area (CA)

The other five organizations, including three public workforce agencies and two FBOs, offer employment/job search services in the selected localities, but were not operating job clubs (or the team was unable to observe the job club) at the time of the site visits. Team members conducted interviews with administrators and staff in these organizations to obtain additional background information about local job club activities and program linkages. These five organizations were: Atlanta Regional Workforce Board; DeKalb Career Center/Georgia Department of Labor (Atlanta, GA); Employment Connections (Cleveland/Akron, OH); Employment Network Ministry at the New Birth Missionary Baptist Church (Atlanta. GA); and Jewish Vocational Service (San Francisco/Bay Area).[15] While information from the interviews with staff in these organizations is incorporated where appropriate, the focus of the analysis summarized in this section of the report (and detailed in the accompanying tables) is on the job clubs observed during the visits.

The following section provides an overview of selected background characteristics of the job clubs visited as part of this study.

Location of Job Clubs and Service Areas. The majority of the job clubs observed were held in facilities located in suburban areas, particularly the FBO-sponsored job clubs that convene sessions in meeting rooms in neighborhood churches. However, a few held their sessions in urban locations – including the Job Forum, which is supported by the San Francisco Chamber of Commerce and meets in their offices in downtown San Francisco, and the Job Partnership of Cleveland's (JPC) Mt. Zion Congregational Church job club site, meeting on the east side of the City of Cleveland.[16] In general, the job club administrators and facilitators viewed their service area as the geographic area from which the bulk of their job club attendees resided or worked, which was typically within a 25- to 30-mile radius of the job club's facility. As discussed in the next section of this report, job club participants typically reflected the demographic characteristics of the geographic areas from which they were drawn, and, for the most part, faced the labor market conditions of the local area served. For example, most of the participants in the Job Partnership of Cleveland's job club at the Mt. Zion Congregational Church were African Americans from the surrounding neighborhoods. However, some facilitators, including those with Christ the King Parish Networking Ministry in California and with Roswell United Methodist Church Job Networking near Atlanta, noted that a number of participants travelled great distances to attend meetings. Facilitators at the Career Network Ministry of the McLean Bible Church in Northern Virginia reported that some attendees regularly commuted for up to an hour to attend their weekly job club sessions.

Local Economic Conditions in Job Club Sites. The economic situation varied across the local areas at the time of the site visits, with the unemployment rate ranging from a low of a little over 4 percent in the areas served by the Career Network Ministry (Washington, DC Metro (MD/VA)) and the SOAR 4 Jobs program (Minneapolis/St. Paul) to a high of over 10 percent for the Neighbors-helping-Neighbors job club's service area in Essex County, NJ (see Table 3-2). The majority of the facilitators felt that local labor market conditions have improved since the 2007-08 economic downturn, resulting in increases in the number of available job openings and reflected by drops in overall attendance at job club sessions from the highs they experienced during and shortly after the recession. However, several facilitators reported that despite the improvements in the economy and the slowly decreasing unemployment rates, there were still many job seekers in need of the services that the job clubs provide. Facilitators also pointed to job seekers who find a job through the job club, are later laid off from that job or leave it looking for a better opportunity, and then return to the job club for help with a new job search. Although the sustainability of the current number of job clubs is unknown if unemployment rates fall further and attendance continues to drop (and if, as a result, the majority of the remaining attendees are the long-term unemployed with their accompanying challenges), the job clubs observed in areas with lower unemployment rates were still thriving at the time of the site visits. Several facilitators indicated that they would continue to operate their job clubs as long as one person showed up for the session looking for help.

Length of Time Job Clubs Have Been in Existence. Of the 16 job clubs visited, five have been in existence for over 15 years - Job Seekers at the Trinity Church of Princeton, Roswell United Methodist Church Job Networking, Career Networking Ministry/McLean Bible Church, ProMatch/Experience Unlimited, and the Job Forum of San Francisco. The oldest, the Job Forum in San Francisco, has been continually operating and holding weekly sessions since 1952. JobSeekers at the Trinity Church in Princeton has been in continual operation for slightly over 30 years, having been organized to address the fallout from the severe economic recession that took place in 1982. However, the majority of the job clubs visited were formed more recently, coinciding with downturns in the economy that resulted in increased numbers of unemployed job seekers. About half of the newer job clubs were formed in the early 2000s, around the time of the 2002-2003 recession and the remainder were started in the late 2000s after the severe economic downturn in 2007-08.

Motivations for Formation of Job Clubs. The majority of the FBO- and CBO-sponsored job clubs observed were launched around the time of and in response to economic downturns and the resulting increase in the number of job seekers looking for guidance and support in finding employment in the surrounding localities. Facilitators cited a number of additional motivations for creation of FBO- and CBO-sponsored job clubs that went beyond the desire to fill an unmet need for new sources of job search assistance for the newly-unemployed. For example, some reported that they wanted to offer a more supportive alternative to the services available through the local public workforce agency. Several identified the need for job search services focused on networking, provided in a "support group format" and aimed at middle-class job seekers who might not seek help through the traditional workforce agency office. Facilitators in some FBO-sponsored job clubs reported that they developed job networking ministries to help others in their congregations and communities, often linking their efforts to the teachings of the church. As one facilitator described her team's motivation for operating the job club, "[we] hear the gospel and try to make a difference." Others started job clubs to fill service gaps in their communities; one facilitator with an FBO-sponsored job club reported that several members of his church formed a job club upon learning that a fellow parishioner was traveling 30 miles to attend weekly job clubs meetings at another church.

2. Numbers and Types of Job Seekers Served by Job Clubs

The literature and several of the stakeholders interviewed for this study suggested that FBO/CBO-sponsored job clubs may attract and serve job seekers who would not otherwise seek job search assistance through public sector workforce agencies and, in some instance, may target or serve somewhat different types of job seekers (e.g., placing more emphasis on serving older workers, technical/managerial workers, congregation members, and those in the immediate surrounding neighborhood of the church or CBO). This section of the report explores patterns of attendance at job clubs visited under this study, including (1) eligibility and targeting criteria used by job clubs, (2) recruitment and referral methods used by job clubs, and (3) numbers and types of job seekers actually attending job clubs.

Table 3-2. Overview of Job Club Sites Visited

Name of Job Club	Organization Sponsoring Job Club	Geographic Area Served	Unemployment Rate for Area Served[17]	Year Club Founded
FBO-SPONSORED JOB CLUBS				
Job Seekers	Trinity Church of Princeton, NJ	Princeton, NJ (within 20-25 miles radius of Princeton)	7.2% (Mercer County)	1982
Job Partnership of Cleveland (JPC)	Mt. Zion Congregational Church	Cleveland, Ohio (principally east side area of Cleveland)	7.0% (Cleveland MSA)	2006
Crossroads Career Network	Snellville United Methodist Church	Snellville, GA (Gwinnett County/northeastern Atlanta suburbs)	7.1%	2002
Job Networking	Roswell United Methodist Church	Roswell, Georgia (northern Atlanta suburbs)	6.2%	1997
SOAR 4 Jobs	St. Odilia Catholic Community	Minneapolis, MN (primarily northeast suburbs/Shoreview area)	4.1%	2002
Career Network Ministry (CNM)	McLean Bible Church	McLean, VA (majority of the attendees are from Northern Virginia)	4.1%	1993[18]
Employment Network Group	Severna Park United Methodist Church	Anne Arundel County, MD (within 10-15 mile radius of Severna Park)	6.2%	2009
CTK Parish Job Networking Ministry	Christ The King (CTK) Parish in Pleasant Hill, CA	East Bay/Contra Costa county area east of San Francisco,	7.3%	2009
CBO-SPONSORED JOB CLUBS				
Neighbors-helping-Neighbors	Neighbors-helping-Neighbors USA, Inc.	26 locations in 8 NJ Counties (note: Cranford, NJ library location visited)	10.1% (Essex Co, NJ)	2011
Community Job Club of Stow	Community Job Club, Inc.	Stow, Ohio (principally suburban areas south of Cleveland and north of Akron, including Stow, Kent, Ravenna)	6.7% (Akron MSA)	2010
Career Transition Group for Women	None – the job club is organized and operated by one volunteer	St. Paul, MN	5.3%	2012[19]
The Job Forum	SF Chamber of Commerce	San Francisco and the surrounding Bay area	5.6%	1951

Name of Job Club	Organization Sponsoring Job Club	Geographic Area Served	Unemployment Rate for Area Served[17]	Year Club Founded
PUBLIC SECTOR- SPONSORED JOB CLUBS				
Jersey Job Club	New Jersey Department of Labor and Workforce Development	23 job clubs offered at American Job Centers across NJ (note: Essex County One- Stop Career Center visited, East Orange, NJ)	10.1% (Essex Co, NJ)	2012
Veterans Networking Group	Hennepin South Workforce Center	Bloomington, MN/southern Hennepin County	4.8%	2003
Arnold Station Job Club	Arnold Career Center/Anne Arundel Workforce Development Corporation	Middle Anne Arundel County (Annapolis, Severna Park, Arnold, MD)	6.2%	2010
ProMatch	NOVA WIB and California Employment Development Department (EDD)	NOVA WIB serves a consortium of seven cities (e.g., Palo Alto, Sunnyvale, Cupertino) in the Northern Silicon Valley.	5.8%	1993

Most of the 16 organizations visited for this study had no eligibility criteria for attendance at their job club sessions, with an overall aim of serving any and all unemployed job seekers within their service area or community. Job clubs also sought to serve new entrants to the labor market (such as recent college graduates) and employed individuals looking to change careers, increase earnings, or move from part- to full-time work (though typically, these groups made up a very small share of job seekers attending job clubs). Most often, FBOs/CBOs simply indicated in their brochures and outreach efforts that "all job seekers are welcome."[20] In the case of FBOs, none of the job clubs limited attendance to church members – and in fact, across the eight FBOs visited, church members represented either no current job club members or only a limited number. Several FBOs indicated that when they started their job clubs they had a higher concentration of church members among the attendees, but that over time congregation members came to represent a smaller (and in some case, none) portion of their total job club attendees. FBOs and CBOs indicated that the vast majority of job club attendees worked or lived within a 20- to 25-mile radius (i.e., a 30- to 45-minute drive) of the facility at which the job club was being held and that outreach and recruitment efforts typically targeted job seekers within that geographic area.

Among the four job clubs operated by public sector organizations, two of the four were open to all job seekers and career changers similar to most of the FBOs/CBOs visited; however, two other public sector-sponsored job clubs were more narrowly focused on specific subpopulations of the unemployed: (1) Hennepin South Workforce Center's Veterans Networking Group was restricted to unemployed and underemployed veterans; and (2) the NOVA WIB/California Employment Development's ProMatch job club required that job seekers interested in attending the job club be eligible and enrolled in the Workforce Investment Act (WIA) program, as well as registered with the CONNECT Job Seeker Center.

The FBO and CBO job clubs visited used similar outreach and recruitment methods as those often used by public sector workforce agencies – dissemination of flyers/brochures about the job club in the community, presentations by job club administrators/facilitators at other public and nonprofit agencies within the community to make staff and job seekers aware of the job club's existence and structure; and increasing use of the FBO/CBO's website and a variety of social media tools (including LinkedIn, Twitter, Facebook, and Meetup Groups). Once established within a community, FBO/CBO job club administrators/facilitators indicated that word-of-mouth became an increasingly important (and low-cost) approach to getting the word out about the job club, with existing and former job club members informing job-seeking family members, relatives, and friends about the job club. With many FBOs/CBOs operating their job clubs on tight budgets (usually with little or no resources available for paid advertisements or to fund marketing/outreach staff), there was extensive reliance upon inexpensive methods of outreach, such as is illustrated by one of the CBO sites visited:

- *Neighbors-helping-Neighbors (CBO-Northern New Jersey). According to the founder/President, NhN uses a variety of outreach and recruitment approaches, with an emphasis on using social media to the fullest extent possible: "We use patch.com, Facebook, and LinkedIn to drive awareness of our group. We ask members to spread the word; we attend community events and make connections with local businesses, Rotary Clubs, chambers (of commerce), Lions Clubs, and Knights of Columbus. We have flyers that we ask all our libraries to post, which include links to our web site. As we are zero-funded and work to be green, we use our website as a focal point of all information. Zero funds forces us to use all forms of free social media. We have been very successful in getting local media coverage around events and other activities. We work with our one-stops, but the support varies from county to county. Word-of-mouth is our single most important advertising -- we keep all the 'success stories' and they are powerful to read and we have them on our website."*

In addition to conducting their own outreach, the FBO/CBO job clubs that were visited relied to varying degrees on referrals from other community organizations and public sector agencies. Several of the FBOs indicated that unemployment within their surrounding community, which, in some instances affected church members, had been an important factor spurring establishment of their job clubs. Hence, some early referrals of church members to FBO-sponsored job clubs came from the pastor or other congregation members, but over a relatively short period of time (once unemployed congregation members had been served) numbers of church members waned and nearly all attendees came from elsewhere in the community. However, churches/congregations sponsoring job clubs continued to make announcements of the job club meetings during church services and posted the schedule and information about upcoming job clubs meetings in weekly church bulletins, newsletters, websites, and on bulletin boards. Therefore, while directly serving relatively few church members, congregations often played an important role in getting the word out about the job club within the community.

Overall, the majority of FBOs and CBOs visited as part of this study, while aware of workforce and training services provided through the American Job Centers (AJCs) in their locality, did not identify AJCs as an important source of referrals. However, most of the FBOs/CBOs visited made staff at AJCs aware of the schedule for job club meetings and requested that AJC staff refer unemployed individuals in need of job club services to meetings. AJCs also sometimes helped to get out the word about upcoming FBO/CBO-sponsored job clubs (and other events associated with these job clubs, such as job fairs) by posting information on their websites or making flyers available in their offices about the job club and informing participants, where appropriate, that such job clubs were a valuable supplemental service available within the community. Several CBOs and FBOs characterized their linkages with local AJCs as "strong" in terms of receiving help from AJCs in getting the word out about upcoming job club meetings. Perhaps more important than helping with outreach and providing referrals, AJCs were available to provide supplemental employment services, and in some instances (if referred job seekers met eligibility requirements and funding was available), training services through programs such as the Workforce Investment Act (WIA) and Trade Adjustment Assistance (TAA). In one case, an Atlanta AJC worked with the Employment Network Ministry of the New Birth Missionary Baptist Church to conduct job fairs in the large church facility.

Table 3-3 highlights the number and types of participants attending job club sessions at the 16 job clubs visited. The job clubs generally attracted job seekers from within a 30- to 45-minute drive of the facility in which the job club was being held – and as such, subpopulations served were broadly reflective of the community served. For example, the job club operated by Job Partnership of Cleveland (JPC) at its Mount Zion Congregational Church site drew mostly active job seekers from the near east side of Cleveland, serving an almost entirely African- American population from the surrounding community. This program, however, attracted job seekers with a variety of characteristics, from those with less than high school degrees to those with postgraduate degrees, laborers and service workers as well as professional and technical workers, and substantial numbers of veterans, as well as ex-offenders re-entering the labor market. It is interesting to note that a majority of the 12 FBO/CBO job clubs visited attracted a significant number of middle-age to older-age job seekers (i.e. age 40 and older), with several of the job clubs visited also tending to attract mostly white-collar professional, middle- management, and technical workers, for example:

- *Neighbor's-helping-Neighbors (CBO-NJ). NhN job clubs, held weekly or bi-weekly in 26 mostly suburban localities across eight New Jersey counties, attracted substantial numbers of older workers (50 years of age older) dislocated from white-collar, professional and technical jobs. Because of its emphasis on peer group sharing during job clubs, NhN also tended to attract and keep job seekers interested in helping others within the group and willing to share their job search experiences with other job seekers.*

- *Community Job Club of Stow (CBO-OH). This job club, open to anyone in the community, mainly draws job seekers from Stow and surrounding communities to the south of Cleveland and north of Akron (including Kent and Ravenna). An outreach brochure notes that the organization offers services for "experienced mature professionals, new grads, veterans, and others who are actively seeking better career opportunities and support in their job search to secure employment faster." The job club seems to attract middle-aged and older workers (with average age of attendees being about 45) – who are termed "mature professionals." Nearly all attendees are white; there is a range of education levels (from high school graduates up to those with post-graduate degrees). There are also quite a few mid-manager and professional workers (such as IT engineers).*

Several facilitators/staff interviewed at FBOs/CBOs felt that some of the job seekers served by their job clubs would not have sought or used the public sector workforce services, but it was not possible to determine the extent to which FBO/CBO-sponsored job clubs served as an alternative to job clubs operated by the public sector. Several of the staff interviewed indicated that it was not unusual for the job seekers they served to attend more than one job club at a time, including those run by FBOs, CBOs, and the public sector.

Table 3-3. Numbers and Types of Job Seekers Attending Job Clubs

Name of Job Club	Organization Sponsoring Job Club	Avg. # of Attendees per Meeting	Types of Job Seekers Typically Attending Job Club
			FBO-SPONSORED JOB CLUBS
Job Seekers	Trinity Church of Princeton, NJ	10-15	Most commonly, participants are middle to upper-middle aged job seekers; significant portion are long-term unemployed older workers
Job Partnership of Cleveland (JPC)	Mt. Zion Congregational Church	20-25	Nearly all participants are African-American from surrounding community, includes about 30% formerly incarcerated and some veterans
Crossroads Career Network	Snellville United Methodist Church	25-40	Most attendees are white and middle-class; about 1/3 are underemployed and/or trying to move out of a "bridge" job
Job Networking	Roswell United Methodist Church	Up to 300	Job seekers range from 20s to 55 plus
SOAR 4 Jobs	St. Odilia Catholic Community	20-30	Most attendees are middle-aged to older job seekers; the majority of current participants are not members of St. Odilia's parish
Career Network Ministry (CNM)	McLean Bible Church	150	Most attendees are seeking white-collar jobs
Employment Network Group	Severna Park United Methodist Church	2-4	Although the types of jobs seekers have varied over time, the majority of attendees are seeking white-collar jobs
CTK Parish Job Networking Ministry	Christ The King Parish in Pleasant Hill, CA	20-60 (at large group general meetings)	Initially job club served some attendees seeking unskilled jobs, but most current attendees are older, white-collar professionals with significant experience in their career fields

Name of Job Club	Organization Sponsoring Job Club	Avg. # of Attendees per Meeting	Types of Job Seekers Typically Attending Job Club
			CBO-SPONSORED JOB CLUBS
Neighbors-helping-Neighbors	Neighbors-helping-Neighbors USA, Inc.	10-15	Attendance reflects job seekers in each workforce area where NhN meetings are held; NhN attracts substantial numbers of older workers (50+) and white-collar, professional/technical workers; with peer group structure, NhN attracts and keeps job seekers interested in networking and helping others in the group
Community Job Club of Stow	Community Job Club, Inc.	16	Nearly all attendees are white; average age is 45; range of education levels represented (high school graduates to post-graduate degrees); substantial numbers of recently dislocated mature technical/professional workers (e.g., IT engineers)
Career Transition Group for Women	None	4-6	All participants are women, primarily from the St. Paul
The Job Forum	San Francisco Chamber of Commerce	5-10	Most attendees are white-collar professionals with college degrees, including some who have just completed college, while others are over 50 and out of work
			PUBLIC SECTOR- SPONSORED JOB CLUBS
Jersey Job Club	New Jersey Dept. of Labor and Workforce Development	10-20 (at Orientation Workshop)	About 60% of active JJC members are UI claimants; attendees reflect job seekers served by the AJC within each locality; referrals come from TANF, TAA,WIA/Wagner-Peyser programs, other AJC partners, correctional system, and job fairs
Veterans Networking Group	Hennepin South Workforce Center	20-25	All participants are veterans; most are from the Bloomington area; most are over 40
Arnold Station Job Club	Arnold Career Center/Anne Arundel WDC	6	Attendees represent a wide range of income and skills levels, although the job club attracts slightly lower-income individuals than the Career Center does overall
ProMatch	NOVA WIB and California EDD	Over 100 at weekly General Membership Meetings	Most attendees are experienced, white-collar professionals over 40 (majority are over 55); most are UI claimants/exhaustees

Table 3-3 (shown earlier) shows the considerable range in the number of job seekers attending individual job club sessions. Most typically, FBOs/CBOs visited as part of this study had between 10 and 30 attendees at job club sessions, though all of the job clubs visited indicated that there was week-to-week variability in numbers of attendees. In some instances, job club attendance would peak when special speakers appeared at the job club or employers were brought in to conduct interviews with job club participants. Among the 12 FBO/CBO job clubs visited, there were three outliers in terms of attendance at job club sessions: (1) Roswell United Methodist Church's Job Networking typically had up to 300 participants at their regular bi- monthly meeting, although they often saw from 350 to 375 attendees when they included job fairs in the program; (2) the McLean Bible Church averaged 150 attendees each week at its Career Network Ministry job clubs (ranging from 125 to 160 each week); and (3) ProMatch, often had over 100 attendees (including around 45 first-time participants) at General Membership meetings. Some job club facilitators indicated that job clubs can become unwieldy and more formal when attendance at individual sessions is in excess of 20 to 25 participants, making it necessary to shift the format of the job club to become more lecture-based and less peer group-driven (unless the larger groups are broken down into smaller blocks of participants or workshops are offered). Several facilitators noted that 10 to 15 attendees is a good number for job club sessions because it allows for personal attention for each attendee, but also provides enough of a group dynamic for discussion and opportunities for productive networking among attendees. Roswell United Methodist Church's Job Networking program compensates for its large size by breaking into multiple workshops for the majority of each session, bringing the entire group of attendees together for dinner and a featured speaker.

It was difficult to obtain unduplicated counts of the number of job club participants served (some organizations did not collect such counts). Annually, in terms of unduplicated counts, it was most common for FBOs/CBOs to serve several hundred participants each year, with several new members (perhaps 3 to 5) joining the job club at each new session. Among the FBOs/CBOs visited, McLean Bible Church's Career Network Ministry was an outlier, serving in excess of 2,000 (unduplicated) job club participants each year. Facilitators of FBOs/CBOs report there is lots of variation in how many times individuals attend job clubs – some attend just once and others linger for a year or longer. Not surprisingly, most job club attendees stop attending job clubs as soon as they get a job.

3. Job Club Structure and Format

Research findings and information collected during interviews with stakeholders suggest that there is significant diversity in the structure of and activities conducted by FBO/CBO-sponsored job clubs. Table 3-4 provides brief descriptions of each of the 16 job clubs visited as part of this study. This section of the report describes the format and content of the job club sessions observed, including: (1) location of meetings; (2) frequency, duration and timing of meetings; (3) participation requirements and patterns of attendance; (4) provision of other workshops and services; (5) use of curriculum to guide job club sessions; (6) agenda and specific content of job club sessions; (7) extent of case management and mentoring of job club attendees; (8) extent of religious/spiritual content in FBO-based job clubs; (9) other services provided; and (10) staffing patterns.

Table 3-4. Overview of General Format of Job Clubs Visited

Name of Job Club	Organization Sponsoring Job Club	Overview of Format of the Job Club
FBO-SPONSORED JOB CLUBS		
JobSeekers	Trinity Church of Princeton, NJ	Weekly facilitated peer support group of job seekers; though congregation provides meeting space, there is no faith/religious content to the job club sessions – the 2-hour weekly job club focuses on facilitated peer group discussions and importance of networking in job search.
Job Partnership of Cleveland (JPC)	Mt. Zion Congregational Church	Mt. Zion Congregational Church is one of 4 Cleveland sites holding a 10- week (3 hours/week) job club using JPC curriculum that infuses faith/bible- based principals ("Keys") with nuts and bolts of effective job search and retention workshop instruction, along with assignment of each participant for 1 year with a volunteer mentor.
Crossroads Career Network	Snellville United Methodist Church	Facilitated career networking/fellowship group that meets once a month for two hours and includes speakers, sharing of job listings, elevator pitches, testimonials and networking. 8-week series of Crossroads Career Network (CCN) workshops and twice-monthly small Christ-Centered Career Groups (C3G) also offered.
Job Networking	Roswell United Methodist Church	Comprehensive job networking/support program with multiple components including: an orientation session for first-time attendees; volunteer-led workshops on various job search topics (e.g., mock interviews, networking); a dinner program with accountability groups (similar to job clubs) for specific groups (e.g., job seekers 21-29, veterans) and job fairs. Also, have volunteer "industry guides" available to take calls/provide advice/network with job seekers.
SOAR 4 Jobs	St. Odilia Catholic Community	Job transition support/networking group that meets twice a month for two hours in a meeting room in a church and includes a presentation by one of a rotating group of speakers for one hour, followed by breakouts in the second hour into small discussion/networking groups to discuss job search progress/share job leads. One group is an orientation session for first-time attendees.
Career Network Ministry (CNM)	McLean Bible Church	Job networking/support group operated by a large group of volunteers; weekly sessions held in church meeting rooms consist of a Resource Hour with orientation sessions for first-time attendees, individual/small group information/assistance sessions as well as a variety of workshops, followed by a large group general meeting with announcements, a 1 to 1.5 hour headline presentation and additional time for networking.
Employment Network Group	Severna Park United Methodist Church	Job networking/support group led by facilitators meets weekly in church; meetings focus on discussions of/recommendations for attendees' job search process and also include 30-minute presentations by one of a rotating

Table 3-4. (Continued)

Name of Job Club	Organization Sponsoring Job Club	Overview of Format of the Job Club
		group of speakers on various job search topics (e.g., government resumes).
CTK Parish Job Networking Ministry	Christ The King Parish in Pleasant Hill, CA	Job networking/support ministry that includes: 1) twice-monthly large group, general meetings with orientation sessions for first time attendees, presentations, testimonials and job search exercises; 2) small group "success teams" that meet weekly and address action items for each participant; and 3) access to the Career Action Network (on-line tool for posting resumes and job listings).
CBO-SPONSORED JOB CLUBS		
Neighbors-helping-Neighbors	Neighbors-helping-Neighbors USA, Inc.	NhN is a network of volunteer peer led job search networking and support groups that follow a community-based approach to help under-employed and unemployed residents get back to work. NhN embraces a 'pay it forward' ethos, asking all associates to contribute to other members by sharing job search techniques, related professional career development resources, personal referrals and generally providing a forum where members feel empowered, energized and focused on the job search. Weekly job clubs typically held in libraries in eight NJ counties.
Community Job Club of Stow	Community Job Club, Inc.	CBO-operated job club meets 2 times a month in local office building in Stow; a facilitator and special speakers presents topics focused on effective job search, resumes, and other employment related topics and there is considerable time for peer sharing and networking. Individual job search assistance and workshops are available outside of the job club on a fee-for-service basis (using a sliding fee scale), including individual career coaching, resume development, and advanced interviewing techniques.
Career Transition Group for Women	None	Networking/support group for women only that meets twice a month for two hours at a library and includes time for each attendee to share job search experiences for feedback/ suggestions/referrals from facilitator and other attendees.
The Job Forum	San Francisco Chamber of Commerce	Job networking/support roundtable forum facilitated by two volunteer panelists who provide customized advice/problem-solving/brainstorming on each attendee's job search process, encouraging discussion, networking, and sharing of job leads among all participants.
PUBLIC SECTOR-SPONSORED JOB CLUBS		
Jersey Job Club	New Jersey Dept. of Labor and Workforce Development	Jersey Job Clubs offers series of workshops for job seekers to be completed in 6 months held at AJCs, including: 4 core workshops lasting 90 minutes each (an Orientation, a Job Search Skills, and Basic/ Advanced Resume Writing Workshops). Several "enrichment workshops" are also offered (Interviewing Skills, Networking Skills, Changing

Name of Job Club	Organization Sponsoring Job Club	Overview of Format of the Job Club
		Employment Landscape, and Skills- Based Volunteering), as well as a weekly job club peer support session.
Veterans Networking Group	Hennepin South Workforce Center	Networking group for veterans that meets twice a month for two hours at the Workforce Center and includes one hour of presentations by speakers and a second hour during which job search progress and job leads are shared.
Arnold Station Job Club	Arnold Career Center/Anne Arundel WDC	Facilitated job club offering support, networking and access to resources that meets twice monthly for two hours in a workforce center and provides learning (through community speakers and instruction led by the Facilitator/Lead Career Advisor on job search topics) as well as networking opportunities; every fourth meeting is devoted to networking only.
ProMatch	NOVA WIB and California EDD	Member-run job search networking/support group that includes: (1) weekly General Membership meetings with speakers, success stories, sharing of job openings, and information about workshops; and (2) required participation (4 hours) in weekly meetings and activities for either program operations or training & development teams that operate various components of the program.

Location of Job Club Meetings. The job clubs operated by FBOs and CBOs were held at community locations made available free-of-charge by either the sponsoring organization or other neighborhood institutions, thereby eliminating any operating costs for meeting rooms but also making the sessions convenient for participants to attend. All the FBO-sponsored job clubs held their main sessions in meeting/conference rooms or fellowship halls in the church or on the church's campus. Christ the King Parish in Pleasant Hill, California, for example, held twice- monthly, large group job club sessions in a conference room on the church grounds (see Exhibit 3-5). Some of their weekly small group "success team" job clubs also met in parish meetings rooms but others were held at nearby locations that were easily accessible to the participants, such as city office meeting rooms and, in one case, a Starbucks coffee shop. Job clubs sponsored by CBOs met in a variety of rent-free locations; two of the CBO job clubs (Career Transition Group for Women and Neighbors-helping-Neighbors) held sessions in community meeting rooms in local public libraries. The Job Forum convened weekly meetings in a conference room in the downtown offices of its sponsor, the San Francisco Chamber of Commerce. The Community Job Club of Stow initially held job club sessions in a local coffee house and a church meeting and, most recently, moved to donated space in a modern office building. The four job clubs sponsored by public workforce agencies operated from AJC/One-Stop Career Centers, thus providing attendees with direct exposure and access to the wide array of services, trained staff and resources available to job seekers at those locations. Due to space limitations, the ProMatch/Experience Unlimited job club held its general membership meetings (which are often attended by over 100 job seekers) in an auditorium in a city-owned building located across the street from the One-Stop Center; however, orientation sessions, workshops and related meetings were held at the One-Stop.

Frequency, Duration, and Timing of Meetings. Nearly all of the 16 job clubs observed held group job club sessions either weekly or twice a month; as also shown in Table 3-5, eight organizations (4 FBOs, 2 CBOs, and 2 Public Workforce Agencies) convened weekly meetings and seven (3 FBOs, 2 CBOs, and 2 Public Workforce Agencies) held meetings twice a month. One of the job clubs visited, Snellville United Methodist Church's Crossroads Career Network, convened its main group networking event once a month. However, some of these organizations operated additional (and typically smaller) job club sessions that met more frequently. In addition to the large group meetings held monthly, the Snellville Crossroads Career Network also sponsored small-group "Christ-Centered Career Group (C3G)" job clubs that met twice- monthly. Similarly, as noted above, Christ the King Parish Job Networking Ministry held large group job club meetings twice a month, but attendees were also invited to participate in small group success team job clubs that met weekly.

Table 3-5. Overview of Job Club Location, Frequency, and Duration

Name of Job Club	Organization Sponsoring Job Club	Location of Job Club	Frequency of Meetings	Average Duration of Job Club
FBO-SPONSORED JOB CLUBS				
Job Seekers	Trinity Church of Princeton, NJ	In church - meeting room.	Weekly	2 hours
Job Partnership of Cleveland (JPC)	Mt. Zion Congregational Church	In church – social hall attached to the church's kitchen.	Weekly (for 10 Weeks)	3 hours
Crossroads Career Network	Snellville United Methodist Church	In church - large fellowship hall/meeting room.	Once a month/second Monday of the month	2 hours
Job Networking	Roswell United Methodist Church	All sessions are held in meeting rooms in the church.	Twice a month, 2nd and 4th Mondays	8.5 hours[21]
SOAR 4 Jobs	St. Odilia Catholic Community	Regular evening sessions are held in the church's community room; occasional special daytime sessions are held elsewhere in the community (e.g., public library).	Twice a month/ second and fourth Mondays	2 hours
Career Network Ministry (CNM)	McLean Bible Church	Orientation sessions for new attendees and individual/small group informational/ assistance sessions are held during the first hour (the Resource Hour) in a large meeting room in the church. Other workshops/ breakout	Weekly; meetings are held Tuesday evenings 50 weeks a year	3.5 hours

Name of Job Club	Organization Sponsoring Job Club	Location of Job Club	Frequency of Meetings	Average Duration of Job Club
		sessions are held in other nearby meeting rooms at the same time. The large group general meeting is held in the large church meeting room.		
Employment Network Group	Severna Park United Methodist Church	Sessions are held in a large meeting room in the church.	Weekly; every Monday morning	2 hours
CTK Parish Job Networking Ministry	Christ The King Parish in Pleasant Hill, CA	The large group general meeting is held in a meeting room on the church campus (30-minute orientation session is held in an adjoining room); small group success teams hold meetings in a variety of convenient locations, including parish meeting rooms, city office conference rooms, and Starbucks.	Large group meetings are held twice monthly on the first and third Thursdays; small group success teams meet weekly	2.5 hours[22]
CBO-SPONSORED JOB CLUBS				
Neighbors- helping-Neighbors	Neighbors-helping-Neighbors USA, Inc.	Public libraries (NhN also has plans to expand to Microsoft stores).	Weekly (a few locations meet every other week, but weekly is preferred)	1.5 hours
Community Job Club of Stow	Community Job Club, Inc.	In modern office building.	Two times a month	2 hours
Career Transition Group for Women	None	In a large meeting room at a community library.	Twice a month – second and fourth Tuesdays of the month	2 hours
The Job Forum	San Francisco Chamber of Commerce	In a meeting room in the San Francisco Chamber of Commerce's offices.	Weekly; every Wednesday evening	2 hours
PUBLIC SECTOR-SPONSORED JOB CLUBS				
Jersey Job Club	New Jersey Dept. of Labor and Workforce Development	American Job Centers (workshops typically held in conference room at AJCs).	Weekly (~6 workshops held weekly at each AJC)	1.5 hours per workshop
Veterans Networking Group	Hennepin South Workforce Center	In workforce center – in a large meeting room with long tables set up in classroom format.	Twice a month – second and fourth Tuesdays of the month	2 hours

Table 3-5. (Continued)

Name of Job Club	Organization Sponsoring Job Club	Location of Job Club	Frequency of Meetings	Average Duration of Job Club
Arnold Station Job Club	Arnold Career Center/Anne Arundel WDC	In a large meeting room in the Arnold Career Center.	Twice a month – second and fourth Thursdays	2 hours
ProMatch	NOVA WIB and California EDD	General Membership Meetings are held in a large auditorium owned by the city and located across the street from the ProMatch and CONNECT Job Seeker Center Offices.	General Membership Meetings are held every Thursday; Individual Team and Business meetings (for everyone) are held on Monday	2.5 hours [23]

The majority (nine) of the job clubs observed held sessions that met for approximately two hours. The shortest meeting was 1.5 hours and the longest session among the traditional job clubs, the Career Network Ministry at the McLean Bible Church, ran for about 3.5 hours with time for networking, a resource hour with individual and small group information sessions and workshops on a variety of job search topics, a group general meeting and a featured presentation. Unique among the job clubs visited, the Roswell United Methodist Church (RUMC) Job Networking Ministry held twice-monthly meetings, offering a comprehensive program of instructional, networking, and support activities and workshops which were scheduled throughout the afternoon and into the evening, starting at 12:30 pm and ending around 9:00 pm. Most job seekers typically participated in some portion of the sessions, including, in some cases, six-to-eight person accountability groups (similar to job clubs) for specific types of job seekers (e.g., veterans, individuals ages 21 to 29) that met for about an hour after the dinner program. Although the job clubs operated by public workforce agencies were held during regular business hours, most of the FBO and CBO job clubs met at the edges or outside of those hours, either early in the morning (as the Severna Park United Methodist Church's Employment Network Group did) or in the late afternoon and early evening, in part to accommodate the schedules of the job seekers but also those of some of the volunteer facilitators. Christ the King Parish's Job Networking group held its large group meetings in the evenings, but scheduled the small group success teams meetings at other times that met the needs of the attendees.

Participation Requirements and Patterns of Attendance. Overall, most of the FBO, CBO, and public workforce agency job clubs observed followed an "open entry, open exit" format for participation in their job club sessions. Attendees at these job clubs did not typically start and end sessions as a cohort, participating in a fixed number of meetings in which a specific list of job search topics was covered sequentially from week to week; rather, they were welcome to join any session at any time. While most of the job clubs followed an agenda or established format (described in more detail below) in each meeting, job club meetings were typically structured as stand-alone sessions that job seekers could attend when, if and as often as they chose. As a result, some job seekers were consistent participants for a period of weeks or months, but others might have sporadic attendance patterns, attending a few meetings, skipping one or two and then returning a few weeks later, depending on the status of their job search process and other commitments. According to facilitators, some job seekers also attended (often encouraged by facilitators) multiple FBO, CBO, and public workforce job club meetings simultaneously, in some cases to address different needs and to find the best fit for their particular job search, but also to cast a wider net for networking opportunities. During job club sessions observed in the Washington, DC Metro and Minneapolis/St. Paul areas, for example, attendees shared their experiences participating in other job clubs currently operating in the community and often referred fellow job seekers to individual facilitators or staff for assistance with specific needs (e.g., a referral to a staff member at a local public workforce center who was particularly skilled in resume development for a specific career field). Job seekers participating in FBO/CBO job clubs might also be concurrently enrolled and participating in workshops and/or other workforce services at the local AJC/One-Stop Center.

Among the FBO/CBO job clubs observed, one diverged from the open-entry, open-exit, standalone format and instead provided a structured sequential program of workshops on job search topics. The Mt Zion Congregational Church Job Partnership of Cleveland's (JPC) program, offered twice a year, was a 10-week, 3 hours per week, series of interrelated workshops that covered the basics of effective job search and retention. A cohort of 20-25 job seekers typically participated in these faith-infused workshops together throughout the 10-week period. One public workforce agency job club model observed – the ProMatch/Experience Unlimited program operated by NOVA WIB and California Employment Development Department – was also structured somewhat differently. Eligible participants were invited to join only as space became available when other members found employment and left the group; after joining, job seekers were required to volunteer their services for four hours per week on program operations or training and development teams that operated the member-run job club program.

Provision of Other Workshops. A few FBO job clubs visited went beyond the traditional job club networking/support sessions and expanded their services to also offer optional workshops or a series of interrelated workshops on relevant job search topics, scheduled either during their regular meetings or on other days and times. Many of these workshops covered topics not dissimilar to those covered in workshops offered at an AJC/One-Stop Center, although FBOs were not typically able to provide computer labs, multiple printers and telephones, etc. For example, the McLean Bible Church's Career Network Ministry operated a number of optional workshops during their 3.5 hour weekly meetings on topics such as LinkedIn, effective resume writing, federal job search, development of the elevator pitch, interviewing and networking. Two examples of other FBOs that offered workshops in conjunction with their job clubs are provided below.

- *Snellville United Methodist Church's Crossroads Career Network (FBO- Atlanta). This program operated two-hour, monthly job club meetings and smaller (4-5 attendees) Christ-Centered Career Groups (C3G) support and accountability groups that met twice a month. In addition, this organization also offered an eight-week series of Crossroad Career Network (CCN) workshops, held on other evenings. This series of workshops, offered five times a year, began with an orientation session*

("Are You at a Crossroads in Your Career?) and included session topics such as "Discovering Your Unique Qualities," "Finding Career Opportunities," and "Interviewing and Evaluating Offers." Facilitators felt that the workshops were the most effective of all of the job club activities they provided.

- **Roswell United Methodist Church (RUMC) Job Networking Program (FBO-Atlanta).** *RUMC's program, also a member of the Crossroads Career Network, provided a comprehensive menu of job networking/support services and activities for job seekers. Twice monthly sessions that ran throughout the afternoon and into the evening offered, in addition to a dinner program, presentations and accountability groups, a variety of volunteer-led (typically professional HR staff/Recruiters) workshops on topics of interest to job seekers (e.g., networking, franchise businesses, strategies for older job seekers.) A condensed version of the Crossroads Career Network Workshop was also offered. At the time of the site visit, 27 workshops were available; according to program administrators, it takes approximately 2 months of regular attendance to complete all workshops.*

One of the four job clubs operated by public workforce agencies, Jersey Job Club, also provided a series of weekly workshops on an array of job search topics in conjunction with a peer support session; sequential attendance at these workshops was not a requirement for participation.

Use of Curriculum to Guide Job Club Sessions. Because their job clubs were designed to be open-entry, open-exit sessions (rather than a set number of meetings covering a specific list of instructional topics and issues), most of the FBO/CBO job clubs (as well as those operated by the public workforce agencies) visited did not use a formal curriculum or facilitator's guide to structure the sequence or the content of the activities and/or the instructional material presented in their job club sessions. Some facilitators noted that they wanted to remain as flexible as possible so they could best address the needs and individual concerns of the attendees at each meeting.

Among the FBO job clubs, only the Mt. Zion Congregational Church followed a standardized curriculum - the Job Partnership, Inc. curriculum - for the 10-week series of workshops that constituted its job club. One of the CBO-sponsored job clubs, the Community Job Club of Stow, also used portions of a curriculum – "Getting Over Job Search Hurdles – Preparation and Positioning" – to guide their sessions, albeit not systematically.[24] Although they did not follow or distribute a curriculum, other FBO and CBO job clubs provided attendees with notebooks, step-by-step guides, handouts and other resources to inform a systematic job search process; facilitators could refer to or draw from these materials during presentations and instructional activities. For example, the McLean Bible Church's Career Network Ministry distributed to each participant a Job Search "Passport" which included a listing of recommended sequential steps in the job search process (e.g., elevator pitch, marketing plan, and networking), as well as a 90+ page handbook, "A Guide to Discovering Your Gifts and Pursuing Your Professional Career Search," which has been updated and revised several times. The Severna Park United Methodist Church's Employment Network Group provided to each participant a book on job search strategies ("So Do You Want a Job or What? Dirty Secrets of Resume Writing and Job Hunting") written by one of the job club's facilitators.

Agenda/Content of Job Clubs. As noted above, most of the job clubs observed followed a standard format, and, in some cases, a fixed agenda, to guide and structure their sessions. The agenda provided below for the Snellville United Methodist Church's Crossroads Career Network monthly networking event is representative of the format used in several of the FBO job club sessions observed:

- Welcome and Opening Prayer
- Facilitated Career Networking and Fellowship
- Presentation – Use of Library Resources in the Job Search
- Testimonial
- Presentation – "Six steps to walking through a crossroads in your career"
- Closing

While many of the job clubs observed shared a number of common elements, the content of the sessions and the number and types of activities often varied based on the size of the group. (See Table 3-4 [earlier] for descriptions of each job club visited.) Most of the job club sessions began with the facilitator providing an introduction to the job club, reviewing the rules and procedures for the session, and sharing general announcements. This was typically followed by introductions of the attendees, which in larger job clubs might be limited to new participants, then moving to delivery of elevator pitches by all members of the group. In smaller job clubs (e.g., The Job Forum, Career Transition Group for Women, Job Seekers) these introductions evolved and expanded into 10-15 minute discussions on the background, employment history and job search goals and experiences of each attendee. These discussions, together with feedback, suggestions, advice, and referrals provided by both the facilitator and the other job seekers in attendance, constituted the bulk of the job club sessions in the smaller job clubs observed. Some of the larger job clubs (including job clubs operated by public workforce agencies) typically included a 45-minute to one-hour presentation by a volunteer speaker (or speakers) on a topic relevant to the job search process, followed by a question-and-answer session. For example, at the SOAR 4 Jobs job club meeting observed by the research team, four employees (one was a member of the church) of a professional staffing firm gave a presentation on "Job Opportunities: Where to Look for Them," which included guidance on job search strategies, trends, sources, approaches, and techniques. Although the content and the format varied considerably across the job clubs, most sessions provided some type of instructional component related to the job search process (e.g., resume development, mock interviews), presented to the entire group or in smaller breakout groups and led either by the facilitator, other volunteers or other job club participants. Time also was set aside to recognize job club participants who found employment and returned to share their success stories, either through a quick report or a longer testimonial by the successful job seeker. Another component of the job clubs' meetings was time for sharing job leads and job listings, ranging from distribution of lists of openings (either in printed format or via email), to discussions among participants during networking time, to the formalized and energetic exchange of information about job openings and jobs sought that was part of the ProMatch group job club meeting. All of the job clubs observed placed a major emphasis on networking as the crucial component for a successful job search, with most job clubs setting aside ample time for group and one-on-one networking opportunities. Although the focus of the job club sessions was clearly on providing strategies and tools for securing a job, it was obvious that the emotional support provided, along with the sense of common purpose and shared experiences, played a critical role for the job club participants. While facilitators were key players in guiding and leading the sessions, the willingness of the participants to trade job leads, provide advice on career decisions, offer referrals to other community resources and offer enthusiastic encouragement contributed to the success of the job clubs.[25]

Case Management and Mentoring for Job Club Attendees. The majority of the job clubs sponsored by FBOs and CBOs did not provide case management or mentoring programs for participants as part of their regular job club activities. Only the Mt. Zion Congregational Church program operated a one-on-one mentoring program, providing participants with volunteer mentors during the 10-week workshop period and continued mentoring for one year after that. Other FBO and CBO job clubs, including SOAR 4 Jobs, the Career Network Ministry, and the Community Job Club of Stow, had volunteers available to provide one-on-one, in-person counseling and assistance with resume preparation and review and interview practice, if requested; several facilitators also reported that they often communicated by phone, email and in-person with participants outside of the regular meetings.

Extent of Religious/Spiritual Content into FBO-Based Job Clubs. Among the eight FBO-operated job clubs observed, were significant differences in the extent to which the sessions, as well as the materials distributed during the meetings, were infused with religious and or spiritual messages. At one end of the spectrum was the JobSeekers job club -- the Trinity Church of Princeton provided a meeting room but there were no prayers or religious references of any kind in the job club session itself. At the next level were the job club sessions (also held in church meeting rooms), which began and ended with prayers but contained little, if any, mention of religion or spirituality during the actual meeting. In one of the job clubs observed, prayers were offered at the opening and closing of the meeting; the only other spiritual references were made by a former participant who quoted a number of biblical passages in his testimonial on his successful job search. A few of the FBO job clubs which opened and closed with prayers did not discuss religious beliefs during their presentations or discussions of jobs search tools and strategies, but they did provide notebooks, brochures and other materials that recommended prayer, worship and bible-study as part of the job search process, often including quotations from scripture. For example, one FBO-sponsored job club distributed eight "Prayers for Those Seeking Work" in handouts that also included the agenda for the session and notes from the last meeting. The McLean Bible Church's Career Network Ministry's Handbook emphasizes the role of God in the job search process, introducing the more traditional guidance on job search with topics such as "Discovering your Spiritual Gifts," supplemented with numerous biblical quotations. Of the job clubs observed, Mt. Zion Congregational Church's JPC job club was the most strongly faith-based program, using a curriculum that infused Bible-based principles with the nuts and bolts of an effective job search. Discussions and instructional activities during the workshop focused on the critical role of religious beliefs and practices in a successful job search process, as well as in long-term job retention.

Provision of Other Services. While the purpose of the FBO and CBO job clubs was to provide assistance and support in finding employment, some of these job clubs were also able to provide additional related support services, although not to the extent that they were available through the public workforce agencies. Some of the larger and more established FBO job clubs (e.g., Career Network Ministry, Roswell United Methodist Church) operated their own "clothes closets" with interview-ready clothing for participants, while others had access to those and other resources (e.g., food pantries) through their sponsoring churches. A few facilitators reported that they were able to provide some participants with limited bus passes or other assistance with transportation through donations from volunteers or church members. Other knowledgeable facilitators familiar with the community network of services were able to steer job seekers to the appropriate public and non-profit agencies for other needs perhaps not directly related to the job search (e.g., housing assistance).

Job Club Staffing. One critical difference between the job clubs sponsored by FBOs and CBOs and those operated by public workforce agencies is the staffing arrangements. Job clubs held at AJC/One-Stop Centers are led by paid professional staff, often with the help of support staff and an array of equipment and tools (e.g., computers, printers) to support the job search. Although a few of the FBO-sponsored job clubs received limited assistance from paid church staff, the vast majority of these clubs were organized, managed, and facilitated solely by unpaid volunteers. Most of the FBO/CBO job clubs rotated a small group of volunteer facilitators or used two or three facilitators to lead each meeting, although one job club had been organized and operated by only one facilitator for the past few years. Larger job clubs such as the McLean Bible Church's Career Network Ministry needed up to 30 volunteers to operate the multiple sessions and breakout groups conducted at a single meeting; staff with the Roswell United Methodist Church's Job Networking program reported that up to 70 volunteers were required for each meeting, including food preparation staff for the job club dinner. JPC's Mt. Zion site had 5 to 10 volunteers available for each job club meeting, including volunteers to help with signing-in participants, several volunteer guest speakers, food servers, mentors, and other volunteers to clean/set up the facility.

Facilitators varied in their level of experience and skills; some were self-taught former participants who wanted to give back. However, a somewhat surprising number of facilitators and workshop leaders were human resources professionals or recruiters for large corporations who volunteered their time. These human resources professionals and recruiters were able to share their expertise and experiences from the perspective of searching for and interviewing job candidates for a range of occupations and job openings. Many of the volunteers at the FBO job clubs were members of the sponsoring church who chose the job club as their opportunity for volunteerism. Although it is difficult to quantify the total number of volunteer hours devoted to the operation of FBO/CBO-sponsored job clubs, it clearly is a large commitment of free labor. Examples of the roles played by volunteer facilitators at two FBO/CBO job clubs are provided below.

- *The Job Forum (CBO – San Francisco). Two volunteer panelists facilitate each job networking/support roundtable meeting, providing customized advice, feedback, and referrals and leading brainstorming sessions on each participant's job search during a two-hour meeting. Approximately 35-40 professionals from business, academia, and nonprofits, many of whom are hiring managers, job coaches, or human resources professionals, rotate as panelists. Networking, discussion and sharing of job leads are encouraged among all attendees.*
- *Severna Park United Methodist Church Employment Network Group (FBO-Washington, DC Metro.) At least two (and sometimes three) volunteers facilitate*

these weekly meetings that include discussions of each attendee's job search progress. One of the facilitators is a professional job search counselor who also volunteers with other area job clubs; the other two are current or former employers/small business owners.

4. Funding and Funding Sources

The FBO/CBO job clubs visited operated with little or no external funding, and most functioned with only a limited budget, particularly when compared to job clubs operated by professional staff within a public workforce center. Even FBO/CBO job clubs such as the McLean Bible Church (serving an average of 150 job seekers each week) operated at extremely low costs, with a total annual budget of $12,000 to $15,000 provided mostly through donations from volunteers. Because they were able to keep their expenses to a minimum, FBOs/CBOs did not require grants or major funders to initiate or maintain their job clubs – and most of the administrators/staff preferred structuring and operating their job clubs so that they would not require outside fund raising or solicitation of government/foundation grants. None of the FBOs visited received government or foundation grants for their job clubs at the time of the visits. The biggest in-kind contribution FBOs and CBOs operating job clubs received was the use of rent- free meeting space. For FBOs, this was usually in the form of a church/congregation meeting room or fellowship hall; for CBOs, free library space on a weekly basis was sometimes utilized. For example, Neighbors-helping-Neighbors mostly relies on meeting rooms made available free- of-charge at public libraries located in 26 communities spread across 8 counties in New Jersey for its weekly or bi-weekly job club meetings. Another CBO-sponsored job club, the Job Forum, is able to hold its weekly sessions in a conference room in the San Francisco Chamber of Commerce's downtown offices, also at no charge.

The other significant in-kind contribution that helped to contain costs, particularly in FBO-sponsored job clubs, was the use of volunteer facilitators and staff to operate job club sessions. For example, the Princeton Job Seekers job club relied upon five volunteers (mostly past Job Seeker participants) who rotated each week to facilitate job club sessions. The lead facilitator of this initiative credited the volunteer arrangement and weekly rotation of facilitator responsibility (i.e., so no facilitator had to cover more than one job club session per month) for the job club's resilience over nearly three decades. Similar to the several other FBO-sponsored job clubs visited as part of this study, the lead facilitator for Job Seekers acknowledged that because there was no external funding for the job club, the provision of a meeting room once a week by the Trinity Church of Princeton at no charge had been a critical ingredient (along with volunteer facilitators) contributing to the group's long-term survival. Donations of space and volunteer time have helped to keep costs for FBO/CBO-sponsored job clubs extremely low compared to the public sector operation of job clubs, which typically operate these job clubs with paid, professional staff.

Several FBO job clubs received additional support in the form of modest financial contributions or staff time from their sponsoring churches and/or members of the congregation to get their job clubs started and to support continued operations. For example, the Snellville United Methodist Church provides its Crossroads Career Network job club with some staff support as well as a small budget, which is used to cover costs such as the annual Crossroads Career Network membership fee and materials for workshops. Christ the King Parish in Pleasant Hill, California also pays the fee required for the Job Networking

Ministry's participants to access the Career Action Network, an online tool for posting resumes and job listings. On a larger scale, the Roswell United Methodist Church's Job Networking Ministry has funded its dinner programs (often attended by 275 - 300 job seekers) over the past five years with a combination of volunteer, private, and corporate donations, including garage sales organized by church members. Several examples of how FBO/CBO sponsored job clubs were able to start-up and continue to operate on very limited budgets follow:

- *Career Transitions Group for Women (CBO-Minnesota). This job club, which was re-started by a volunteer after it was discontinued by a local nonprofit organization providing services for women, does not receive funding or contributions from any outside sources. There are virtually no expenses associated with operating this job club that meets twice a month in a meeting room at a neighborhood public library at no cost. There is a single facilitator, who estimates that she donates about 12 hours each month to plan and facilitate the job club. The facilitator pays for name tags and, occasionally, printing costs for informational materials. During the job club session observed during the site visit, one participant suggested that attendees chip in a few dollars to offset the facilitator's expenditures.*

- *Community Job Club of Stow (CBO-Ohio). This job club was formed on and continues to operate on a shoestring. Initially, a church offered free meeting space and provided an $800 grant to offset printing, refreshment, and other costs. With the support of a local real estate developer, this job club was able to move to new space free-of-charge inside a modern office building in Stow, which offers both a meeting area (for the job club) and office space for the lead facilitator and volunteers. Currently, with no expense for either office or staffing, this organization spends a total of about $180/month to operate its job club, which includes $80/month to cover cost of phone/Internet; and $100/month to cover cost of office supplies, refreshments, and other miscellaneous costs. The executive director donates her time for planning and attending job club sessions. To help offset operational costs, the organization has received $1,000 from an individual donor and $250 from the local Lions Club. Additionally, the organization offers fee-for-service assistance to job club participants (in-person services tailored to individual needs, such as resume development, help with job search, etc.). For example, the organization is planning to offer an "active interviewing" workshop at $10-15 per workshop in 2014. Finally, the organization is looking for grants from foundations and government to help with covering future operating costs.*

- *SOAR 4 Jobs- St. Odilia Catholic Church (FBO-Minnesota). Operating for over 10 years in a Minneapolis suburb, this job club holds two-hour meetings twice a month while incurring virtually no out-of-pocket costs. Sessions are held in a meeting room made available by the church at no cost; the church also provides space for a resource room with books, handouts and other informational resources for job seekers, either donated or purchased by the church. The job club team also has access to the services of the church's secretary and the copying equipment and supplies. A small group of volunteers rotate as facilitators; two volunteers also provide one-on-one counseling and assistance (e.g., resume preparation, interview practice) for participants, if requested. Volunteers supply the refreshments for the job club meetings. In addition, special presentations on topics of interest to job seekers are held during working hours at other no-cost locations in the community (e.g., public libraries) on an occasional basis.*

5. Job Club Participant Data Collection and Views on Evaluation

FBO and CBO-operated job clubs visited as part of this study collected and maintained minimal (and in most instances, virtually no) participant-level data, including data on job club participant demographic characteristics, job club services utilized, or individual outcomes (such as job placement/retention, hours worked, wage rates, or earnings). While there was some variation across FBOs/CBOs visited in the types of participant-level data maintained, overall, the identifying information and job club participant-level data maintained pales when compared to data maintained by public sector organizations (such as AJCs) operating job clubs, and particularly, in comparison to data currently collected on UI claimants and participants enrolled in the WIA, Wagner-Peyser, and TAA programs. Appendix E provides two tables that provide for each of the 12 FBOs and CBOs visited as part of this study (1) an overview of the types of data collected on job club participants (Table E-1) and (2) an overview of the use of participant data forms and management information systems (MIS), as well as views on the potential for future evaluation of job clubs (Table E-2).

Few of the FBOs/CBOs visited collected much beyond using an attendance sign-in sheet, which typically included the date of the job club, job club attendee's name, occupation/job interest, and basic contact information (such as an e-mail address and phone number). Several FBO/CBO-sponsored job clubs did not even keep track of ongoing attendance at each job club session, collecting only the names and e-mail addresses of each first time attendee at a job club session. While stressing the need to keep paperwork and administrative tasks to an absolute minimum, several FBO/CBO facilitators/leaders indicated that it was important to collect basic contact information on job club attendees so they could (with the permission of attendees) share this information (typically name and e-mail address, and possibly telephone number) among job club attendees to spur networking among active job club participants, and especially to share job leads that job seekers might come across during their own job search activities. In addition, facilitators for some job clubs noted that they collected this information so they could alert current and former job club attendees of upcoming networking and job search events, including job fairs and presentations by speakers.

Several of the FBO/CBO representatives interviewed during visits viewed their lack of paperwork requirements imposed on job cub participants as a strength and an attractive feature of their job clubs when compared to job clubs (and other workforce services) offered through the public workforce system in their locality. FBO/CBO administrators/facilitators did not want to unnecessarily burden participants with intake forms or other reporting requirements (such as whether a job club participant was employed at a certain point in time after they began attending the job club). None of the FBO/CBO administrators interviewed indicated that they would be comfortable asking participants to provide Social Security Numbers (SSNs) as part of the intake process. Further, FBOs/CBOs sponsoring job clubs were not eager to collect additional background/intake data on job club participants, in part, because they did not want to be viewed as bureaucratic (or in similar terms as a public workforce organization) and because they feared that asking for such confidential data might be viewed as intrusive, inappropriate, and/or dampen interest in job club participation. Further, beyond collecting names, contact information, and job interest, FBO and CBO representatives did not feel that they had a need or justifiable use for collecting additional information; most did not maintain hardcopy case files or automated client data systems in which to securely store any personal information collected (such as SSN, date of birth, etc.). Given the volunteer staffing and shoe-string budgets that most of the CBO/FBO job clubs operated under, FBOs/CBOs also expressed concerns about the staff time and effort involved in collecting additional and more detailed information from participants and inputting such data into an automated data system. Some FBO/CBO administrators/facilitators also were unsure about the appropriateness of prying into personal details (e.g., asking about age, race/ethnicity, ex-offender status, barriers to employment, etc.).

There were, however, a few FBO/CBO organizations visited which went beyond a simple sign-in/attendance sheet and had job club participants complete an intake form or participation agreement form, although these forms were streamlined in comparison to those normally used in the public workforce system for job club participants and those served by WIA or the Wagner Peyser programs. For example, Stow's Community Job Club (a CBO-based job club) has participants complete a two-page intake form prior to attending their first job club, providing the following data items:

- contact information – address, phone, email address;
- current/past employment information -- current employment status, current/last position held, length of time in current/past job, current/last annual income, name/address of current/last employer, reason for unemployment (e.g., laid-off, quit, etc.);
- education (type of degree, certifications);
- number living in household (including number under age 18);
- current marital status;
- type of industry sector and position/occupation being sought;
- challenges faced in job search;
- interest in volunteering at Community Job Club (including type of volunteer activity and hours willing to volunteer per week);
- how the job club participant heard about the Community Job Club;
- family income and primary source of income; and
- information about type of occupation/job the individual is interested in obtaining.

In part, the collection of additional data at this particular site was intended to support more individualized job placement assistance that is offered (some of which is provided on a fee- for-service basis), as well as to target job club session topics and discussions on the specific needs of those attending each job club session. A second site that collected more detailed participant-level data at the time of intake was the Jobs Partnership Cleveland's (JPC) Mt. Zion Congregational Church site, which also uses a two-page intake form (referred to as a "student profile") that collects the following data items:

- contact information – address, phone, email address;
- emergency contact information;

- current/past employment information -- current employment status, and if employed, whether it is full/part-time, name of employer, job title, job duties/responsibilities, date of employment, and current salary;
- marital status and name of spouse;
- household composition, including number living in household, and then a breakdown of the name, relationship, age and sex of each household member);
- housing arrangement;
- primary language spoken in household;
- church affiliation;
- explanation of family issues that need to be addressed (e.g., housing employment, social service referrals, chemical dependency, medical, etc.);
- whether individual has been convicted of felony, and if so, charges and length of time served;
- barriers to employment;
- whether there have been gaps between employment, and if so, why;
- whether participant has need for any special assistance to obtain/sustain employment; and
- whether the participant has dependencies on drugs, alcohol, smoking, or other type (with explanation).

The background information collected on the JPC/Mt. Zion intake form was used by workshop instructors as well as mentors to whom each JPC/Mt. Zion participant was assigned, to assess individual barriers to employment and target assistance and outside referrals for support services on the specific needs of each participant over the 10 weeks of workshops. As is discussed later in this section, despite collecting this more detailed background information during the intake process, these two sites do not enter data from these forms into an automated participant tracking data system for analytical purposes (though some data are entered onto an Excel spreadsheet at the two sites), but rather are used for case management purposes and guiding service delivery.

None of the FBO or CBO job clubs visited had an automated participant data system to systematically capture receipt of services or outcomes for each participant. With regard to service utilization, some FBOs/CBOs maintained a listing of attendees at job club sessions (typically on an Excel spreadsheet or in a Microsoft Word file). For example, in several sites, administrators could provide a count of the total number of job club attendees for the year (and in some instances, for several years or even since inception of the job club), most recent month, or an individual session. Some FBOs/CBOs also were able to provide an unduplicated count of the number of individuals attending job club sessions over the past year. Although most FBO/CBO job clubs did not have the staff or resources to examine attendance patterns or participant characteristics in any detail, one facilitator conducted an analysis of area codes for evening phone numbers to determine the geographic areas from which the majority of attendees were drawn. None of the FBOs/CBOs visited maintained data on referrals of participants to the public workforce system or other service providers (or received confirmation that referred participants had been enrolled or received services from other providers).

While most of the FBOs/CBOs encouraged participants to share their "success" stories when they obtained a job – including coming to a job club session for a "victory lap" to discuss their placement and the job search activities that helped in securing the new position – none of the FBOs/CBOs visited systematically collected job placement or job retention data (i.e., job placement date, wage amount, and number of hours working per week). Collection of job placement/retention data tended to be anecdotal, with some participants emailing or calling the facilitator or fellow job club participants to inform them of their good fortune. In many instances, job club participants would attend one or several job club sessions and then simply stop coming – without letting the facilitator know whether they were successful or unsuccessful in finding a job. Though interested in job placement outcomes for job club participants, FBOs/CBOs visited as part of this study lacked the staffing, procedures, and data systems to track and systematically collect placement or retention data. They also did not in many cases feel it was appropriate to follow-up with participants to find out what had happened or to check in with participants periodically (e.g., six months after they leave the job club) to determine whether they had been able to retain the job. The lack of systematic collection of job placement/retention data, however, did not stand in the way of some FBOs/CBOs boasting of their success in assisting job club attendees to secure and keep jobs (and in some instances, making claims of achieving a specific job placement rate). Finally, in interviews, FBO/CBO job club administrators/facilitators – while interested in better understanding their job placement results – did not feel it was feasible for their organizations (given staffing/funding constraints and their emphasis on minimal paperwork burden for participants and mostly volunteer staff) to expand efforts to collect additional data on participant characteristics, service utilization, or outcomes.

With regard to evaluation, none of the FBO, CBO, or public sector job clubs visited had been part of a formal evaluation effort, and there was little enthusiasm for rigorous (random assignment-type) impact studies or even implementation or outcomes evaluation efforts. Among the reasons that FBOs/CBOs have not been involved in rigorous evaluation efforts and were generally pessimistic about prospects for being part of future impact/outcome evaluation efforts were the following:

- Lack staff time and expertise to collect/maintain/analyze data to support outcome/impact type studies;
- Unwillingness to burden staff or participants with more extensive/intrusive data collection;
- Concern that asking participants for identifying information (such as SSN) or other sensitive participant background/characteristics data, would be perceived as inappropriate and dampen participant interest in the program;
- Concerns about costs of entering/maintaining data in an automated system, as well as concerns over safeguarding participant data in manual and automated data files; and
- Unwillingness to randomly assign individuals to treatment and control groups – CBOs/FBOs would be loath to deny job club services to job seekers in need within their communities.

Some FBO/CBO administrators/facilitators recognized that it could potentially be useful to collect systematic outcome data for job club participants, for example, from the standpoint of being able to better inform church leaders of the success of their initiatives and to potentially attract additional funding from church members or even foundations for their efforts. They also acknowledged that while they felt reassured by their many past successes in helping job seekers to secure a job, there might be a need for more systematic analysis of both job placement and job retention outcomes. While pessimistic about their prospects for increasing data collection or being part of more rigorous outcome/impact evaluation efforts, FBOs/CBOs indicated that they would need considerable technical assistance related to developing and implementing data collection forms (e.g., intake, service receipt, and outcomes forms), data collection procedures, and automated systems if they were to be part of more rigorous evaluation efforts. Given the lack of automated participant tracking systems, an effort to make available a low-cost/low- burden model of participant forms and a simplified automated participant tracking system that could be used on a stand-alone PC might be of interest to some FBOs/CBOs operating job clubs.

C. Conclusions

Although the exact number of job clubs currently being operated by FBOs and CBOs is unknown, information obtained during the stakeholder interviews as well as the site visits indicates that the number is likely growing (or, at the very least, not decreasing) reflecting the continued demand for the networking and peer support services provided by job clubs. For example, a 17-page spreadsheet (updated on 11/5/13) providing locations and meeting times for FBO and CBO (as well as public workforce agency) job clubs in the Minneapolis/St. Paul metro area included information for over 80 job clubs. Despite an overall decrease in the unemployment rate since the height of the 2007-08 economic downturn, the FBO/CBO job clubs continue to hold regularly-scheduled meetings and fill a need not currently being met by the job clubs operated by public sector job clubs. Although some of the job club facilitators indicated that overall attendance has fallen in recent years, they reported that they are willing to continue providing services as long as there are some participants who come to the meetings seeking help. While DOL's Center for Faith-based and Neighborhood Partnerships on-line job clubs registry is helpful in identifying a sample of job clubs operating across the country, there is no existing data source that provides an accurate count of the ebb and flow of FBO/CBO job clubs nationwide or by locality.

Findings from the interviews with stakeholders and facilitators during the site visits indicate that job clubs operated by FBOs, CBOs, and public workforce agencies are alike in many ways, with all of them emphasizing the critical importance of networking, offering ongoing peer support and sharing of similar experiences among participants, as well as providing instruction and guidance on the basics of the job search process (e.g., elevator pitches, resume development, interview practice). Noteworthy differences between the FBO/CBO job clubs and those operated by public workforce agencies are related to staffing patterns and available resources for program operations and services. While public workforce agency job clubs are led by paid professional staff, sometimes supported by the full complement of workshops, activities, and other services typically available through the AJC/One-Stop Center, FBO/CBO job clubs, in most cases, operate with limited budgets or no funding whatsoever. Meeting space is usually provided free-of-charge by the sponsoring church or community organization and teams of volunteers plan, manage and facilitate all aspects of the job clubs. Although the exact number of volunteer hours devoted to the operation of FBO/CBO job clubs is not known, the total amount of labor contributed by these volunteers is likely huge – and of great value to large numbers of job seekers seeking support and assistance. As discussed in the next section, additional implementation studies featuring site visits to a stratified random sample of FBO/CBO job clubs could provide a more detailed and representative account of the features of such job clubs in comparison to job clubs operated by AJC and other public sector agencies.

Although the focus of this study was on traditional job clubs (i.e., regularly-scheduled group meetings designed to enhance job search skills and provide ongoing support to individuals as they search for jobs), it is evident that many FBOs and CBOs have expanded their services for job seekers to include activities and instructional sessions that go beyond those of traditional job clubs. Some of the FBOs and CBOs visited during the site visits offered job clubs as only one component of a more comprehensive menu of services for job seekers that also included smaller "accountability groups" that met until all job seekers found employment, individual or a series of instructional workshops, one-on-one job search assistance and guidance, additional networking sessions, access to websites with job listings/jobs sought and job fairs. The New Birth Missionary Baptist Church's Employment Network Ministry in Atlanta, for example, does not operate regularly scheduled job club meetings but instead has sponsored large job fairs and also links job seekers in the congregation with volunteer church members who can provide individual job search assistance.

Finally, the site visits shed considerable light on the extent to which FBOs and CBOs sponsoring job clubs collect data on program participants and the extent to which they have in the past and are likely in the future to embrace rigorous evaluation. Key findings with respect to data collection and evaluation are the following:

- FBO/CBO-sponsored job clubs rarely collect in-depth information on participants, activities, and outcomes -- while collecting name and other contact information, CBOs and FBOs do not typically collect other identifying information, such as SSNs, that would enable an evaluator to link individual data to administrative data such as Unemployment Insurance (UI) wage records;
- Many FBOs/CBOs (and all the ones visited for this study) do not maintain automated management information systems that provide information about participants' background characteristics, services received, or outcomes; and
- FBOs and CBOs are generally opposed to participating in an evaluation that involves random assignment and often do not have excess demand for their services – hence, for most FBOs/CBOs, random assignment would mean turning away job seekers who could have been served.

As discussed in the next section, these factors are likely to present substantial challenges to future efforts to implement experimental and non-experimental impact evaluations at FBOs/CBOs in order to rigorously evaluate the outcomes/impacts of their job clubs.

SECTION 4. ALTERNATIVE EVALUATION DESIGNS FOR POTENTIAL FUTURE RIGOROUS STUDY OF FBO/CBO-SPONSORED JOB CLUBS

As was discussed earlier in the literature review (see Section 2), while public sector-sponsored job clubs have been rigorously evaluated through randomized controlled trial (RCT) impact studies in the past, no such studies have been conducted of FBO/CBO-sponsored job clubs. If feasible, future experimental and/or non-experimental evaluation efforts would help to better understand the impacts and cost-effectiveness of FBO/CBO-sponsored job clubs, particularly given the low cost and considerable reach of these initiatives in serving job seekers who may not be served by the public workforce system. This section examines a range of experimental and non-experimental approaches to future evaluations of FBO/CBO-operated job clubs, with a particular focus on whether it would be feasible to rigorously estimate net impacts of FBO/CBO-sponsored job clubs. This section is divided into the following sections: (a) an overview of potential outcomes and explanatory variables that could be the focus of rigorous evaluation; (b) an assessment of the potential for experimental research designs; (c) an exploration of the potential for non-experimental research designs; (d) discussion of the potential for process/implementation evaluations; and (e) conclusions and recommendations for future evaluations of FBO/CBO-sponsored job clubs. Before considering alternative research designs, it is important to reiterate that there are some serious constraints on conducting rigorous experimental/non-experimental evaluations of FBO/CBO-sponsored job clubs, which have been highlighted in earlier sections of this report (particularly Section 3):

- FBOs/CBO job clubs rarely collect in-depth information on job club participant characteristics, activities and services received, and employment/earnings outcomes;
- CBOs and FBOs rarely collect identifying information, such as SSNs, that would enable an evaluator to link individual data to administrative data such as Unemployment Insurance (UI) wage records;
- FBOs/CBOs (and all the ones visited for this study) do not typically maintain automated management information systems that track participants' background characteristics, services received, and outcomes; and
- FBOs and CBOs are unlikely to give consideration to participation in an evaluation that involves random assignment and often do not have excess demand for their services – hence, for most FBOs/CBOs, random assignment would mean turning away individuals who could have been served.

All these factors are likely to confound efforts to implement experimental and non-experimental impact evaluations at FBOs/CBOs – and may, in fact, make it impossible to conduct rigorous evaluations. Finally, even if it is possible to overcome these hurdles, the small number of participants served by most FBO/CBO job clubs is likely to make it challenging to rigorously estimate impacts, unless such impact studies combine observations across sites and/or the enrollment period for the evaluation lasts several (or even many) years. With these constraints in mind, this section examines a range of potentially feasible research designs.

A. Potential Outcome and Explanatory Variables for Experimental and Non-Experimental Evaluations of FBO/CBO- Sponsored Job Clubs

Potential outcome measures that should be collected for each job club participant to support an impact evaluation are the following:

- Employment status following participation in the job club (e.g., at 3, 6, 12, and 24 months from the first date of attendance at the job club or from the date of exit);
- Hourly wage rates and hours worked following participation in the job club (e.g., at 3, 6, 12, and 24 months from the first date of attendance at the job club or from the date of exit); and
- Quarterly earnings for up to three years after the first date of attendance or alternatively, after participation in the job club concludes[26].

While some impact evaluations use analysis of variance (ANOVA) to compare outcomes for treatment and control group participants (e.g., the difference in means for the earnings between the treatment and control groups), often multivariate techniques such as multiple regression are used to compare outcomes after adjusting for a set of explanatory, or control, variables. There are several important reasons for using explanatory variables in multivariate models, including the following:

- to increase the precision of estimated program effects;
- to control for "confounding factors" in non-experimental designs that would otherwise result in biased estimates of program effects;
- to estimate interactions between individual characteristics (as captured by the explanatory variables) and program effects; and
- to generally improve understanding of the determinants of outcomes for intervention participants.

Among the potential explanatory variables (collected on each job club attendee) that would likely be needed and should be considered for collection to support experimental and nonexperimental evaluation efforts are the following:

- Demographic variables (e.g., age, gender, race/ethnicity, disability status, etc.);
- Educational attainment and credentials;
- Previous work history and earnings (e.g., occupation, hours worked, wages/earnings, number of month unemployed prior to attending job club);
- Programmatic inputs (e.g., job club workshop sessions/hours attended, receipt of one- on-one assistance; completion of resume by the end of job club; receipt of other job club-related assistance; and receipt of other job readiness and training assistance from the Employment Service, Workforce Investment Act (WIA) program, and the local public workforce system/American Job Centers); and
- Environmental-specific factors (e.g., economic characteristics of the labor market to which the job club participant is seeking employment).

Given the lack of participant data, service utilization, and outcome data currently being collected by FBOs/CBOs, as well as the lack of automated data systems and unwillingness to burden staff and participants with additional data collection, it is likely that considerable effort (accompanied by technical assistance) would be needed by interested FBOs/CBOs to collect even a portion of these data items. It is likely to be necessary if such rigorous studies were to be conducted that the funder would need to carefully recruit FBOs/CBOs and make certain of their willingness and capacity to implement new data collection forms and/or data systems. Based on our observations and analysis, it is unlikely that most FBOs/CBOs would be willing to obtain identifying information (i.e., SSNs) that has been used in past rigorous evaluation studies of public sector training initiatives to match participants with Unemployment Insurance wage record data (or National Directory of New Hires Data, NDNH). Overall, based on discussions conducted with stakeholders and with FBO/CBO administrators/staff during site visits, DOL, foundations, and others interested in funding such rigorous studies would need substantial cooperation on the part of FBOs/CBOs to overcome the very substantial hurdles to mounting experimental and non- experimental impact studies, which are the focus of the next two sections of this report.

B. Potential Experimental Research Designs for Evaluating FBO/CBO Job Clubs

Randomized social science experiments are a type of controlled experiment that happens outside a laboratory environment; they use the same random assignment methods as are used for experiments in the physical and biological sciences. A substantial number of social science experiments have been conducted over the past 50 years. Experimental methods are used because they have a high degree of credibility, as randomization assures that those who experience the policy change (the experimental group) are like, in all important ways, those who do not experience it (the control group), except for the difference in treatment/policy itself. Randomized experiments can only be effective if the treatment is significantly different from the services received by the control group. The sample size must also be adequate to assure that differences in outcomes between the treatment and control groups are due to the treatment rather than chance.[27]

The experimental method has weaknesses, but it should be noted that the weaknesses apply to non-experimental evaluations as well. A common weakness is that the results of the experiment may not generalize to types of individuals other than those enrolled in the experiment, or to different areas with different economic and programmatic environments, or to policies that differ slightly from those tested in the experiment. In evaluation terminology this is the "external validity" problem. The severity of this problem can be reduced if a large number of experiments are conducted in multiple sites, on different populations, and with different policy features. Despite these weaknesses, the strengths of experiments are great. Even if the results may not be completely generalizable and even if they do not always capture all the relevant effects of the program, they provide more credible evidence than other methods.

1. Types of Experiments

There are two ways to conduct random assignment experiments. The first involves denial of services to a control group in order to test the treatment. The second involves enhancing the treatment such that the offer of the normal treatment becomes the control group, while the enhanced treatment becomes the treatment for the experimental group.

Denial of services becomes more practical when resources are limited and the offer of the treatment is presented as a lottery in which the winners receive the treatment.[28] Even in these cases, however, resistance often develops to the implementation of the experiment. For example, the latest evaluation of the Job Corps involved denial of services – treatment group members were offered Job Corps slots, while controls were not – and strong objections were made by youth who were denied participation in the Job Corps program during the enrollment period for the experiment. This denial of service could be a serious obstacle to overcome with respect to implementation of random assignment to rigorously evaluate job clubs operated by FBO/CBOs, in part, because FBO/CBO staff and volunteers would likely be reluctant to deny job seekers within their community needed assistance. There is an added challenge that such organizations would have heightened concerns over being perceived within their communities as denying services to needy job seekers, and that such denial of services would cut against the grain of the underlying mission of churches and other non-profit organizations to serve their communities. Particularly in the case of churches and congregations, there may be a strong resistance to incorporating random assignment (and denial of services) because of faith or spiritual beliefs related to not turning away anyone within the community in need of help.

"Bump ups" of services as an experimental method may be met with less resistance. The treatment group is offered enhanced services, while the control group continues to be offered the traditional services. For example, during the operation of eight Unemployment Insurance experiments, the control group was offered traditional job search assistance and training services. The treatment groups, on the other hand, were either offered enhanced job search assistance and training, or they were offered additional services such as relocation services, reemployment bonuses, or self-employment assistance. In no case was there an objection by members of the control groups about not being offered enhanced services (Wandner 2010). Although FBOs/CBOs are unlikely to object to an experimental evaluation where both groups receive a treatment, none of the sites visited offered, or had intentions of offering, more than one treatment, and none of the sites (with the possible exception of McLean Bible Church) included sufficient observations for an experiment to be likely to achieve statistically significant impact estimates.

2. Applying Experimental Methods to the Rigorous Evaluation of FBO/CBO-Sponsored Job Clubs

Given the recent history of experimental evaluations of employment and training initiatives in the United States and the ability of such studies to generate rigorous net impact estimates of intervention effects (e.g., on employment and earnings), it is sensible to consider using an experimental research design in evaluating the job clubs operated by FBOs and CBOs. Implementing an experimental design involves random assignment to treatment (i.e., eligibility to attend the job club) and control (i.e., no attendance at the job club) groups is likely problematic for most FBOs/CBOs (perhaps all) because of the necessity of denying some job seekers access to the job club services. While it may be possible to convince a select group of larger FBOs or CBOs to be part of such an experimental study, discussions with stakeholders and site visits conducted under this study suggested a low probability of recruiting any such organizations to an experimental study featuring total denial of services to control group members.

The only potentially realistic experimental design option would appear to be a study involving an enhancement of services. This approach would make sense if there were an interest on the part of the participating organization (and the evaluation sponsor) in enhancing the current job club that is being offered. Such enhancements could be accomplished by extending the time/or intensity of a job club (e.g., offering a job club that meets once a week and another one that meets 2 or 3 times a week, or adding a supplementary series of workshops to a basic job club meeting that only the treatment group would receive). It could also be of use, for example, in testing the effectiveness of a new curriculum (or added components to a curriculum) versus an existing curriculum. However, such a design does not make sense if the objective is to evaluate the net impact of the current job club model versus the absence of attending the job club. If there is a desire to estimate the impact of the current program relative to no program, non-experimental methods would in most likelihood have to be used (and these are explored in the next section of this report).

C. Potential Non-Experimental Research Designs for Evaluating FBO/CBO Job Clubs

As described in the previous section, the use of randomized controlled trials (RCTs) is only really feasible for evaluating job club programs for a differential impact analysis where the RCT is used to compare the impacts of alternative treatments rather than the impact of the program compared to no treatment. In this section, two potential non-experimental evaluation impact approaches are explored – an instrumental variables approach known as "randomized encouragement" and propensity score matching (PSM) – and we offer our assessment of the likely appropriateness of each of these non-experimental approaches. Additionally, it should be noted, several other non-experimental research designs – before/after, regression discontinuity, and interrupted time series designs – were examined but were found to be inappropriate or infeasible for assessing impacts of FBO/CBO-sponsored job clubs.

1. Instrumental Variables Using "Randomized Encouragement"

Given the difficulties of using the more common evaluation approaches, it is worth considering the use of an instrumental variables approach known as "randomized encouragement."[29] In this approach, potential FBO/CBO job club users would be divided into a treatment and control group using random assignment. The treatment group would then be encouraged to participate in a FBO/CBO job club by providing them with information about the program and perhaps a small allowance to defray the costs of attending, while the control group would receive nothing. Note that in the randomized encouragement model, the treatment is not randomly assigned, but the encouragement to participate is; we use the terms treatment group and control group to refer to encouragement status, not job search club participation status. Assuming that data on actual participation in the job club can be obtained, two-stage least squares, a form of instrumental variables estimation, can be used to estimate the impact of job club participation on the outcomes of interest. If the encouragement has the desired effect of increasing participation in the program, then the conditions for use of instrumental variables are met, namely that the instrument is correlated with the treatment variable of interest (participation in a job club), but is not related to the outcome variable of interest in any other way (which is assured by the random assignment to encouragement status).

The evaluation would be conducted as follows. First, a pool of potential job club users must be identified and randomly assigned to encouragement treatment or control status. If a state unemployment insurance (UI) office were willing to participate, targeted claimants could be assigned to encouragement status at the time of their initial claim or at some other pre-designated time, e.g., after the sixth week of the claim. Those in the treatment group would receive an inducement to enroll in a FBO/CBO job club, while those in the control group would receive no inducement. The inducement would include, at a minimum, information on the job club(s) of interest including the time and location of meetings. Stronger encouragement could include financial inducements such as a transportation allowance to attend the job club. The FBO/CBO job clubs participating would have to agree to provide the names and Social Security numbers of treatment and control group members who participate to the entity evaluating the program. The evaluation would make use of encouragement status, participation status, information on the individual from the UI claim application and wage records to estimate the impact of the job club on employment and earnings using two-stage least squares.

There are, however, both practical and statistical issues that must be investigated before it can be determined if this approach would be an appropriate choice for an evaluation. On the practical side, one key problem is that the strategy requires the FBO/CBO job clubs that are to be evaluated to provide the evaluator with the participation status of all claimants randomly assigned to treatment and control encouragement status. As noted previously, FBO/CBO job clubs are generally reluctant to collect Social Security numbers, but that would be the most accurate way to identify members of the treatment and control groups who participate in the job club. A second potential problem is that the state Unemployment Insurance agency may balk at providing any form of encouragement to attend a private sector job club, particularly a faith- based job club.

The randomized encouragement model is subject to the dangers noted by Angrist and Krueger (2001) and Murray (2006). First, the instrument, random encouragement, may be a "weak instrument" in the sense that there is not a strong correlation between encouragement and participation; in this situation the evaluation is likely to produce very imprecise estimates or biased estimates. Second, the two-stage estimator is only asymptotically unbiased, so for small samples, it may produce biased estimates of the impact. Third, two-stage least squares may produce biased estimates of the standard errors, although there are approaches available to correct for this. Another limitation of this proposed approach is that it is applicable only for Unemployment Insurance claimants. There is no way to tell if the impacts estimated would apply to other groups of potential job club participants.

As is apparent from the limitations described above, the randomized encouragement approach is not ideal. However, given the unlikelihood of being able to perform random assignment on job club status and the difficulties in developing an appropriate propensity score matching approach (discussed in the next section), a randomized encouragement evaluation approach is worth exploring.

2. Propensity Score Matching (PSM)

Propensity score matching (PSM) is a commonly used method of developing a comparison group that is similar on characteristics that affect program participation and outcomes of interest. The primary motivation for using PSM is that those receiving the treatment of interest may differ systematically from those not receiving the treatment, so rather than compare all who receive the treatment with all who do not, one needs to restrict the comparison group to those who are as similar as possible to those who receive the treatment.

One way to obtain treatment and comparison groups that are similar is to match them on observed characteristics. As there are generally a large number of characteristics that could be matched on, and it would be difficult or impossible to match exactly on continuous variables, Rosenbaum and Rubin (1985) developed propensity score matching as a means to construct a comparison group that is similar to the treatment group where, instead of attempting to match on a large number of characteristics, the match is performed on a single variable, namely the propensity (probability) of participating in the treatment. Although there are many variations on propensity score matching, the basic approach follows the steps described by Caliendo and Kopeinig (2008):

- Using data for treatment group members and those who have not received the treatment, estimate a statistical model that produces an equation predicting the probability that a person with various characteristics will receive the treatment.[30]
- Select a matching mechanism to determine which individuals who do not receive the treatment will be assigned to the comparison group.[31]
- Check the data to make certain that the treatment and comparison group samples span the same range in their probabilities of receiving the treatment, and eliminate cases where there is no overlap.
- Determine if the quality of the match is adequate, and if it is not, refine the equation for estimating propensity scores until adequate matches are obtained.[32]
- Estimate the impact using analysis of variance, regression analysis, or difference-in-difference regression analysis.
- Conduct sensitivity analysis to determine if variations in matching or analysis affect the estimated impacts.

The primary weakness of propensity score matching is that it relies on the strong assumption that all the variables that affect treatment status and the outcome variable are included in the match. Moreover, it is impossible to test whether this assumption is met. There is some disagreement in the research community as to how well results from propensity score matching are similar to the results from RCTs.

None of the studies that have analyzed impact estimates using propensity score matching conclude that the approach is always valid. Barnow (2010) notes that most of the studies find that propensity score matching works best when certain conditions are met:

- It is important to only include observations in the region of common support, where the probabilities of participating are nonzero for both treatment group members and comparison group members,

- Data for the treatment and comparison groups should be drawn from the same data source, or the same questions should be asked of both groups.
- Comparison group members should be drawn from the same geographic area as the treatment group.
- It is important to understand and statistically control for the variables used to select people into the treatment group and to control for variables correlated with the outcomes of interest.
- Differences in difference estimators appear to produce less bias than cross section matching in several of the studies, but it is not clear that this is always the case.

There are several reasons why propensity score matching is unlikely to be useful for evaluating FBO/CBO-sponsored job clubs. First, propensity score matching requires a rich set of variables that can explain how eligible individuals are selected for treatment and comparison group status; yet, FBOs/CBOs rarely collect any data on the characteristics of their participants, making it unlikely that suitable matching characteristics could be found. Second, these organizations do not collect outcome data and are generally unwilling to collect Social Security numbers that could be used to obtain outcome data from other sources such as state unemployment insurance wage records. Third, most FBO/CBO programs have few participants, typically less than 30 at any given time; thus, in most instances, the impact evaluation would be likely to have too few observations to generate statistically significant findings. Finally, Cook, Shadish, and Wong (2008) have noted that propensity score matching tends to work best when the selection process is well understood and the selection variables are available for the analysis; at this time we know little about how individuals select into such programs. Thus, while technically feasible, it is unlikely that in evaluating FBO/CBO job clubs propensity score matching can be used to isolate the effects of the job club from other factors that affect employment and earnings. Overall, we do not recommend that PSM be used as a method for estimating impacts of FBO/CBO job club attendance.

D. Potential Process/Implementation Evaluation Designs for Evaluating FBO/CBO-Sponsored Job Clubs

A process or implementation evaluation[33] involves the systematic collection and synthesis of information on the program environment and processes. A recent World Bank publication (Gertler et al., 2011) provides a working definition of "process evaluation":

> ...A process evaluation is an evaluation that tries to establish the level of quality or success of the processes of a program; for example, adequacy of the administrative processes, acceptability of the program benefits, clarity of the information campaign, internal dynamics of implementing organizations, their policy instruments, their service delivery mechanisms, their management practices, and the linkages among these.

Similarly, Holcolmb and Nightingale (2003) note the "term implementation analysis is used as an umbrella term referring to a range of studies that address the ways public policies are developed and implemented – from the early stages when legislation is formulated and regulations developed, to the actual delivery of services at the grass roots level, and all administrative, political, and operational stages in between." With regard to assessing FBO/CBO-sponsored job clubs, a process/implementation evaluation could be initiated as a stand-alone study or as a component of a comprehensive impact evaluation effort. Such process/implementation evaluations – which provide contextual information to support analyses of program outcomes, impacts, and costs – would be complementary to the various types of experimental/non-experimental evaluations of the job clubs discussed earlier. Additionally, such studies may also provide feedback that can be helpful in identifying differences across job clubs operated by the public sector, CBOs, and FBOs, as well as in efforts to refine the curriculum or instructional methods across job clubs.

A first step in planning a process evaluation of FBO/CBO-based job clubs would be to determine the key evaluation questions that would be the focus of the effort, and then to tailor the types of data collection and analysis activities to address each of the questions. Once the overall purpose and key evaluation questions have been determined, the next step in the planning process is to identify specific types of data collection to be undertaken. Common data collection methods employed in process evaluation, which could be readily applied to assessment of FBO/CBO-sponsored job clubs, include: (1) site visits; (2) focus groups with job club participants; (3) customer satisfaction surveys with job club participants; and (4) implementation of participant tracking systems. Each of these major types of data collection activities are briefly discussed below in relation to evaluating FBO/CBO-sponsored job clubs (anticipating that a detailed process/implementation study design would be completed prior to conduct of any such evaluation effort).

1. Site Visits

An overall goal of observational visits is to determine how job clubs actually operate and the variation in structure, curriculum, instructional methods, etc. that are present across FBO/CBO job clubs. Such visits could also be used to examine the environmental context, including other services available within the local area, economic conditions in the local area, and the extent to which and how the FBO/CBO-operated job club is connected to the public workforce system/American Job Centers.

During the planning phase for such site visits, it will be critical to determine the number of job clubs to be observed and how job clubs will be selected. If the findings from the study are to be used to determine how FBO/CBO-sponsored job clubs operate generally, a representative sample is desirable and can be selected by picking, a (possibly stratified) random sample of job clubs. In addition to selecting FBO/CBO job clubs for site visits, it also might be useful to conduct visits to job clubs operated by public sector organizations in the same localities (to provide a comparison). If such job clubs do not exist, local workforce agencies in the same localities could be visited to learn more about why these organizations do not offer a job club and the extent to which the public sector workforce agency collaborates with the FBO/CBO job club(s) in its locality and to gain views from public sector officials on these FBO/CBO- sponsored job clubs. There is no exact number of site visits that should be selected, with the number to be conducted governed by available budget, the extent of variability in the implementation of job clubs, and the extent to which there is a desire to capture diversity of FBO/CBO implementation by type of workshop (e.g., religiously/spiritually infused versus more secularly based job clubs), numbers attending the job club, geographic location, and other characteristics. A good starting point might be to conduct site visits at 10 to 15 FBO/CBO job clubs, then gauge the extent of variation/diversity in implementation of the job clubs and extent to which job clubs are meeting the needs of job seekers. An observational site visit guide(s) should be developed to ensure that site visitors are observing job clubs on the same factors/dimensions and using the same scale for their ratings on factors. It will also be critical to provide training for site visitors prior to conducting the visits to ensure there is similarity across sites in terms of how interviews are conducted, how site program components/activities (such as job club meetings) are observed and rated, and analyses and other products that emerge from each visit. In planning for site visits, separate discussion guides should be developed to guide discussions with different types of respondents (e.g., job club administrators, facilitators, etc.).[34] During visits, semi-structured interviews should be conducted with program administrators /facilitators to gain their input on their approach to facilitating job club sessions, the time allocated to various job club modules/activities, the challenges in conducting job clubs (e.g., issues with regard to the curriculum, the views on the workshop facility/equipment, etc.), and suggestions for improving job club activities or curriculum. During each visit, it will be important for the two- or three-person site visit team to observe the job club session or series of workshops, as a job club attendee would view the session. Following each visit, a brief site visit report or detailed tables on FBO/CBO site characteristics should be prepared, intended to support and facilitates cross-site analyses/synthesis.

2. Focus Groups with Job Club Participants

As part of the site visit, or separately, focus groups[35] could be conducted with job club participants to obtain their perspectives on the job club they attended. Focus groups would provide an excellent and relatively low-cost opportunity to collect job club attendee perspectives about the structure, substantive content, delivery, and helpfulness of the job club in helping each attendee in planning a job search and securing a job. Krueger and Casey (2010) note the importance of conducting focus groups for a variety of evaluation efforts: "...Focus groups are a wonderful method for gathering information for formative and summative evaluations. But don't limit your use of focus groups to the time after a program is implemented or completed. Focus group interviews are also valuable for getting information in the design phases of programs, policies, and even evaluations."

Such focus groups would likely provide further explanations of what might be observed during site visits to job clubs, as well as what might be found in analyses of customer satisfaction surveys and administrative data on participant outcomes, and other data collection activities. For example, focus groups with job club attendees may help in better understanding how participants react to each job club session/module and which are felt to be most/least important or helpful (and why), views on the job club facility, what exercises/activities were found to be most helpful, whether participants were able to complete their resume, and what participants would change about the workshop.

The steps involved in planning focus groups are relatively similar regardless of the types of individuals included in the group. The first planning step involves determining the scope and purpose of the focus groups, particularly in terms of the study questions each group can effectively address. Once the objectives of each focus group are determined, the next step would involve determining the number and location where each focus group would occur. The number of focus groups to conduct is somewhat subjective, though in all likelihood a good starting point would be to conduct five to seven focus groups (each involving eight to 12 participants). A third planning step involves the development of discussion guides to provide structure to focus groups and ensure that critical topics are covered. Krueger (2010) notes the importance of not only defining questions that are to be addressed but also the sequencing of questions:

> …The questions used in a focus group interview are carefully sequenced so that they focus more and more specifically on the key topic of the study. That is, the questions progressively direct participants into discussing the topic in greater detail and more depth. In other interview environments the researcher might ask the most important questions first or use an informal, unstructured approach to interviewing. These strategies are not used in focus group interviews.

Once planning for the visits has been completed and agreement has been gained on where each of the focus groups should occur, the activities involved in conducting the focus groups are likely to include the following:

- **Recruitment of Focus Group Participants.** A strategy is needed for identifying and selecting job club participants for the focus groups. Selection should be conducted to produce to the extent possible a representative cross-section of workshop participants (i.e., so that focus group attendees are not "cherry-picked"). One potential cost-effective approach is to conduct focus groups at the conclusion of the observational site visits, and to randomly select eight to 12 participants from the roster of job club attendees over the past month or quarter. When selecting individuals to attend focus groups it is important to take into consideration the likelihood of no-shows (e.g., it may be necessary to select/invite 15 to 20 job club attendees to yield 8 to 12 focus group participants). To help encourage participation in the focus groups by those selected, it may also be necessary to offer an incentive payment (e.g., typically between $25 and $50), especially to recruit individuals who may have attended job clubs in the past but are now employed.
- **Identify an Appropriate Facility for the Focus Group.** It may be possible to conduct the focus group in the conference room where the job club is held or another nearby conference room on/near the organization sponsoring the job club. There also are professional focus group facilities (which are located throughout the country), as well as conference rooms at American Job Centers or other public employment agencies that could potentially host focus group sessions.
- **Conduct the Focus Group.** Within a focus group setting, a moderator guides the discussion, making sure to incorporate all of the focus group participants in the discussion. The moderator utilizes a discussion guide, but listens carefully to responses and follows up with questions to further probe participant responses. Krueger (2010) emphasizes the important role that the moderator plays in engaging focus group participants. Questions are usually open-ended and intended to generate a variety of viewpoints. Typically, focus group discussions last about 90 minutes, during which it is possible to cover six to eight major topics. Focus groups provide an ideal opportunity to gauge where views of group members converge or diverge and to probe in considerable detail the perspectives of focus group members. Krueger (2010, p. 381) notes the importance of obtaining a range of perspectives from focus group participants. Focus groups are often video- or audio-taped. In the absence of a

video/audio recording, it is essential to keep careful notes of the dialogue throughout the session.

- **Summarize the Results of the Focus Group.** Immediately following each focus group, it is important to draft a summary of the focus group discussion. This synthesis should capture the main points made by participants on each of the subjects covered, including points of consensus and disagreement among focus group members. If available, this synthesis can be supplemented with an video or audiotape of the focus group session.[36]

3. Customer Satisfaction and Participant Follow-up Surveys

Customer satisfaction surveys are one method available to determine and track job club attendees' engagement in and perspectives on an FBO/CBO-sponsored job club. Such a survey could be conducted periodically (once yearly or quarterly) or on job club participants once they exit the workshop. Such surveys can be conducted by having participants complete a form (manually), by sending out a mailing, by telephone, or Internet. Using an Internet application, it is possible to easily (and at very low cost) deliver the survey to participants and, depending upon the software used, it is possible to instantaneously tabulate results by question as survey responses are completed. The advantage of in-person completion of the survey (for example, the last 10 minutes of a job club meeting) is that response rate is likely to be high (though the particular meeting may not be representative of meeting held throughout a year or quarter). In developing customer satisfaction surveys, care should be taken to ensure that the survey is not overly burdensome (e.g., can be completed in not more than about 10 to 15 minutes). Often a 5- point Likert scale is used in customer satisfaction surveys. The instrument should also include several qualitative open-ended questions that allow for more detailed identification of strengths, weaknesses, and ways in which curriculum or facilitation of the job club could be enhanced. While conducting a customer satisfaction survey at the conclusion of the workshop is useful for gauging participant views about the job club curriculum and facilitation, it might be useful to supplement such a customer satisfaction survey with a follow-up survey at six or 12 months after the participant begins or concludes attendance at the job club. Often the date of first attendance is a more solid date for timing follow-up surveys, as participants sometimes disappear and then re-engage with job clubs – making it difficult to fix a date of exit. However the issue with using begin date is that it is possible that a participant will not have become employed and is still attending the job club six months or a year after beginning the job club.

4. Job Club Participant Tracking System

The FBO/CBO-sponsored job clubs visited as part of this study did not employ automated management information or participant tracking systems to support systematic and in- depth analysis of participant characteristics, services received, or employment/earnings outcomes. With a few exceptions, they also did not use detailed (manual) participant forms to collect data on job club participants at the time of entry into the program or during their participation, with the exception in some instances of documenting attendance at job club sessions. Most FBO/CBO administrators and staff indicated that their organizations did not need extensive data about job club attendees and that they did not want to burden staff or participants with completing additional forms and/or entering participant data into automated data systems.[37] However, it is possible that some FBOs and CBOs operating job clubs, similar to their public sector counterparts, would be interested in and benefit from collecting some additional participant-level data. Such collection of participant-level data could benefit sponsoring organizations from the standpoint of monitoring and assessing program performance, as well as (if interested) reporting on program results. For interested FBOs and CBOs, it might be useful to consider implementing two participant tracking forms: (1) a participant intake form to capture characteristics of new job club participants (e.g., several demographics, education and employment background, career/job interests, and potential barriers to employment), and (2) a service receipt and employment/earnings outcomes tracking form. Examples of two fairly streamlined forms that interested job clubs could potentially implement are provided in Appendix F. (Note: The two forms in Appendix F are samples, which can and should be tailored to individual job club requirements, operations, and capabilities.). The collection of outcome data (on employment and earnings) could be timed to either the date job seekers start or exit from the job club (with the sample forms in Appendix F using date of exit from the job club). Finally, the sample forms (and other participant-level data collected) could be entered into automated participant data systems to facilitate data analysis and reporting, including using software applications that operate on stand-alone personal computers (such as Microsoft Access, STATA, SPSS-PC) or more complex web-based or mainframe software applications.[38]

E. Recommendations for Future Evaluation of FBO/CBO Job Clubs

Overall, for reasons stated earlier and throughout this section – particularly FBO/CBO inability/unwillingness to collect significant amounts of data on job club participants and reluctance to consider random assignment of job seekers to treatment or control groups – the prospects for rigorous (experimental) evaluation of FBO/CBO-sponsored job clubs appear to be bleak. It is a remote possibility that a select group of FBOs/CBOs could be enticed to be part of an enhancement/bump-up type experimental study, though such a study would not be helpful in determining the net impact of enrollment versus non-enrollment in a job club – but rather would only explore incremental effects of some added feature to an existing job club. Such a study would need to carefully select among CBO/FBOs serving sufficient numbers of job seekers (likely to be in the neighborhood of 400 to 500 job seekers, unless pooling of samples is possible across sites) and provide substantial levels of technical assistance to ensure that: (1) an appropriate point of randomization is established, (2) treatment group members receive the enhanced services in an appropriate dosage and that there is no contamination of individuals assigned to the control group, (3) participating organizations collect data elements necessary to support the analysis part of the study (including necessary personal identifiers, services received, and if appropriate outcomes, all of which organizations may be reluctant to collect), and (4) a participant tracking system is designed and implemented to support random assignment and secure maintenance of participant characteristics, services, and outcomes. With respect to non-experimental study designs, while before/after, regression discontinuity, and interrupted time series research designs do not appear appropriate or feasible, there is some potential for using "randomized encouragement" and propensity score matching (PSM). Most promising of these two non-experimental methods is the random encouragement approach, though as discussed earlier in this section such an approach is likely to run into a host of implementation challenges.

Building on this exploratory study, perhaps the most promising (and feasible) next step from an evaluation perspective would be to conduct more detailed process/implementation study of FBO/CBO job clubs, possibly in conjunction with AJC job clubs to better define what the distinctions are. A process/implementation study would be applicable to periodic efforts to assess and track implementation of the job clubs over time, as well as to identify strengths and weaknesses/challenges of the job clubs from varying perspectives (e.g., job club attendees, job club facilitators, and other organizational administrators/other staff). The strength of such studies is in obtaining contextual information for understanding the environment in which interventions occur, as well as in gaining rich qualitative perspectives on the intervention. Through not providing estimates of impacts of attendance at job clubs (on employment and earnings), such studies can be complementary to experimental/non-experimental studies and help to provide explanations for participant outcomes/impacts. Such information, particularly if collected over time, can help to identify ways in which job clubs are exceeding or falling short of expectations from various perspectives, and identify potential approaches to improving workshop content, facilitation, facilities, and participant outcomes.

APPENDIX A. JOB CLUB EVALUATIONSTAKEHOLDER DISCUSSION GUIDE

Introduction: I am (we are) researchers from the Capital Research Corporation, Inc., a private research organization based in Arlington, VA, which conducts policy-related research on a variety of social welfare and economic issues. Our telephone interview here today is part of an evaluation focusing on job clubs being administered by community-based and faith-based organizations. This project is being conducted by Capital Research Corporation and George Washington University, under contract to the U.S. Department of Labor. As part of this evaluation, we are conducting an initial round of telephone interviews with 7 to 9 individuals knowledgeable about faith-based organizational involvement in job clubs. We would like to take about one hour of your time to discuss your knowledge of job clubs. In our discussions, we have a particular interest in comparing job clubs sponsored by public sector organizations (such as local workforce investment boards or One-Stop Career Centers) with job clubs sponsored by faith-based and community-based organizations. [If your organization sponsors/operates job clubs, we are both interested in learning about your job club, as well as your wider perspectives on job clubs operated by public, community-based, and faith-based organizations.] Before beginning the interview, I (we) want to thank you for agreeing to participate in the study. I (we) know that you are busy and we will try to be as focused as possible. Before we start, I want to let you know that though we will be taking notes during this interview, when we write our reports and discuss our findings, information from all interviews is compiled and presented so that no one person can be identified. Do you have any questions before we begin?

1. Before we begin, we'd like to get some general information about you –
   a. Name
   b. Organization
   c. Contact information (address, telephone, e-mail)

    d.   Title/Role at Organization

    e.   For how long and in what capacity have you been involved with or studied job clubs (e.g., researcher, program developer, implementer, etc.) and faith based organizations.

2.   Over the past decade, do you believe that the number of faith-based and community-based organizations sponsoring job clubs has increased, stayed the same, or decreased? What about the number of people participating in such job clubs? If there has been a change in either the number of job clubs or the number of participants, what factors are responsible for the increase/decrease? Please discuss and identify any literature/resource that provides data/statistics on the number of faith-based/community-based job clubs in existence or that have formed over the past five years.

3.   What types of community-based and faith-based organizations sponsor such job clubs? Why do they hold these clubs?

4.   What are the targeted subpopulations (if any) served by faith-based and community-based organizations? Do the subpopulations targeted or served by faith- and community-based organizations differ from the subpopulations targeted/served by public sector sponsored job clubs – and if yes, how?

5.   We are particularly interested in identifying differences in the ways in which job clubs operated by faith-based and community-based organizations serve their participants versus those operated by public sector organizations, such as local workforce investment boards, America's Job Centers (or One-Stop Centers), or welfare agencies. Please discuss differences in terms of the following dimensions:

    a.   How often and for how long job clubs meet

    b.   Size/numbers attending job club sessions

    c.   Duration/intensity of job club involvement for participants

    d.   Patterns of attendance/extent of attrition from job clubs

    e.   Curriculum used and topics covered during job clubs

    f.   Kinds of instructional methods used (e.g., lecture, small group instruction, peer group discussion, web-based/computer-based instruction

    g.   Types of instructors/facilitators used

    h.   Extent of case management/peer support/mentoring provided

    i.   Job development/placement assistance provided

    j.   Additional services provided (e.g., transportation, clothing, referral to job training, other support services)

    k.   Inclusion of social and recreational activities

    l.   Inclusion of religious and spiritual activities

    m. Activities that occur once the participant finds a job (e.g., are they encouraged to continue to attend job club sessions?)

6.   To what extent and how do FBO/CBO-sponsored job club interact/partner with the public workforce development system/America's Job Centers? For example, are there referrals to and from the workforce development system? Are FBO/CBO job club participants encouraged to visit and use America's Job Centers/workforce development resources? If so, what public sector workforce services do job club participants use?

7. What types of data do faith-based and community-based organizations typically collect on job club participant characteristics, services received, and outcomes? For example, are automated data systems being used to track participant characteristics, services received, and outcomes? Do you have any knowledge of how data collection differs between FBO/CBO job clubs and government-sponsored job clubs?

8. What outcome measures (if any) are being used to assess job club performance in faith- and community-based job clubs and, if known, how do these compare to those collected by public sector organizations conducting job clubs? Some possibilities include:
   - Number of participants attending job club sessions
   - Number of participants dropping out of the job club prior to obtaining a job
   - Average number of job club sessions attended (and range)
   - Job placement outcomes
   - Job retention outcomes
   - Earnings/hourly wages/hours worked
   - Other outcome measures, such as improved self-esteem or upgrading of skills/educational credentials

9. Are you familiar with any past or current studies or research that focused on outcomes for participants of faith- or community-based job clubs? If so, please discuss and provide references for evaluations/literature that are specifically focused on this topic.
   a. Are you aware of any faith-based or community-based organizations operating a job club that has been the focus of a formal evaluation? If yes, what type of evaluation was conducted (e.g., implementation/process evaluation, outcome evaluation, quasi- experimental or experimental net impact evaluation, cost-effectiveness/cost-benefit study)?
   b. Do you think it would be possible to conduct an evaluation involving randomized controlled trials (experimental) to systematically examine job club impacts on participants (i.e., which would involve random assignment of job club candidates to treatment and control groups, similar to experiments currently used to test new medical treatments)?
   c. Do you have any suggestions with regard to how a future evaluation could be conducted to more systematically gather data on the outcomes of FBO/CBO job clubs?

10. Finally, is there any other information regarding the operations or potential effectiveness of FBO/CBO job clubs that you haven't shared/we haven't discussed? Thank you for your time.

APPENDIX B. JOB CLUB EVALUATIONSITE VISIT INTERVIEW GUIDE FBO/CBO- OPERATED JOB CLUBS

Introduction: I am (we are) researchers from the Capital Research Corporation, Inc., a private research organization based in Arlington, VA, which conducts policy-related research on a variety of social welfare and economic issues. Our visit here today is part of an evaluation focusing on job clubs being administered by community-based and faith-based organizations. This project is being conducted by Capital Research Corporation and George Washington University, under contract to the U.S. Department of Labor. A major aim of the evaluation effort is to identify lessons learned from your experiences in conducting job clubs for unemployed and underemployed individuals. As part of this evaluation, we are conducting site visits to six localities across the United States, during which we are interviewing administrators and staff involved in providing job club services. We are here to learn about your job club model, including how you recruit individuals to attend your job club, the services job club participants receive, how participation in your job club helps participants find and keep jobs, and how your job club activities are related to other services and activities your organization provides. Our aim is to learn from your experiences, not audit or judge your programs.

Privacy Statement: Before beginning the interview, I (we) want to thank you for agreeing to participate in the study. I (we) know that you are busy and we will try to be as focused as possible. We have many questions and are going to talk to many different people, so please do not feel as though we expect you to be able to answer every question. And, we understand that your participation in this discussion is voluntary and you may choose to not answer questions you don't wish to. In addition, before we start, I want to let you know that though we take notes at these interviews, information is never repeated with the name of the respondent. When we write our reports and discuss our findings, information from all interviews is compiled and presented so that no one person can be identified. Do you have any questions before we begin? [Respond to questions.]

A. General Job Club Organization and Environmental Context

1. Before we begin, we'd like to get some general information on you and verify some information about your organization.
   a. Organization name
   b. Contact information (address, telephone, fax, e-mail)
   c. Website address
2. Obtain the following information on each respondent involved in the interview (note: request a business card from each interviewee):
   a. Name
   b. Organization
   c. Contact information (address, telephone, e-mail)
   d. Title
   e. Position/role in the organization and in the job club
   f. How long the individual has been involved in organization and the job club
3. Please provide background on your organization:
   a. Type of organization operating the job club (e.g., CBO, church or congregation, 501-c-3)
   b. In addition to the job club, what other types of services does your organization provide for unemployed or underemployed job seekers?
      • Other networking events (please describe.)
      • Resource room?

- Job readiness, resume, interviewing, other types of workshops
- One-on-one job placement assistance
- Job development assistance
- Job fairs
- Training services
- Other types of assistance

   c. Other relevant features about the organization that have affected the job club implementation/operations

4. What is the geographic area from which you principally draw your job club participants? Please generally describe the economic environment for this service area --
   a. Unemployment rate/availability of job openings in area served (generally and for particular population attending job club).
   b. Other local economic conditions that may affect the job club's ability to recruit and retain participants and the ability of job club participants to find employment (e.g., in- or out-migration of major employers, major layoffs, and natural disasters)

B. Job Club Objectives and Start-Up

1. When was your job club established?
2. Why did your organization establish the job club? If the job club has been in existence for several years, why does your organization continue to offer the job club?
3. What are the main goals of your job club? Have these goals changed since the establishment of your job club?
4. Please discuss start-up and early implementation experiences of your job club --
   a. Did your organization start from scratch or draw upon the curriculum or experiences of another existing model?
   b. Who took the lead in establishing your job club?
   c. What challenges did your organization run into in planning and initiating your job club?
   d. What factors facilitated project start-up?
   e. What factors were barriers to starting the job club?
   f. What organizations did you work most closely with during the design and start-up of your job club?

C. Outreach, Intake, and Assessment Activities for the Job Club

1. What methods does your organization use to recruit unemployed/underemployed individuals to attend your job club? Possibilities include:
   - Announcement to the congregation/general membership of organization
   - Distribution of flyers, posters, or other educational/informational

- Informational websites
- Toll-free informational hotlines
- Outreach campaigns using media (e.g., TV, radio, newspaper, ads on buses/bus shelters)
- Orientation workshops/presentations in the community (e.g., at nonprofit organizations, America's Job Centers/One-Stops, other workforce development agencies, neighborhood centers, libraries)
- Word-of-mouth
- Web-based recruitment (using Twitter, blogs, Facebook, LinkedIn)

2. Has your organization worked with any other organizations to obtain referrals to your program? Possibilities include:
   - Churches/congregations/faith-based organizations
   - Community/nonprofit organizations
   - Workforce system (One-Stops)
   - Courts/correctional system
   - Other

3. Is recruitment for your job club broadly targeted on all unemployed/underemployed individuals in your service area or is it targeted on unemployed/underemployed individuals with specific characteristics? Possibilities include:
   - Only members of a congregation
   - Specific neighborhoods/geographic areas
   - Low-income/disadvantaged individuals
   - Adults only
   - Youth only
   - Formerly incarcerated individuals
   - Separating/retiring active duty military personnel
   - Unemployed/underemployed veterans
   - Trade-affected/dislocated workers
   - Older workers/seniors
   - Persons with disabilities
   - Unemployed white-collar workers
   - Individuals dislocated from various manufacturing and service sectors

4. Has your job club experienced recruitment challenges (e.g., inability to find/recruit enough interested individuals for your job club)? If so, what challenges have been encountered and how have each of these challenges been addressed? Some possible challenges include:
   - Had difficulty finding unemployed/underemployed individuals
   - Economic conditions have improved so there is not as much need for a job club in the locality
   - Some of the outreach strategies didn't result in many applicants
   - Partner organizations did not provide enough referrals
   - Some applicants had difficulty getting to job club facility (e.g., transportation difficulties)
   - Didn't have enough resources for recruitment

- Other similar programs competing for the same pool of participants: provide description of the other organizations

5. What incentives and services (if any) have been used to encourage participation and/or retention in the job club? Possible incentives include:
   a. Bus passes/tokens
   b. Food provided at job club
   c. Supportive services
   d. Other

6. Can anyone attend your job club, or is there a process by which individuals are assessed to be eligible or appropriate to attend your job club? If there is a process, who determines eligibility or whether an individual is appropriate to participate in your job club? What, if any, criteria are used to select among candidates recruited? *(ask for copies of any assessment materials)*
   Possible criteria includes:
   - Be unemployed/underemployed
   - Be referred from other specific organizations or agencies
   - Attend an orientation session
   - Complete a program application
   - Complete an interview with program staff
   - Meet income or other requirements
   - Meet education level requirement (e.g., high school diploma)
   - Take/pass a standardized skills assessment test (e.g., TABE, ABLE, BESI, WorkKeys)
   - Take/pass grantee's own customized skills assessment test
   - Other, please specify

7. Are there any efforts to determine the specific service needs of job club participants? If so, how are the service needs of job club participants determined? Please take us briefly through the assessment process, noting any formal assessment tests that you use prior to or during participation in your job club (e.g., TABE, interest inventories, substance abuse screening).

8. Is an individual service strategy or employment development plan created for each participant *(note: request a blank copy of the form used)*? If yes, please briefly describe this plan or process.

D. Description of the Job Club Services/Activities

1. Where (at what location) does the job club meet? Are there multiple locations? Does the location for your job club vary (e.g., from week-to-week)?

2. How often does the job club meet (weekly, bi-weekly, once a month)? For how many hours/minutes is the job club scheduled to meet? Is the actual duration of the job club about the same duration as it is scheduled (e.g., does it run over)? Is the actual duration of each job club variable or about the same?

3. In addition to formal club meetings, do job club members interact with staff or volunteers for assistance at other times or in other situations? If so, please describe purpose and frequency.

4. How is the job club structured? Do individuals start and end as a cohort or is there open entry/open exit to the job club? Is there, for example, a 6- or 10-week series of workshops during which a curriculum is presented systematically from week to week, or is each job club meeting a stand-alone workshop? Is there a separate series of workshops offered at other days/times? Do participants come and go as they please from session to session (e.g., attend a few sessions, skip several, come back) or are they expected to stay engaged in sessions until they secure a job? Once they obtain a job, can and do they continue to attend the job club?

5. What is the typical attendance at the job club (i.e., total number attending and percentage of members attending)? [Note: If available, please provide a table with the number of attendees of each job club held over the past 12 months). Is there much variation in number of job club attendees each session (minimum/maximum attendees over the last 12 months)? What is the maximum number of attendees that can be handled for a given session? Does anyone ever get turned away because too many show for a particular job club session? What, if any, is the ideal number (or range) of attendees for a given job club session?

6. Is a curriculum used to guide the job club workshop sessions? If yes, could you provide us with a copy of the curriculum and discuss the following –
    *   What is the name of the curriculum? Who developed the curriculum? Was the curriculum purchased or obtained from another organization? Was the curriculum developed in-house? If so, describe the curriculum development process.
    *   Please discuss source(s) of the curriculum – and if more than one source was used, discuss how and the process by which the curriculum was developed.
    *   Please provide an overview of the curriculum – an outline of curriculum modules/key substantive topics covered, amount of time devoted to each module/topic
    *   What kinds of instructional methods are used (e.g., lecture, small group instruction, peer group discussion, web-based/computer-based instruction).

7. How is each job club meeting structured? Is the structure/activities of each meeting basically the same each time or is there substantial variation across job club meetings? Does the structure/activities depend on who is in attendance at each job club meeting? Can you please provide an overview of a typical job club meeting, including overall duration and sequencing/amount of time devoted to specific activities? Please discuss specific types of activities that are included in your job club, such as:
    *   instruction on job readiness and effective job search strategies;
    *   discussions about targeting certain occupations or industry sectors for employment;
    *   time set aside for job club members to plan their job search activities for an upcoming period and to identify specific job leads (through searches on the

Internet on job boards and employer websites, discussion among job club members, reviews of classified advertisements, and other networking activities);

- assistance on resume and cover letter development/refinement;
- discussions among job club participants about challenges and opportunities with respect to job search activities;
- invitations to employers to share information on their industry sectors and potential job openings;
- conduct of mock (practice) or actual interviews with employers for jobs;
- speakers presenting on specific topics; and
- testimonials from former/current participants.

8. To what extent are job club sessions/workshops facilitated by a staff member? Who plays the role of the facilitator (e.g., staff, volunteer)? Is the facilitator the same from job club session to job club session? What role does the facilitator play (e.g., providing instruction/lectures, guiding group discussion, working one-on-one or in small groups with participants)?

9. Is there any kind of mentoring/case management component for participants that accompanies (or is offered in addition to) the job club? If there is a mentoring/case management component --
   - Who provides mentoring/case management services?
   - What are the credentials of mentors/case managers?
   - When does the mentoring/case management occur?
   - How is the match made between the participant and the mentor/case manager? What is the caseload for the case manager/mentor?
   - How long does mentoring/case management last (e.g., 6 months, year, until an individual finds a job, etc.)? Is there variation in duration? How often does mentor/case manager meet in-person with participant (minimum, maximum, average)? What other types of contacts occur between participant and mentor/case manager (telephone, email, texting) and how often? What constitutes "completing" mentorship/case management?
   - What activities occur after a person obtains a job?

10. To what extent and how does the FBO/CBO-sponsored job club interact/partner with the public workforce development system/America's Job Centers? State DOL/ES career centers? For example, are there referrals to and from the workforce development system? Are FBO/CBO job club participants encouraged to visit and use America's Job Centers/workforce development resources? If so, what public sector workforce services do job club participants use?

11. What are the patterns of attendance at job clubs among participants (e.g., attend each job club until the participant finds a job, attend session and skip several and then attend)? Once individuals begin attending the job club do they continue to attend until they obtain a job? How much attrition is there before job placement? What are the specific reasons for dropping out/attrition prior to obtaining a job? Has job club taken any steps to reduce attrition and, if yes, what specific steps have been taken?

12. Once a participant obtains a job, are they encouraged to continue to attend job club sessions? What additional services, if any, are provided to those successful in obtaining jobs (e.g., job retention services, transportation services, clothing, referral

to training and other workforce services, and other support services)? Are participants that find a job encouraged to upgrade their skills and credentials so they can move to better paying jobs? Do participants that find a job come back to the job club to share their experiences?

E. Job Club Participant Characteristics and Outcomes

1. What types of data are being collected on job club participant characteristics, services received, and outcomes? What specific information do you collect (e.g., name, email address)? For example, is an automated data system being used to track participant characteristics, services received, and outcomes? If available --
   - Please provide copies of the participant forms being used (e.g., intake, assessment, services receipt/tracking, participant outcome forms).
   - Please provide documentation of the automated data system being used (e.g., systems manual, software program being used, whether it is a web-based application, sample screen shots and reports).
2. What outcome measures (if any) are being used to assess job club performance, and if available, please provide data on the following outcomes for the past year for job club attendees (or three years, if possible) –
   - Number of participants attending job club sessions
   - Number of participants dropping out of the job club prior to obtaining a job
   - Average number of job club sessions attended (and range)
   - Job placement outcomes
   - Job retention outcomes
   - Earnings/hourly wages/hours worked
   - Other outcome measures, such as improved self-esteem or upgrading of skills/educational credentials
   - Discuss how each of these outcome measures are obtained (e.g., telephone calls conducted with participants/employers and the intervals at which data are collected).
3. Of the strategies or services that you provide through your job club program, which do you feel are most/least effective in helping job club participants to obtain jobs? Are there ways in which your job club has fallen short of its goals for helping participants cope with unemployment and obtain jobs? If yes, how? Are there other approaches, strategies, or services that you believe would contribute to better employment outcomes for the job club participants you serve?
4. How does your job club differ from activities provided by the public workforce system? Please describe the major similarities and differences in philosophy, approach, characteristics of customers served, services provided, and outcomes.
5. Has your job club been the focus of a formal evaluation? If yes, what type of evaluation was conducted (e.g., implementation/process evaluation, outcome evaluation, quasi-experimental or experimental net impact evaluation, cost-effectiveness/cost-benefit study)? Please provide final or interim reports that may have been produced under the evaluation effort(s)?

6. If your job club has *not* been the subject of an evaluation in the past, would you be willing to be part of a future evaluation? Do you think your organization (or other FBO/CBOs) would be willing to be part of a randomized controlled trial (experimental) evaluation to systematically examine job club impacts on participants [i.e., which would involve random assignment of job club candidates to treatment and control groups, similar to experiments currently used to test new medical treatments)?

7. Do you have any suggestions with regard to how a future evaluation could be conducted to more systematically gather data on the outcomes of FBO/CBO job clubs?

F. Job Club Staffing

1. Please describe your organizational structure and staffing arrangement for your job club (if available, please provide an organizational chart)
   - Paid administrators/staff involved in the job club initiative (i.e., role, number, and hours per month or FTE)
   - Number of volunteers (i.e., role, number, and hours per month or FTE)
   - Were there any new hires brought on for the job club initiative
   - What is the experience and/or credentials of administrators/staff/volunteers involved in job clubs
   - How much turnover has there been in job club staff (past 12 months)

2. What kinds of training/staff development activities have been provided for job club staff? Please describe the extent and types of training/staff development activities, including who has conducted the training. Are there areas in which you feel there should have been more staff development/training? If yes, what are those areas?

G. Job Club Costs/Expenditures

1. If available, what are the costs associated with developing and implementing FBO/CBO job clubs?

2. What are the major ongoing costs/expenditures for the program? If available, please provide a line item budget and line item expenditures report for the most recent year (e.g., breaking down total expenditures for items such as project staff, rent, equipment purchase or rental, subcontracts, etc.)? Note: If expenditure data are not available, please estimate the resources for job clubs over the past year (e.g., staff, volunteers, cash and in-kind donations, technology, facilities/space)?

3. What kinds of funding have been used to pay for the costs of the job club?
   a. Donations from congregation/budget line item from the sponsoring organization
   b. Foundation grants
   c. Government funding (describe if federal, state, or local and whether funding is grant or contract)
   d. Other sources

H. Closing Questions

1.   What are your organization's plans for the next several years with regard to the job club? Will the job club be expanded? Are there sufficient resources to sustain the initiative in the coming years? What sources of funding are likely to be used to sustain your job club?
2.   To what extent do you think your program could be replicated in other localities? What features of your job club are most amenable to replication? What features of the project are least amenable to replication? How does location, the target population served, or other distinctive features of your program make it either non-transferable or limit transferability?
3.   To date, what do you consider your most important accomplishments under your job club project? What do you believe to be the main lessons learned from your job club?

I. Checklist of Items to Collect from Site (If Available)

-   Background information about the locality
-   Background information about the organization
-   Additional documentation/reports detailing job club services/activities
-   Diagram showing how participants flow through the job club
-   Budget/expenditures data for the past 12 months

APPENDIX C. JOB CLUB EVALUATION SITE VISIT INTERVIEW GUIDE – WORKFORCE INVESTMENT BOARD (WIB)/AMERICAN JOB CENTER (AJC) OPERATED JOB CLUBS

Introduction: I am (we are) researchers from the Capital Research Corporation, Inc., a private research organization based in Arlington, VA, which conducts policy-related research on a variety of social welfare and economic issues. Our visit here today is part of an evaluation focusing on job clubs being administered by community-based and faith-based organizations. This project is being conducted by Capital Research Corporation and George Washington University, under contract to the U.S. Department of Labor. As part of this evaluation, we are conducting site visits to public sector, faith-based, and community-based organizations conducting job clubs in six local workforce areas. With regard to our visits to WIBs/American Job Centers, we are interested in learning about (1) if your organization operates a job club, details about how this job club operates and the services it offers, and (2) whether your organization has linkages with faith-based or community-based organizations and the nature of these linkages.

Privacy Statement: Before beginning the interview, I (we) want to thank you for agreeing to participate in the study. I (we) know that you are busy and we will try to be as focused as possible. We have many questions and are going to talk to many different people, so please do not feel as though we expect you to be able to answer every question. And, we understand that your participation in this discussion is voluntary and you may choose to not answer questions you don't wish to. In addition, before we start, I want to let you know that though we take notes at these interviews, information is never repeated with the name of the respondent. When we write our reports and discuss our findings, information from all interviews is compiled and presented so that no one person can be identified. Do you have any questions before we begin?

A. Background on Organization and Collaboration with Local Job Clubs

1. Before we begin, we'd like to get some general information on you and verify some information about your organization.
   a. Organization name
   b. Contact information (address, telephone, fax, e-mail)
   c. Website address
2. Obtain the following information on each respondent involved in the interview (note: request a business card from each interviewee):
   a. Name
   b. Organization
   c. Contact information (address, telephone, e-mail)
   d. Title
   e. Position/role in the organization
3. Please provide background on your organization]:
   a. Type of organization (e.g., government agency, nonprofit established to operate the AJC, for-profit, etc.
   b. Geographic area served
   c. Major sources of funding (funding from federal/state/city agencies, foundations, fee for service)
   d. Types of clients/customers served or targeted
   e. Major programs/initiatives operating
   f. What types of services does your organization provide for unemployed or underemployed job seekers?
      • Job club?
      • Resource room?
      • Job readiness, resume, other types of workshops
      • One-on-one job placement assistance
      • Job development assistance
      • Job fairs
      • Training services
      • Other types of assistance

Note: If Wib/American Job Center Does *Not* Operate a Job Club, Skip Sections B-G and Go to Section H (Additionally: Find Out Why the Organization Does Not Offer a Job Club).

B. Job Club Objectives and Start-Up

1. When was your job club established?
2. Why did your organization establish the job club? If the job club has been in existence for several years, why does your organization continue to offer the job club?
3. What are the main goals of your job club?
4. Please discuss start-up and early implementation experiences of your job club --
    a. Did your organization start from scratch or draw upon the curriculum or experiences of another existing model?
    b. What challenges did your organization run into in planning and initiating your job club?

C. Outreach, Intake, and Assessment Activities for the Job Club

1. What methods does your organization use to recruit unemployed/underemployed individuals to attend your job club? Possibilities include:
    - Distribution of flyers, posters, or other educational/informational
    - Announcements provided with unemployment insurance checks
    - Informational websites
    - Toll-free informational hotlines
    - Outreach campaigns using media (e.g., TV, radio, newspaper, ads on buses/bus shelters)
    - Orientation workshops/presentations in the community (e.g., at nonprofit organizations, other workforce development agencies, neighborhood centers, libraries)
    - Word-of-mouth
    - Web-based recruitment (using Twitter, blogs, Facebook, LinkedIn)
2. Has your organization worked with any other organizations to obtain referrals to your program? Possibilities include:
    - Churches/congregations/faith-based organizations
    - Community/nonprofit organizations
    - Courts/correctional system
    - Other
3. Is recruitment for your job club broadly targeted on all unemployed/underemployed individuals in your service area or is it targeted on unemployed/underemployed individuals with specific characteristics? Possibilities include:
    - Specific neighborhoods/geographic areas
    - Low-income/disadvantaged individuals
    - Unemployment insurance claimants
    - Welfare recipients
    - Adults only
    - Youth only
    - Formerly incarcerated individuals

- Separating/retiring active duty military personnel
- Unemployed/underemployed veterans
- Trade-affected/dislocated workers
- Older workers/seniors
- Persons with disabilities
- Unemployed white-collar workers
- Individuals dislocated from various manufacturing and service sectors

4. Has your job club experienced recruitment challenges (e.g., inability to find/recruit enough interested individuals for your job club)? If so, what challenges have been encountered and how have each of these challenges been addressed? Some possible challenges include:
   - Had difficulty finding unemployed/underemployed individuals
   - Economic conditions have improved so there is not as much need for a job club in the locality
   - Some of the outreach strategies didn't result in many applicants
   - Partner organizations did not provide enough referrals
   - Some applicants had difficulty getting to job club facility (e.g., transportation difficulties)
   - Didn't have enough resources for recruitment
   - Other similar programs competing for the same pool of participants: provide description of the other organizations

5. What incentives and services (if any) have been used to encourage participation and/or retention in the job club? Possible incentives include:
   a. Bus passes/tokens
   b. Food provided at job club
   c. Supportive services
   d. Other

6. Can anyone attend your job club, or is there a process by which individuals are assessed to be eligible or appropriate to attend your job club? If there is a process, who determines eligibility or whether an individual is appropriate to participate in your job club? What, if any, criteria are used to select among candidates recruited? *(ask for copies of any assessment materials)*
   Possible criteria include:
   - Be unemployed/underemployed
   - Be registered/enrolled with the Wagner-Peyser program or the Workforce Investment Act
   - Be referred from other specific organizations or agencies
   - Attend an orientation session
   - Complete a program application
   - Complete an interview with program staff
   - Meet income or other requirements
   - Meet education level requirement (e.g., high school diploma)
   - Take/pass a standardized skills assessment test (e.g., TABE, ABLE, BESI, WorkKeys)
   - Take/pass grantee's own customized skills assessment test

- Other, please specify

7. Are there any efforts to determine the specific service needs of job club participants? If so, how are the service needs of job club participants determined? Please take us briefly through the assessment process, noting any formal assessment tests that you use prior to or during participation in your job club (e.g., TABE, interest inventories, substance abuse screening).

8. Is an individual service strategy or employment development plan created for each participant (note: request a blank copy of the form used)? If yes, please briefly describe this plan or process.

D. Description of the Job Club Services/Activities

1. Where (at what location) does the job club meet? Are there multiple locations? Does the location for your job club vary (e.g., from week-to-week)?

2. How often does the job club meet (weekly, bi-weekly, once a month)? For how many hours/minutes is the job club scheduled to meet? Is the actual duration of the job club about the same duration as it is scheduled (e.g., does it run over)? Is the actual duration of each job club variable or about the same?

3. In addition to formal club meetings, do job club members interact with WIB/One-stop staff for assistance at other times or in other situations? If so, please describe purpose and frequency.

4. How is the job club structured? Do individuals start and end as a cohort or is there open entry/open exit to the job club? Is there, for example, a 6- or 10-week series of workshops during which a curriculum is presented systematically from week to week, or is each job club meeting a stand-alone workshop? Is there a separate series of workshops offered at other days/times? Do participants come and go as they please from session to session (e.g., attend a few sessions, skip several, come back) or are they expected to stay engaged in sessions until they secure a job? Once they obtain a job, can and do they continue to attend the job club?

5. What is the typical attendance at the job club (i.e., usual number attending each session)? Is there much variation in number of job club attendees each session (minimum/maximum attendees over the last 12 months)? What is the maximum number of attendees that can be handled for a given session? Does anyone ever get turned away because too many show for a particular job club session? What, if any, is the ideal number (or range) of attendees for a given job club session?

6. Is a curriculum used to guide the job club workshop sessions? If yes, could you provide us with a copy of the curriculum and discuss the following –

   - What is the name of the curriculum? Who developed the curriculum? Was the curriculum purchased or obtained from another organization? Was the curriculum developed in-house? If so, describe the curriculum development process.

   - Please discuss source(s) of the curriculum – and if more than one source was used, discuss how and the process by which the curriculum was developed.

- Please provide an overview of the curriculum – an outline of curriculum modules/key substantive topics covered, amount of time devoted to each module/topic
- What kinds of instructional methods are used (e.g., lecture, small group instruction, peer group discussion, web-based/computer-based instruction).

7. How is each job club meeting structured? Is the structure/activities of each meeting basically the same each time, or is there substantial variation across job club meetings? Does the structure/activities depend on who is in attendance at each job club meeting? Can you please provide an overview of a typical job club meeting, including overall duration and sequencing/amount of time devoted to specific activities? Please discuss specific types of activities that are included in your job club, such as:
    - instruction on job readiness and effective job search strategies;
    - discussions about targeting certain occupations or industry sectors for employment;
    - time set aside for job club members to plan their job search activities for an upcoming period and to identify specific job leads (through searches on the Internet on job boards and employer websites, discussion among job club members, reviews of classified advertisements, and other networking activities);
    - assistance on resume and cover letter development/refinement;
    - discussions among job club participants about challenges and opportunities with respect to job search activities;
    - invitations to employers to share information on their industry sectors and potential job openings;
    - conduct of mock (practice) or actual interviews with employers for jobs;
    - speakers presenting on specific topics; and
    - testimonials from former/current participants.

8. To what extent are job club sessions/workshops facilitated by a staff member? Who plays the role of the facilitator (e.g., staff, volunteer)? Is the facilitator the same from job club session to job club session? What role does the facilitator play (e.g., providing instruction/lectures, guiding group discussion, working one-on-one or in small groups with participants)?

9. Is there any kind of mentoring/case management component for participants that accompanies (or is offered in addition to) the job club? If there is a mentoring/case management component --
    - Who provides mentoring/case management services?
    - What are the credentials of mentors/case managers?
    - When does the mentoring/case management occur?
    - How is the match made between the participant and the mentor/case manager? What is the caseload for the case manager/mentor?
    - How long does mentoring/case management last (e.g., 6 months, year, until an individual finds a job, etc.)?
    - What activities occur after a person obtains a job?

10. What are the patterns of attendance at job clubs among participants (e.g., attend each job club until the participant finds a job, attend session and skip several and then

attend)? Once individuals begin attending the job club do they continue to attend until they obtain a job? How much attrition is there before job placement? What are the specific reasons for dropping out/attrition prior to obtaining a job? Have you taken any steps to reduce attrition from the job club, and, if yes, what specific steps have been taken?

11. Once a participant obtains a job, are they encouraged to continue to attend job club sessions? What additional services, if any, are provided to those successful in obtaining jobs (e.g., job retention services, transportation services, clothing, referral to training and other workforce services, and other support services)? Are participants that find a job encouraged to upgrade their skills and credentials so they can move to better paying jobs? Do participants that find a job come back to the job club to share their experiences?

E. Job Club Participant Characteristics and Outcomes

1. What types of data are being collected on job club participant characteristics, services received, and outcomes? What specific information do you collect (e.g., name, email address)? For example, is an automated data system being used to track participant characteristics, services received, and outcomes? If available --
   - Please provide copies of the participant forms being used (e.g., intake, assessment, services receipt/tracking, participant outcome forms).
   - Do you collect any data beyond what is required for Wagner-Peyser and WIA reporting? If so, what?

2. What outcome measures (if any) are being used to assess job club performance, and if available, please provide data on the following outcomes for the past year for job club attendees (or three years, if possible) –
   - Number of participants attending job club sessions
   - Number of participants dropping out of the job club prior to obtaining a job
   - Average number of job club sessions attended (and range)
   - Job placement outcomes
   - Job retention outcomes
   - Earnings/hourly wages/hours worked
   - Other outcome measures, such as improved self-esteem or upgrading of skills/educational credentials
   - Discuss how each of these outcome measures are obtained (e.g., telephone calls conducted with participants/employers and the intervals at which data are collected).
   - Do you look at how job club participants do on the Common Measures used to measure performance for the Wagner-Peyser and WIA programs?

3. Of the strategies or services that you provide through your job club program, which do you feel are most/least effective in helping job club participants to obtain jobs? Are there ways in which your job club has fallen short of its goals for helping participants cope with unemployment and obtain jobs? If yes, how? Are there other

approaches, strategies, or services that you believe would contribute to better employment outcomes for the job club participants you serve?

4. If there are other job clubs operated by FBOs/CBOs in your local workforce area, how does your job club differ from activities provided by these FBOs/CBOs? Please describe the major similarities and differences in philosophy, approach, characteristics of customers served, services provided, and outcomes.

5. Has your job club been the focus of a formal evaluation? If yes, what type of evaluation was conducted (e.g., implementation/process evaluation, outcome evaluation, quasi-experimental or experimental net impact evaluation, cost-effectiveness/cost-benefit study)? Please provide final or interim reports that may have been produced under the evaluation effort(s)?

6. If your job club has *not* been the subject of an evaluation in the past, would you be willing to be part of a future evaluation? Do you think your organization would be willing to be part of a randomized controlled trial (experimental) evaluation to systematically examine job club impacts on participants [i.e., which would involve random assignment of job club candidates to treatment and control groups, similar to experiments currently used to test new medical treatments)?

7. Do you have any suggestions with regard to how a future evaluation could be conducted to more systematically gather data on the outcomes of participants of your job club?

F. Job Club Staffing

1. Please describe your organizational structure and staffing arrangement for your job club (if available, please provide an organizational chart)
    *   Paid administrators/staff involved in the job club initiative (i.e., role, number, and hours per month or FTE)
    *   Number of volunteers (i.e., role, number, and hours per month or FTE)
    *   What is the experience and/or credentials of administrators/staff/volunteers involved in job clubs
    *   How much turnover has there been in job club staff (past 12 months)
3. What kinds of training/staff development activities have been provided for job club staff? Please describe the extent and types of training/staff development activities, including who has conducted the training. Are there areas in which you feel there should have been more staff development/training? If yes, what are those areas?

G. Job Club Costs/Expenditures

1. If available, what are the costs associated with running a job club? If available, please provide a breakdown or estimate of the major costs of running a job club by major cost (e.g., breaking down total expenditures for items such as project staff, rent, equipment purchase or rental, subcontracts, etc.)? If available, please provide an overall estimate of the costs of running your job club for the last 12 months.
2. What kinds of funding have been used to pay for the costs of the job club?

e.   Government funding (describe if federal, state, or local and whether funding is grant or contract)

f.   Other sources

H. Questions about Linkages with FBO/CBO-Operated Job Clubs in the Local Workforce Area

1.   Knowledge of and your organization's linkages with faith-based/community-based organization (FBO/CBO) job clubs in the workforce area:

a.   Are you aware of other FBO/CBO job clubs operating in your local workforce area?

b.   If FBO/CBO job clubs exist in your locality, does your job club interact/partner with these FBO/CBO-operated job clubs in your local workforce area? For example, are there referrals to and from other job clubs operating in your local area? Do job club participants attending other FBO/CBO visit and use America's Job Centers/workforce development resources? If so, what public sector workforce services do job club participants of FBO/CBO use?

2.   We are particularly interested in identifying differences in the ways in which job clubs operated by faith-based and community-based organizations serve their participants versus those operated by public sector organizations, such as local workforce investment boards, America's Job Centers (or One-Stop Centers), or welfare agencies. Please discuss differences in terms of the following dimensions:

a.   How often and for how long job clubs meet

b.   Size/numbers attending job club sessions

c.   Duration/intensity of job club involvement for participants

d.   Patterns of attendance/extent of attrition from job clubs

e.   Curriculum used and topics covered during job clubs

f.   Kinds of instructional methods used (e.g., lecture, small group instruction, peer group discussion, web-based/computer-based instruction

g.   Types of instructors/facilitators used

h.   Extent of case management/peer support/mentoring provided

i.   Job development/placement assistance provided

j.   Additional services provided (e.g., transportation, clothing, referral to job training, other support services)

k.   Inclusion of social and recreational activities

l.   Inclusion of religious and spiritual activities

m.   Activities that occur once the participant finds a job (e.g., are they encouraged to continue to attend job club sessions?)

Checklist of Items to Collect from Site (If Available)

- Background information about the locality
- Background information about the organization
- Additional documentation/reports detailing job club services/activities
- Diagram showing how participants flow through the job club
- Budget/expenditures data on your organization's job club

APPENDIX D. REFERENCES

Angrist, J. D. & Krueger, A. B. (2001). "Instrumental Variables and the Search for Identification: From Supply and Demand to Natural Experiments." *Journal of Economic Perspectives. 15*(4), 69-85.

Azrin, N. H., Flores T. & Kaplan, S. J. (1975). "Job-Finding Club: A Group-Assisted Program for Obtaining Employment." *Behavioral Research and Therapy, 13*, 17-27.

Azrin, N. H. & Philip, R. A. (1979). "The Job Club Method for the Handicapped: A Comparative Outcome Study." *Rehabilitation Counseling Bulletin, 23*, 144-155.

Azrin, N. H., Philip R. A., Thienes-Hontos, P. & Besalel V. A. (1980). "Comparative Evaluation of the Job Club Program for Welfare Recipients." *Journal of Vocational Behavior, 16*(2) 133-145 (April).

Azrin, N. H., Philip R. A., Thienes-Hontos, P. & Besalel V.A. (1983a). "Follow-up on Welfare Benefits Received by Job Club Clients." *Journal of Vocational Behavior, 18*(3) 253-254 (June).

Azrin, N. H., Besalel, V. A., Wisotzek I., McMorrow & Bechtel, R. (1983b). "Behavioral Supervision Versus Information Counseling of Job Seeking in the Job Club." *Rehabilitation Counseling Bulletin*, 214-218 (March).

Barnow, B. S. (2010). "Setting Up Social Experiments: The Good, the Bad, and the Ugly." *Journal for Labour Market Research*, Vol. *43*, No. 2, 91-105.

Bishop, J., Barron, J. & Hollenbeck, K. (1993). *Recruiting Workers: How Recruitment Policies Affect the Flow of Applicants and Quality of New Workers*. Columbus OH: The Ohio State University, The National Center for Research in Vocational Education (September).

Bloom, H. S. (1995). "Minimum Detectable Effects: A Simple Way to Report the statistical Power of Experimental Designs." *Evaluation Review, 19*(5) 547-566.

Boddie, S. C. & Cnaan, R. (Eds.). (2006). *Faith-Based Social Services: Measures, Assessments, and Effectiveness*. Binghamton, NY: Haworth Pastoral Press. Simultaneously published as *Journal of Religion and Spirituality in Social Work, 25*, 3 and 4.

Bortnick, S. M. & Ports, M. H. (1992). Job Search Methods and Results: Tracking the Unemployed, *Monthly Labor Review*, December 1992, *115* (12), 29–35.

Brown, A. (1997). "Work First: How to Implement and Employment-Focused Approach to Welfare Reform, Technical Report. New York: March 1997.

Caliendo, M. & Kopeinig, S. (2008). "Some Practical Guidance for the Implementation of Propensity Score Matching." *Journal of Economic Surveys. 22*(1), 31-72.

Career Network Ministry Handbook. (2009). *A Guide to Discovering Your Gifts and Pursuing Your Professional Career Search*. McLean, VA.

Chaves, M. (1999). *Congregations' Social Service Activities*. Washington, DC: Urban Institute. Chaves, M. & Tsitos, W. (2001). *Congregations and Social Services: What They Do, How They Do It, and With Whom*. Washington, DC: Aspen Institute.

Chaves, M. & Anderson, S. L. (2008). "Continuity and Change in American Congregations: Introducing the Second Wave of the National Congregations Study." *Sociology of Religion, 69*, 4.

Cook, T. D., Shadish, W. R. & Wong, V. C. (2008). "Three Conditions Under Which Experiments and Observational Studies Produce Comparable Causal Estimates: New findings from Within-study Comparisons." *Journal of Policy Analysis and Management.*, *27*(4), 724-750.

De Jong, F. J. & Horn, C. (2008). "Opening the Black Box of Faith-Based Social Services: Measuring Program Components and Treatment Dose." In Joshi, P., Hawkins, S. & Novey, J. (Eds.), *Innovations in Effective Compassion: Compendium of Research Papers Presented at the Faith-Based and Community Initiatives Conference on Research, Outcomes, and Evaluation.* RTI International.

DeVita, C. J. & Kramer, F. D. (2008). *The Role of Faith-Based and Community Organizations in Hurricane-Related Human Services.* For the U.S. Department of Health and Human Services, Assistant Secretary for Planning and Evaluation. Urban Institute.

Diamond, P. A. (2010). "Unemployment, Vacancies, Wages." Nobel Prize Lecture, December 2010.

Diette, T. M., Goldsmith, A. H., Hamilton, D. & William, D., Jr. (2012). "Causality in the Relationship between Mental Health and Unemployment." In *Reconnecting to Work: Policies to Mitigate Long-Term Unemployment and Its Consequences*, Appelbaum, L. D., (Ed.). Kalamazoo, MI: W.E. Upjohn Institute for Employment Research, 63-94.

Elliott, J. R. & Sims, M. (2001). "The Impact of Neighborhood Poverty and Race on Job Matching among Blacks and Latinos." *Social Problems*, *48*(3) 341-361 (August).

Falcon, L. M. (1995). "Social Networks and Employment for Latinos, Blacks and Whites." *New England Journal of Public Policy*, *11*, 17-28.

Falcon, L. M. & Edwin, M. (1996). The Role of Social Networks in the Labor Market Outcomes of Latinos, Black and Non-Hispanic Whites." Paper presented at the Russell Sage Foundation Conference on "Residential Segregation, Social Capital and Labor Markets," New York, NY.

Fischer, R. L. (2008). "In God We Trust, All Others Bring Data: Assessing the State of Outcomes Measurement for Faith-Based and Community-Based Programming." In Joshi, P., Hawkins, S. & Novey, J. (Eds.), *Innovations in Effective Compassion: Compendium of Research Papers Presented at the Faith-Based and Community Initiatives Conference on Research, Outcomes, and Evaluation.* RTI International.

Gais, T. (2008). *Understanding the Roles of 'Faith' and Faith-Based Organizations in the Delivery of Drug Treatment Services.* Presented to Administration for Children and Families/Office of Planning, Research and Evaluation Research and Evaluation Conference, Albany, NY.

Gais, T. L. & Arria, A. (2010). *Faith-Based and Substance Abuse Treatment Services: Patient Characteristics and Outcomes.* Albany, NY: Nelson A. Rockefeller Institute of Government.

Gais, T. L., Arria, A. & Caldeira, K. (2010). *Understanding the Roles of Faith and Faith Based Organizations in the Delivery of Drug Treatment Services: An Analysis of Merged Program and Client Data.* Albany, NY: Nelson A. Rockefeller Institute of Government.

Gertler, P. J., Martinez, S., Premand, P., Rawlings, L. B. & Vermeersch, C. M. (2011).*Impact Evaluation in Practice.* Washington, DC: The World Bank.

Goldman, B. (1981). *Impacts of the Immediate Job Search Assistance Experiment: Louisville WIN Research Laboratory Project.* New York, NY: Manpower Demonstration Research Corporation.

Goldman, B. (1989). "Job Search Strategies for Women on Welfare," in *Job Training for Women: The Promise and Limits of Public Policies,* eds. Sharon L. Harlan and Ronnie J. Steinberg, Philadelphia: Temple University Press.

Gould-Stuart, J. (1982). *Welfare Women in a Group Job Search Program: Their Experiences in the Louisville WIN Research Laboratory Project.* New York NY: Manpower Demonstration Research Corporation.

Granovetter, M. (1973). "The Strength of Weak Ties," *American Journal of Sociology,* May 1973, *78* (6), 1360–1380.

Granovetter, M. (1983). "The Strength of Weak Ties: A Network Theory Revisited," *Sociological Theory,* 1983, *1,* 201–233.

Gray, D. (1983). "A Job Club for Older Job Seekers: An Experimental Evaluation." *Journal of Gerontology, 38* (3), 363-368.

Green, J. C. & Sherman, A. L. (2002). *Fruitful Collaborations: A Survey of Government-Funded Faith-Based Programs in 15 States.* Charlottesville, VA: Hudson Institute.

Green, G. P., Tigges, L. M. & Diaz, D. (1999). "Racial and Ethnic Differences in Job Search Strategies in Atlanta, Boston and Los Angeles." *Social Science Quarterly, 80*(2), 263-278.

Hartmann, T. A. (2003). *Moving Beyond the Walls: Faith and Justice Partnerships Working for High-Risk Youth.* Philadelphia, PA: Public/Private Ventures.

Holcomb, P. A. & Nightingale, D. S. (2003). "Conceptual Underpinnings of Implementation Analysis" in Lennon, Mary Claire and Corbett, Thomas, Editors. *Policy into Action: Implementation Research and Welfare Reform.* Washington, DC: The Urban Institute Press.

Holcomb, P., Pavetti, L., Ratcliff, C. & Riedinger, S. (1998) "Building an Employment Focused Welfare System: Work First and Other Work-Oriented Strategies in Five States, Technical Report." Washington D.C.: Urban Institute, June.

Holzer, H. J. (1987). "Informal Job Search and Black Youth Unemployment." *American Economic Review,* 77, 446-452.

Holzer, H. J. (1988). "Search Method Use by Unemployed Youth." *Journal of Labor Economics,* 6(1) 1-20 (January).

Jacobson, J., Marsh, S. & Winston, P. (2005). *State and Local Contracting for Social Services Under Charitable Choice.* Washington, DC: Mathematica Policy Research.

Johnson, B. R., Tompkins, R. B. & Webb, D. (2002). *Objective Hope. Assessing the Effectiveness of Faith-Based Organizations: A Review of the Literature.* Philadelphia, PA: University of Pennsylvania Center for Research on Religion and Urban Civil Society.

Johnson, T. R., Dickinson, K. P., West, R.W. (1983). McNicholl, S. E., Pfiester, J. M., Stagner, A. L. & Harris, B. J. (1983). *A National Evaluation of the Impact of the United States Employment Service.* A Report to the United States Department of Labor. Menlo Park, CA: SRI.

Johnson, T. R., Dickinson, K. P. & West, R. W. (1985). "An Evaluation of the Impact of ES Referrals on Applicant Earnings." *Journal of Human Resources, 20*(1), 117-137.

Kennedy, S. S. & Bielefeld, W. (2003). *Charitable Choice: First Results from Three States*. Indianapolis, IN: Indiana University/Purdue University, Center for Urban Policy and the Environment.

Klepinger, D. H., Johnson, T. R., Joesch, J. M. & Benus, J. M. (1998). "Evaluation of the Maryland Unemployment Insurance Work Search Demonstration." Unemployment Insurance Occasional Paper 98-2. Washington, DC: Employment and Training Administration, U.S. Department of Labor.

Klepinger, D. H., Johnson, T. R. & Joesch, J. M. (2002). "Effects of Unemployment Insurance Requirements: The Maryland Experiment." *Industrial and Labor Relations Review, 56*(1), 3-22 (October).

Klerman, J., Koralek, R., Miller, A. & Wen, K. (2012). *Job Search Assistance Programs – A Review of the Literature*. Report prepared by Abt Associates, Inc. OPRE Report #2012-39, Washington DC: Office of Planning, Research and Evaluation Administration for Children and Families, U.S. Department of Health and Human Services.

Kramer, F. D. (2010). "The Role for Public Funding of Faith-Based Organizations Delivering Behavioral Health Services: Guideposts for Monitoring and Evaluation." *American Journal of Community Psychology, 46*, 342-360 (October).

Kramer, F. D., Nightingale, D. S., Trutko, J. W. & Barnow, B. S. (2003a). "Employment and Training Services Provided by Faith-Based Organizations: An Exploratory Study and Issues for Consideration in the Use of Public Funds," in Riley, J., Branch, A., Wandner, S. & Gordon, W. (Eds.). *A Compilation of Selected Papers from the Employment and Training Administration's 2003 Biennial National Research Conference*. U.S. Department of Labor.

Kramer, F. D., Wittenberg, D.C., Holcomb, P. A. & Nightingale, D. S. (2003b). "Performance-Based Contracting to Achieve Employment Goals: Lessons from Programs for Welfare Recipients." Washington, D.C.: The Urban Institute.

Krueger, A. B. & Mueller, A. (2011). *Job Search, Emotional Well-Being and Job Finding in a Period of Mass Unemployment: Evidence from High-Frequency Longitudinal Data*. Washington, DC: Brookings Institution.

Krueger, A. B. & Mueller, A. (2010). "Job Search and Unemployment Insurance: New Evidence from Time Use Data." *Journal of Public Economics*, April 2010, *94* (3–4), 298–307.

Krueger, A. B. & Mueller, A. (2011). *Job Search, Emotional Well-Being and Job Finding in a Period of Mass Unemployment: Evidence from High-Frequency Longitudinal Data*. Washington, D.C.: Brookings Institution.

Krueger, R. A. & Casey, M. A. (2010). "Focus Group Interviewing" in Wholey, J. S., Hatry, H. P. & Newcomer, K. E. (Ed.). *Handbook of Practical Program Evaluation (Third Edition)*. San Francisco, California: Jossey-Bass.

Marx, J. & Leicht, K. (1992). "Formality of Recruitment to 229 Jobs: Variation by Race, Sex, and Job Characteristics." *Social Science Research, 76*, 190-196.

McCall, J. J. (1970). "The Economics of Information and Job Search" *Quarterly Journal of Economics, 84* (1), 113-126.

Ministry of the Hills. (2011). *Empowering Job Seekers*.

Monsma, S. V. (2004). *Putting Faith in Partnerships: Welfare-to-Work in Four Cities*. Ann Arbor, MI: University of Michigan Press.

Monsma, S. V. (2006). "The Effectiveness of Faith-Based Welfare-to-Work Programs: A Story of Specialization." In S.C. Boddie & R.A. Cnaan (Eds.), *Faith-Based Social Services:Measures, Assessments, and Effectiveness.* Binghamton, NY: Haworth Pastoral Press.

Monsma, S. V. & Smidt. C. E. (2009). *An Evaluation of the Latino Coalition's Reclamando Nuestro Futuro (Reclaiming our Future) Program.* Paul Henry Institute for the Study of Christianity and Politics, Calvin College. Prepared for the US Department of Labor.

Mortensen, D. & Pissarides, C. (1994). "Job Creation and Job Destruction in the Theory of Unemployment." *Review of Economic Studies, 61* (3), 397–415.

Murray, M. P. (2006). "Avoiding Invalid Instruments and Coping with Weak Instruments." *Journal of Economic Perspectives. 20*(4), 111-132.

Noyes, J. L. (2008). *Measuring the Role of Faith in Program Outcomes: Key Conceptual and Methodological Challenges.* Discussion Paper prepared for the Institute for Research on Poverty Working Conference, Measuring the Role of Faith in Program Outcomes. Madison, WI.

Oates, J. & Tom, P. (2011). "Training and Employment Notice: Encouraging Partnerships between the Workforce Investment System and Job Clubs to Meet Career and Employment Needs." Washington, DC: U. S. Department of Labor, May 20, 2011.

Orr, L. (1999). *Social Experiments: Evaluating Public Programs with Experimental Methods.* Thousand Oaks, California: Sage Publications.

Pissarides, C. (2000). *Equilibrium Unemployment Theory (2nd ed.).* Cambridge, Massachusetts: MIT Press.

Rosenbaum, J. E., DeLuca, S., Miller, S. R. & Roy, K. (1999). "Pathways into Work: Short- and Long-Term Effects of Personal and Institutional Ties." *Sociology of Education,* 72(3) 179-196 (July).

Rosenfeld, C. (1977). "Job Search of the Unemployed, May 1976." *Monthly Labor Review* (November) 39-43.

Smith, J. A. & Todd, P. E. (2005). "Does Matching Overcome LaLonde's Critique of Nonexperimental Estimators?" *Journal of Econometrics. 125*, 305-353.

Stiglitz, G. J. (1961). "The Economics of Information" *Journal of Political Economy, 69* (3), 213-225.

Stiglitz, G. J. (1962). "Information in the Labor Market" *Journal of Political Economy, 70* (5), 94-105.

U.S. General Accounting Office. (2002). *Charitable Choice: Federal Guidance on Statutory Provisions Could Improve Consistency of Implementation.* Publication No. GAO-02-887.

Wandner, S. A. (2010). *Solving the Reemployment Puzzle: From Research to Policy.* Kalamazoo MI: W. E. Upjohn Institute for Employment Research.

West, S. G., Naihua, D., Pequegnat, W., Gaist, P., Des Jarlais, D. C., Holtgrave, D., Szapocnik, J., Fishbein, M., Rapkin, B., Clatts, M. & Mullen, P. D. (2008). "Alternatives to the Randomized Controlled Trial." *American Journal of Public Health,* 98(8), 1359-1366.

Wolfhagen, C. & Goldman, B. S. (1983). *Job Search Strategies: Lessons from the Louisville WIN Laboratory.* New York: Manpower Demonstration Research Corporation.

APPENDIX E. OVERVIEW OF PARTICIPANT DATA COLLECTION AND EVALUATION OF JOB CLUBS BASED ON SITE VISITS

Appendix E - Table 1. Data Items Collected by FBOS/CBOS on Job Club Participants

Name of Job Club	Organization Sponsoring Job Club	Attendance at Job Club/Sign in Sheet?	Data Collected on Job Placement?	Data Collected on Wage at Placement?	Data Collected on Hours Worked at Placement?	Data Collected on Retained in Job?
FBO-SPONSORED JOB CLUBS						
JobSeekers	Trinity Church of Princeton, NJ	Yes (sign-in sheet) with name, e-mail address, phone #, occupation looking for	No (only if participants report back to the facilitators)	No	No	No
Job Partnership of Cleveland (JPC)	Mt. Zion Congregational Church	Yes	Yes (collected by mentor for up to 1 year after class)	No	No	No
Crossroads Career Network	Snellville United Methodist Church	Yes (Name, email address, phone number and job interest are collected so as to inform attendees of upcoming events.)	No (only if participants report back to the facilitators)	No	No	No
Job Networking	Roswell United Methodist Church	Name, e-mail address, and telephone number are collected for follow-up purposes. Attendance is not tracked.	No, although attendees who find jobs are encouraged to return and talk about their success	No	No	No
SOAR 4 Jobs	St. Odilia Catholic Community	Yes. Name, phone, email address, current/prior	No – only if participants report back during a job	No	No	No

Name of Job Club	Organization Sponsoring Job Club	Attendance at Job Club/Sign in Sheet?	Data Collected on Job Placement?	Data Collected on Wage at Placement?	Data Collected on Hours Worked at Placement?	Data Collected on Retained in Job?
		company, current/prior position and field/position seeking are collected and distributed as a networking tool for participants. Attendance is tracked in an Excel spreadsheet.	club session			
Career Network Ministry (CNM)	McLean Bible Church	Name, address, phone number, email address, how heard of CNM, whether attendee at MBC, whether member of LinkedIn/ Meet Up and career field of interest are collected from first time attendees on Participant Information and Agreement Form. Attendance is not tracked.	No, but some participants (approximately25-30%) share that information during general meeting	No	No	No
Employment Network Group	Severna Park United Methodist Church	Name and email address are collected from first time attendees but attendance is not tracked	No (but some participants may provide placement information)	No	No	No
CTK Parish Job Networking Ministry	Christ The King Parish in Pleasant Hill, CA	Name, phone number, email address, career field of interest, job search challenges and distance	Job placement data for those who participate in a success team is tracked; however, the	No	No	No

Appendix E - Table 1. (Continued)

Name of Job Club	Organization Sponsoring Job Club	Attendance at Job Club/Sign in Sheet?	Data Collected on Job Placement?	Data Collected on Wage at Placement?	Data Collected on Hours Worked at Placement?	Data Collected on Retained in Job?
		willing to commute for job are collected from first-time attendees at orientation. Attendance at large group meetings is not tracked; some facilitators track attendance for their success teams.	number who found a job after attending a large group meeting but who did not join a success team is not known			
CBO-SPONSORED JOB CLUBS						
Neighbors-helping-Neighbors	Neighbors- helping-Neighbors USA, Inc.	Yes (collect name, e-mail address, town, type of job seeking)	Not systematically, but try to get participants to call/leave word of placement	No	No	No
Community Job Club of Stow	Community Job Club, Inc.	Yes (sign-in sheet)	No (only if participant reports back to executive director)	No	No	No
Career Transition Group for Women	None	Yes – there is a sign-in sheet for name, email address, area of job interest and whether individual is a first-time attendee	No – only if individual reports back to the facilitator	No	No	No
The Job Forum	San Francisco Chamber of Commerce	Name, e-mail address and referral source are collected on sign-in sheet.	No, although some individuals may contact	No	No	No

Name of Job Club	Organization Sponsoring Job Club	Attendance at Job Club/Sign in Sheet?	Data Collected on Job Placement?	Data Collected on Wage at Placement?	Data Collected on Hours Worked at Placement?	Data Collected on Retained in Job?
		Attendance is not tracked as job seekers typically attend only a few sessions.	panelists when they find a job			

Appendix E - Table 2. Overview of Use of Participant Data Forms, Mis, and Evaluation by FBO/CBO-Sponsored Job Clubs

Name of Job Club	Organization Sponsoring Job Club	Are Data Forms Completed on Job Club Attendees (Other than Attendance List)?	Participant Data System/ MIS Used?	Is Customer Satisfaction Survey Used?	Has Job Club Been Evaluated in Past?
FBO-SPONSORED JOB CLUBS					
JobSeekers	Trinity Church of Princeton, NJ	No	No	No	No
Job Partnership of Cleveland (JPC)	Mt. Zion Congregational Church	Yes (3-page intake form completed with characteristics and career interests)	Yes (by JPC)	Yes	No
Crossroads Career Network	Snellville United Methodist Church	No	No	No, but evaluation forms are distributed at meetings	No
Job Networking	Roswell United Methodist Church	No	No	No	No
SOAR 4 Jobs	St. Odilia Catholic Community	No	No	No – but an evaluation form is distributed at the close of every meeting	No

Appendix E - Table 2. (Continued)

Name of Job Club	Organization Sponsoring Job Club	Are Data Forms Completed on Job Club Attendees (Other than Attendance List)?	Participant Data System/ MIS Used?	Is Customer Satisfaction Survey Used?	Has Job Club Been Evaluated in Past?
Career Network Ministry (CNM)	McLean Bible Church	No, other than the Participant Information and Agreement Form described above.	No	No	No
Employment Network Group	Severna Park United Methodist Church	No	No	No	No
CTK Parish Job Networking Ministry	Christ The King Parish in Pleasant Hill, CA	No.	No	No	No
CBO SPONSORED-JOB CLUBS					
Neighbors- helping-Neighbors	Neighbors-helping-Neighbors USA, Inc.	No	No	No	No
Community Job Club of Stow	Community Job Club, Inc.	Yes (2-page application completed (includes contact information, past employment education, # in household, family income, type of occupation/job sought)	No	No	No
Career Transition Group for Women	None	No	No	No	No
The Job Forum	SF Chamber of Commerce	No	No	No	No

APPENDIX F. SAMPLE JOB CLUB PARTICIPANT FORMS FOR TRACKING PARTICIPANT CHARACTERISTICS, SERVICES RECEIVED, AND OUTCOMES

Form 1: Job Club Participant Intake Form

Name (Last Name, First, MI):	Participant Identifier (e.g., SSN or ID#):
Street Address, City: State: Zip:	Email Address: Facebook Page Address: Linked-In Address:

Home Phone:
 	
Work Phone:
 	
Cell Phone:
	Alternative Contact:
	  Name: Relationship:
	
	  Phone:
	
	  E-mail:

Race – Individual considers herself/himself to be one or more of the following (check all that apply): ___Yes ___No White ___Yes ___No Black/African American ___Yes ___No Asian ___Yes ___No American Indian/Alaskan Native ___Yes ___No Native Hawaiian of Other Pacific Islander Individual is Hispanic/Latino: ___Yes ___No	Gender: ____Male ____Female Birthdate (MM/DD/YYYY): ____/____/_____ Special Client Characteristics (at Time of Enrollment): ___Yes ___No Individual with Disability ___Yes ___No Ex-Offender ___Yes ___No Veteran Unemployment Insurance Compensation Recipient: ___UI Claimant ___UI Exhaustee ___Not Claimant/Exhaustee

Education Information:
 	
School Status at Program Entry (**Please check One**)
_____Currently In School   _____Currently Not In School
 	
Highest Level of Education Completed (**Please Enter One**)
_____ No Education
_____ Grade (**enter** 1 to 12)
_____ Years of college/full-time technical/vocational school
          (**enter** 1 to 4)
_____ Education beyond Bachelor's Degree
	Degree or certificates Received (**check all that apply**):
	___Yes ___No No Degree or Certificate
	___Yes ___No Attained High School Diploma
	___Yes ___No Attained GED or equivalent
	___Yes ___No Attained Certificate of
	                          Attendance/Completion
	___Yes ___No Attained Other Post-secondary Degree
	                          or Certification
	___Yes ___No Baccalaureate Degree (4-year)
	___Yes ___No Occupational Skills Licensure, Certificate
	                          or Credential

Employment and Earnings Information:
Currently employed? ___Yes ___No
If currently working, for last week of employment:
  Number hours worked for week:____
  Hourly wage: $_____ per hour
If not working, for most recent job (for last week of employment):
  Number hours worked for week:____
  Hourly wage: $_____ per hour
  Reason for leaving last job:
  ___Laid-off ___Left Voluntarily ___Fired ___Other
Occupation/last job held:
 	
Type of job seeking/career field of interest:
	Do the following make it hard to find or keep a job…
	___Yes ___No Health problems or disabilities
	___Yes ___No Lack of access to reliable transportation
	___Yes ___No Lack of a resume
	___Yes ___No Trouble reading or writing
	___Yes ___No Problems speaking English
	___Yes ___No Lack of a green card
	___Yes ___No Lack of child care
	___Yes ___No Other:_____

Comments on type of job sought or help needed in obtaining job (use back or additional pages, if needed):	**Forms Completed by (Staff Name/Initials):** Date: ____/____/_____

Form 2: Job Club Participant Services Received, Exit/Follow-Up Form

First Name:		Last Name:	

Job Club Services Received:
(Note: Update at Time of Exit from Job Club)
 	
Job Club Attendance: *Service Never Received*
  # of Job Clubs Attended: _____
  Total # of Hours of Job Club Attended: _____
    Date of First Job Club: ___/___/___
    Date of Last Job Club: ___/___/___
		Other Employment Services: *Service Never Received*
		___Job Readiness Workshop(s)/Assistance –
		       # of total hours:____
		___Help with Resume Development (Review/Updating)
		___Practice/Mock Job Interviews
		___Job Development/Placement Services
		       Was participant placed in a job? __Yes __No
		___Job Retention Services
		___Referral to Education/Occupational Training Services
		___Case Management/Mentoring
		___Other: _____	

Outcome and Exit Information:
 	
Date of Exit (MM/DD/YY): ___/___/___
 	
Exit Reason (Check One):
___Completed job club/services
___Dropped out before completing job club/services
___Other: _____
		Employment Status Exit:
		___Employed ___Not Employed ___Unknown
		
		If employed at Exit:
		  Occupation: _____
		  # of hours worked per week: ___
		  Hourly Wage: $_____	

Employment Status 6 Months After Exit:
___Employed ___Not Employed ___Unknown
 	
If employed at 6 Months After Exit:
  # of hours worked per week: ___
  Hourly Wage: $_____
		Employment Status 12 Months After Exit:
		___Employed ___Not Employed ___Unknown
		
		If employed at 12 Months After Exit:
		  # of hours worked per week: ___
		  Hourly Wage: $_____	

Additional Case Notes/Comments:		**Forms Completed by (Staff Name/Initials):** Date: ___/___/___	

APPENDIX G. POLICY BRIEF – PROMISING PRACTICES IDENTIFIED IN JOB CLUBS OPERATED BY FAITH- AND COMMUNITY-BASED ORGANIZATIONS

Over the past several decades, job search support groups, commonly referred to as "job clubs," have evolved into one of several important activities used by the public workforce system and faith- and community-based organizations to enhance worker readiness and employability, as well as to provide ongoing support to unemployed and underemployed individuals as they search for jobs. The U.S. Department of Labor's (DOL) Chief Evaluation Office (CEO) contracted in September 2012 with Capital Research Corporation, Inc. and George Washington University to conduct an assessment of job clubs sponsored by faith-based and community-based organizations (FBOs/CBOs). The overall purpose of this evaluation effort was to systematically describe the key characteristics of job clubs being offered by a range of faith- and community- based organizations, document how they differ from and are similar to the job clubs operated by publicly-funded workforce agencies (such as at American Job Centers [AJCs]), and identify potential approaches that might be used for more rigorous formal evaluation of impacts and effectiveness. This evaluation effort, conducted over a 20-month period, included three main research activities: (1) a literature review; (2) an "environmental scan," with a particular focus on conducting interviews with key stakeholders knowledgeable about job clubs and site visits to FBO/CBOs sponsoring job clubs in six localities; and (3) identification and exploration of alternative evaluation designs for future rigorous study of FBO/CBO job clubs. A few promising practices of faith-based and community-based organizations operating job clubs that were identified during the completion of the environmental scan merit further consideration and study. These are highlighted below.

Practice #1: Establishment of Strong Linkages with AJCs/One-Stops. Among the job clubs visited as part of this study, there was a wide range in terms of the strength of the collaboration between the FBO/CBO job clubs and the local public workforce agency. Facilitators in some FBO/CBO job clubs had few or no cross-referrals of job seekers and weak to no linkages with staff at the local AJC/One-Stop. Other facilitators for FBO/CBO job clubs, as well as staff at public workforce agencies, however, reported very successful connections with their counterparts, which appeared to benefit job seekers. For example, job club staff at the Arnold Station Job Club in Maryland worked closely with the facilitators for the Severna Park United Methodist Church's Employment Network Group, attending each other's job clubs and even sharing the services of one volunteer facilitator. The Minnesota Department of Employment and Economic Development posts the schedule for all ongoing FBO/CBO- operated job clubs on the Positively Minnesota website; a 17-page spreadsheet listing information for all existing job clubs (including those at the Workforce Centers) is also maintained for the entire Minneapolis/St. Paul area. A mutually-beneficial relationship with local One-Stop Center staff (who attended and made presentations at job club meetings) was also reported by facilitators at Christ the King (CTK) Parish Job Networking Ministry in Pleasant Hill, CA.

Practice #2: Expansion to Include Other Job Search Services in Addition to Traditional Job Clubs. Although the focus of this study was on traditional job clubs (i.e., regularly-scheduled group meetings designed to enhance job search skills and provide ongoing support to individuals as they search for jobs), many FBOs and CBOs have expanded their services for job seekers to include activities and instructional sessions that go beyond job clubs. Some of the FBOs and CBOs visited during the site visits offered job clubs as only one component of a more comprehensive menu of services for job seekers that also included individual or a series of instructional workshops, one-on-one job search assistance and guidance, additional networking sessions, and job fairs. Many of these workshops covered topics not dissimilar to those covered in workshops offered at an AJC/One-Stop Center, although FBOs/CBOs were not typically able to provide computer labs, multiple printers and telephones, etc. For example, the McLean Bible Church's Career Network Ministry operated a number of optional workshops during their 3.5 hour weekly meetings on topics such as LinkedIn, effective resume writing, federal job search, development of the elevator pitch, interviewing and networking. Roswell United Methodist Church (RUMC) Job Networking Program, a member of the Crossroads Career Network, provided a comprehensive menu of job networking/support services and activities for job seekers. Twice monthly sessions that ran throughout the afternoon and into the evening offered, in addition to a dinner program, presentations and accountability groups, and a variety of volunteer-led (typically professional HR staff/Recruiters) workshops on topics of interest to job seekers (e.g., networking, franchise businesses, strategies for older job seekers.) The New Birth Missionary Baptist Church's Employment Network Ministry in Atlanta does not operate regularly scheduled job club meetings but instead has sponsored large job fairs and also links job seekers in the congregation with volunteer church members who can provide individual job search assistance.

Practice #3: Supplementation of Traditional Job Club Large Group Meetings with Smaller Support Group Sessions. In addition to the large group job clubs meetings that typically met in the evenings and provided job search instruction and presentations by speakers, some of the FBOs and CBOs visited as part of this study also operated additional (and typically smaller) job club sessions that met more frequently, often serving as an additional support or "accountability" group for a few job seekers. In some cases, these smaller groups were made up of job seekers with similar goals or interests who often agreed to continue meeting until all participants found employment. For example, in addition to the large group job club sessions held monthly, the Snellville Crossroads Career Network also sponsored small-group "Christ- Centered Career Group (C3G)" job clubs that met twice-monthly. Similarly, Christ the King Parish Job Networking Ministry held large group job club meetings twice a month, but attendees were also invited to participate in small group success team job clubs that met weekly, providing an additional layer of support with a more individualized focus. As one of the components of its comprehensive job networking support program, Roswell United Methodist Church also convened multiple accountability groups for job seekers with specific needs (e.g., job seekers ages 21-29, veterans.)

Practice #4: Increased Reliance on Social Media as an Outreach Tool and an Ongoing Communication Strategy. While strongly encouraging job club participants to take advantage of social media in their own networking and job search efforts, many FBO/CBO job club facilitators were also moving towards increased usage of these tools for both outreach to new job seekers and as a means to inform and stay connected with current participants. For example, the Neighbors-helping-Neighbors job club in New Jersey reported using social media "to the fullest extent possible", relying on patch.com, Facebook, and LinkedIn to "drive awareness" of their group in the community. Other job clubs also used Twitter as well as Facebook and LinkedIn to share information about upcoming networking events, speakers and presentations. McLean Bible Church's Career Network Ministry also used Meetup as to tool to alert job seekers about upcoming job search workshops and to enable them to register for the sessions.

Practice #5: Use of Online Networking Tools. One of the FBO sites visited as part of this study, Christ the King Parish Job Networking Ministry, provided its job club participants with access to the Career Actions Network, a web-based service that enables registered users to post both resumes and job listings. An online networking tool, this website connects job seekers with employment opportunities and also provides a mechanism for employed individuals as well as employers willing to share their knowledge and "insider" connections to share information about available, and in some cases, hidden job openings.

End Notes

[1] N.H Azrin, R.A. Philip, P Thienes-Hontos, V.A. Besalel. 1980. "Comparative Evaluation of the Job Club Program for Welfare Recipients." *Journal of Vocational Behavior* 16(2) 133-145 (April). N.H Azrin, R.A. Philip, P Thienes-Hontos, V.A. Besalel. 1983. "Follow-up on Welfare Benefits Received by Job Club Clients." *Journal of Vocational Behavior* 18(3) 253-254 (June). Gray, Denis. 1983. "A Job Club for Older Job Seekers: An Experimental Evaluation." *Journal of Gerontology* 38 (3) 363-368. Also: "Improving Job-Seeking Skills of Adolescents with Handicaps Through Job Clubs." *Career Development for Exceptional Individuals.* 1988

11(2):118-125. "Assisting Unemployed Older Workers to Become Reemployed: An Experimental evaluation." *Research on Social Work Practice* 1994 4(1): 3-13."Retraining the Older Worker: Michigan's Experience with Senior Employment Services." *Journal of Career Development* 1986 13(2):14-22.

[2] Section 2 of this report provides a literature review, which includes more in-depth discussion of key findings from the literature on job clubs.

[3] Specifics about the methodology for the environmental scan, including selection of locations and specific FBO/CBO job clubs for visits is included in Chapter 3 of this report.

[4] Portions of Sections A and B focusing on job search theory and research results on job clubs are based on a recent review of job search theory and findings by Klerman et.al. (2012).

[5] In 1962, the Gordon Committee, a presidential appointed committee on employment and unemployment statistics, recommended that the Bureau of Labor Statistics (BLS) begin to ask job search questions as part of the Current Population Survey (CPS), which is an important source of monthly U.S. unemployment and employment statistics. Explicit job search questions were added to the CPS in 1967.

[6] Research also found international differences in job search. De Graff and Flap (1988) found that many more American men used personal social contacts to find jobs than Dutch or German men. Other studies examined search methods used in countries including Germany, Italy, Spain and Taiwan (Lin 1999).

[7] However, over the past decade, there have been substantial changes in the focus and content of job club sessions to keep up with changes in the ways in which job seekers network and search for jobs. For example, job club curriculum is now typically infused with instruction on how to effectively use the Internet and various social media tools (especially LinkedIn, Facebook, Twitter, and YouTube) to build/expand the job seeker's network, conduct research on occupations and obtain relevant labor market information, and search for and make application for job openings.

[8] Possible concerns with the analysis include failure to control for participant characteristics, which could be important given the small sample size, and the fact that participants who attended four sessions or less (and their matched pair person) were excluded from the analysis. (The published article does not indicate what proportion of the treatment group was excluded because of this criterion.) Also, the control group received no job search services, so while the study establishes that group job search is superior to no counseling, it does not compare group job search to individualized services. Finally, the study was carried out in a single small town in Southern Illinois, so there could be external validity concerns.

[9] Starting in April 1980, the Louisville group job search program was piloted and researchers conducted case studies using informal interview techniques. Researchers also attended the group job search program sessions as participant-observers (Gould-Stuart 1982).

[10] The CFBNP directory of job clubs is available at: https://partnerships.workforce3one.org/page/resources/1001107639349545113

[11] See the CFBNP website for examples of curriculum available at (see especially the "Resources" tab): https://partnerships.workforce3one.org/page/resources/1001109738191140636

[12] Monsma notes that these findings are similar to those from another study of faith-based and secular welfare-to-work programs (Bielefeld, Littlepage and Thelin, 2003 cited in Monsma 2006), in which the non-faith-influenced programs provided twice the number of hard skills services than the faith-influenced programs.

[13] The term faith-based arose during welfare reform in the 1990s.

[14] If the public sector organization ran a job club (which occurred in four of the six localities visited), then the site visit team interviewed administrators/staff about the job club and observed the job club (similar to the visits conducted with the FBO/CBO job clubs that were the main focus of the study).

[15] Tables presented in this section of the report provide data for the 16 sites where job clubs were observed during the site visits. Data on the other five organizations where no job clubs were observed is not included.

[16] The Mt. Zion Congregational Church was the focus of the site visit; but the sponsoring organization – Job Partnership of Cleveland – also helped to administer and provide technical assistance to two other job club at the time of the site visit.

[17] Unemployment rate is for service area of job club at the time of the site visit.

[18] CNM – The job club was estimated by CNM administrators to have been formed about 20 years ago (at the time of the visit in 2013).

[19] Career Transition Group for Women – Job club in its current form started in 2012, but this job club started at the initiating organization in 2003.

[20] With the exception of one CBO - the Career Transition Group for Women, which to date had served only female job seekers and primarily targeted outreach on serving female job seekers – the FBO/CBO job clubs visited indicated that all types of job seekers attended their sessions.

[21] RUMC Job Networking sessions are 12:30-9:00 PM -- workshops range from 45 minutes to 3.5 hours; dinner program is 1.5 hours; keynote speaker presentation is 1 hour.

[22] CTK Parish: Large group meetings are 2.5 hours (including ½ hour for networking at beginning and end); small group success teams are 2 hours.

[23] ProMatch: General Membership Meeting: 2.5 hours; Individual Team/Business Meeting: 4 hours

[24] The two FBO-operated job clubs that offered the Crossroads Career Network Workshop, Snellville United Methodist Church Crossroads Career Network and Roswell United Methodist Church Job Networking, followed a modified version of the Crossroads Career Workshop curriculum.

[25] During the ProMatch general membership job club session, for example, one self-described "introverted engineer" shared the story of how he was reluctant to pursue a "cold call" with an employer, but pushed himself to do so because he was unwilling to disappoint the other group members who had encouraged him.

[26] It is possible to track employment and earnings outcomes from either the date of first attendance or at the time of exit from the job club. With regard to exit date, it often can be difficult to determine the exact date of exit for job club attendees because attendance patterns may be erratic, with participants missing sessions and then attending after several weeks, then missing sessions, and so on. The start of job club attendance is generally easier to establish, but it is possible that individuals will still be attending job clubs at 3, 6 or even 12 months after their start date. In random assignment experimental studies, often the date of random assignment is used to time subsequent points of follow-up data collection.

[27] During the planning phase of experimental studies it is important to determine the "minimum detectible effect" (MDE) to ensure appropriate sample size. The concept of minimum detectable effect (MDE) was identified by Bloom (1995) and others as a practical way to summarize the statistical power of a particular evaluation design. Orr (1999) describes the MDE as "the smallest true impact that would be found to be statistically significantly different from zero at a specified level of significance with specified power."

[28] Such denial of services may be more readily accepted by program operators and policy makers when there is excess demand for the services (e.g., a waiting list), so that in the absence of the experiment some individuals who might qualify for services cannot be served because of a lack of available resources to serve them. In this case (when there is excess demand for services than can be supplied), even with random assignment to treatment and control groups the same or similar numbers of individuals may be served as would be the case if an experiment was not used.

[29] See West et al. (2008) for a description of randomized encouragement.

[30] Typically logistic regression analysis is used where the dependent variable is treatment status.

[31] Caliendo and Kopeinig (2008) and Smith and Todd (2005) suggest a number of matching strategies. The simplest approach is one-to-one matching, where for each treatment group person, a comparison group person is selected on the basis of having the closest propensity score; a variation on this approach is many-to-one matching. Other approaches include kernel density matching and local linear regression matching where all or most of the nonparticipants are included in the analysis but those who are poor matches are assigned zero or low weight in the analysis. Other refinements to the matching procedure include methods in which cases where there are no good matches are excluded and selection of observations with or without replacement.

[32] One approach to determine if the groups are similar is to use t-tests to determine if the treatment and matched comparison groups have statistically significant differences on each of the explanatory variables.

[33] Holcomb and Nightingale (2003) observe that "research that describes and explains how programs, policies, and procedures are translated into operation goes by different names: implementation research, process analysis, management research, organizational analysis, case study research, or simply qualitative research." In this memorandum we primarily use the term "process" or "implementation" research.

[34] Appendix B provides the discussion guides used during interviews with the FBO/CBO administrators/staff for this exploratory study. These guides serve as a sample of the structure and types of instruments that could be used – and may provide a starting point for developing such instrumentation.

[35] A focus group is defined as "a small group of people whose response to something (as a new product or a politician's image) is studied to determine the response that can be expected from a larger population." (Source: www.merriam-webster.com/dictionary)

[36] For more detail on focus groups and the step-by-step instructions in planning and conducting focus groups see: Kreuger (2010).

[37] See Section 3 for a more detailed discussion of concerns of FBOs/CBOs toward implementing additional data collection forms and automated participant tracking systems.

[38] If such participant forms or participant-level systems are implemented it is essential to also design and implement security procedures to protect participant confidentiality.

In: Faith- and Community-Based Organizations
Editor: Glenn P. Bagley

ISBN: 978-1-63321-578-8
© 2014 Nova Science Publishers, Inc.

Chapter 2

THE ROLE OF FAITH-BASED AND COMMUNITY ORGANIZATIONS IN POST-KATRINA HUMAN SERVICE RELIEF EFFORTS[*]

Carol J. De Vita and Fredrica D. Kramer

EXECUTIVE SUMMARY

By almost any measure—geographic reach of the storm, population displaced, destruction of property, costs of disaster relief, and prospective costs of rebuilding—the effects of hurricanes Katrina and Rita represent the largest single natural disaster on U.S. soil in the past 100 years. The events also produced one of the largest disaster response efforts by nongovernmental, charitable organizations, including both faith-based and community organizations (FBCOs).

Purpose and Methods

To obtain detailed data on FBCOs' contributions to relief efforts following hurricanes Katrina and Rita and learn how these groups might help in future disasters, the Urban Institute conducted a two-year study for the Office of the Assistant Secretary for Planning and Evaluation, U.S. Department of Health and Human Services. The study included a telephone survey of 202 FBCOs that provided hurricane-related human services in the Gulf Coast region and in-depth, field-based case studies of eight organizations in Louisiana and Mississippi that provided such services.

The telephone survey offers quantitative data on the types of FBCOs that participated in relief and recovery efforts, the services provided, individuals served, and the monetary and human resources and networks and collaborations used to provide relief and recovery

---

[*] This is an edited, reformatted and augmented version of a final report issued by the U.S. Department of Health and Human Services, Office of the Assistant Secretary for Planning and Evaluation, December 2008. The report was prepared under contract.

services. Information was collected between November 2007 and February 2008 from a stratified random sample of FBCOs in the Gulf Coast region. Of the 202 respondents, 120 self-identified as faith-based organizations and 82 as secular nonprofits. Most of those who identified as faith-based were religious congregations, though a small number (14) were professional human services providers.

The case studies used in-depth, field-based interviews with the leaders of the study organizations and others with whom they interacted or who may have influenced the assistance provided. Site visits were conducted between May and July 2008. The purpose of the case studies was to understand how eight organizations in different communities and with different purposes before the storms responded to the disaster. The case studies explored what motivated these organizations to respond as they did, how they related to the larger web of disaster responders, and whether the efforts of these generally smaller or nontraditional responders will be sustainable over time or replicable in future disasters. Because the cases selected involved relationships among many organizations, the studies illustrate a complex network of actors, including public and private agencies, and generally a melding of faith-based and secular organizations.

The study addresses five broad research questions: (1) what are the characteristics of FBCOs that provided disaster-related human services; (2) what services were provided, and to whom; (3) what resources (monetary, material, and human) were used to deliver services; (4) what networks facilitated the ability of FBCOs to deliver services; and (5) what lessons can be learned from these relief efforts?

Major Findings from the Survey

Characteristics of the FBCOs
- FBCOs responding to the survey represented a wide range of local organizations. Some had operating budgets of less than $500; others more than $1 million. Faith-based organizations that responded to the survey were considerably older (median age 55 years) than secular nonprofits (25 years).
- Half the FBCOs in the survey used paid staff to deliver relief and recovery services, but the number of paid staff was relatively small (median of five). More than three-quarters of FBCOs used volunteers, with the median number of volunteers around 20. For most FBCOs in the survey, the volunteer workforce increased substantially after the hurricanes.
- Two-thirds of the FBCOs surveyed had no prior experience giving disaster relief assistance after a hurricane. This was especially true of secular nonprofits and those located a greater distance from the direct impact of the storms.

Types of Services
- Roughly 70 percent of survey respondents provided immediate relief services, such as food, water, clothing, and temporary shelter. A large proportion of faith-based groups, predominantly congregations, provided these services, as did FBCOs in geographic locations outside the storms' direct impact.

- In contrast, fewer FBCOs provided long-term recovery services, such as housing rehabilitation, mental health counseling, or job training. Less than half the respondents indicated involvement in any of these services, and less than 25 percent provided child care or job training. The notable exception is in housing rehabilitation: nearly 60 percent of congregations in the survey engaged in sustained housing rehabilitation. Secular nonprofits tended to provide relief and recovery services for a longer period than faith-based organizations. Again, with the exception of housing rehabilitation services, faith-based organizations tended to end their services within three months after the storm, whereas secular nonprofits were more likely to stay for a year or more.

People Served

- Records were not often kept on the number of clients served during the crisis, so survey respondents provided a rough estimate of the number of individuals helped. About a quarter of respondents reported serving fewer than 50 people, while almost a fifth reported serving more than 1,000. These numbers could represent multiple visits by the same individual, as might be characteristic for some emergency services.
- Providing demographic information on people served is even more difficult than providing numeric counts. Nearly a third of survey respondents declined to provide even an estimate. Of those who did, recipients were most frequently described as low- income and families with children.

Funding Relief/Recovery Services

- Estimating the amount of money spent on relief and recovery services was difficult. More than a third of survey respondents could not tell us an amount, in part because they did not keep records. Of those respondents that provided information, the median budget for relief/recovery work was $6,667.
- For most respondents, donations from individuals were the most common source of financial support. Faith-based organizations were more likely than secular nonprofits to receive individual donations. In contrast, secular nonprofits were about three to four times more likely than faith-based groups to have received financial support from government.

Networks and Collaborations

- Two of every three respondents worked with other groups to provide post-hurricane services. Nearly half reported that the collaborations were new, and another fifth reported a combination of new and old relationships. Most collaborations involved sharing resources such as space, equipment, and supplies.
- Relatively few respondents worked with state and local governments; however, secular nonprofits were twice as likely as faith-based groups to do so (23 percent versus 10 percent). Only about 7 percent of FBCOs worked with federal agencies. Faith-based organizations, mostly congregations, were most likely to work with other faith-based groups, while nonprofits were most likely to work with other nonprofits.

Perceptions of the Relief/Recovery Effort

- Perceptions of what went well in providing services after the storms differed by type of organization. Most faith-based respondents cited the people who were helped, while secular nonprofits pointed to the collaborations.
- Among the most common challenges mentioned were insufficient supplies and services, poor communication, and poor service coordination.

Major Findings from the Case Studies

Characteristics of Case Study Organizations

- Although half the case study organizations were secular and half were faith based, their collaborations represent a mix of faith-based and secular organizations. While religious faith may have provided a personal motivation for some organizations' leaders, staff, or volunteers, the reasons for involvement were often indistinguishable between religious and secular organizations.
- Disaster responses in the case studies appear often to owe as much to chance as to deliberate planning. With one exception, none of the organizations studied had previously engaged in disaster response planning, and they made decisions in response to challenges created by the storms.

Catalysts for Response

- The magnitude of the disaster was the primary reason that FBCOs studied responded, and raises the question of who and how many would respond in future disasters. The level of devastation, the influx of evacuees to communities along the exit routes, and the inundation of cash, material donations, and volunteers both inspired engagement and demanded management and coordination (e.g., to sort, store, and distribute goods and to house, feed, triage, or supervise volunteers) on a level never before needed. Chance rather than prior disaster experience or preconceived plan explained the direction that the responses often took.
- The storms' magnitude also focused attention on the personal and social dimensions of the disaster, including permanent loss of housing, widespread family dislocation and emotional trauma, and the particular vulnerabilities of low-income minority populations, issues not addressed in depth or at all in previous disasters. For many, these factors would worsen over time. The storms and flooding also created a vacuum in the human service delivery system and a serious challenge to serving the swelling numbers who needed assistance with resources already strained before the disaster.
- Traditional models for disaster response were severely challenged, overwhelmed, or dysfunctional, motivating newcomers to disaster response to try to help, and spawning new approaches to both relief and recovery. Traditional responders did not have the trained staff, resources, or protocols to provide more than limited assistance, and they were frequently ill prepared for the long-term need for shelter or the extent of psychological trauma in wide portions of the population.

Mechanics of Response

- Case study organizations together provided emergency aid, donations management, volunteer housing and coordination, case management, and direct human services; most provided some aspect of almost all these services. All the organizations used both paid staff and volunteers in their relief work. Seven of the eight organizations were supported by some public funding.

- Finding and maintaining staff was a challenge for some organizations studied. The order for total evacuation meant that public employees who were not exempt would be unavailable in the critical first days after the storms; even first responders might be unavailable if their families had not been provided for through pre-arranged plans. Several organizations in New Orleans reported losing a majority of their staff because housing and basic infrastructure in the city had not returned.

- Volunteers were important to the disaster response but could also create challenges, including the need for housing, feeding, careful supervision, and debriefing, as well as liability concerns. FBCOs using outside volunteer professionals, such as physicians and nurses, had no way, beyond basic licensing, of evaluating their quality or competence. Volunteers might come with truckloads of goods but had no place to stay and little money. As "demucking" of houses was completed, it became hard to match volunteer skills with tasks required for rebuilding. Some respondents suggested that some other FBCOs were in "over their heads" (for example, taking on shelters or feeding responsibilities with inadequate experience or resources) or less able to integrate their work with other relief efforts under way.

- The inability to communicate readily created a major challenge to locating staff, congregants, volunteers, and partners to restart operations. Some FBCOs studied developed creative ways to use the Internet, including organizations' own web sites, email networks, and official government sites, to generate large responses from social and professional networks and the general public, and to match organizational needs with volunteer skills and interest. One FBCO set up a 211 information number outside the impact area to help hurricane victims find services they had used in New Orleans. Another equipped a van with satellite communications to bring help to devastated areas and allow hurricane victims and first responders to communicate their whereabouts to others.

- Leaders in several case study organizations illustrated attributes of particular value in the crisis. Leaders were often high-energy people able to donate large amounts of time, sometimes pro bono, in part because their own lives had not returned to normal. Several brought expertise, such as in management, housing operations, logistics training, or human service delivery, and in working in stressful circumstances. Others used connections to community and political institutions to catalyze funding and craft services based on unique understandings of services and populations. Because this disaster presented new and larger issues than experienced in the past, leaders had to learn to change approaches as populations and needs changed over time. Several leaders of case study organizations seemed to understand the limits of their expertise and connected with others in the area to broaden their services and skill sets.

- Familiarity with local areas and perceived legitimacy were keys to overcoming distrust of severely traumatized individuals. Traditional responders were often unfamiliar with local conditions and local facilities and services, and any knowledge gained on the ground was lost as new teams were rotated in.

- All the cases studied involved inter-organizational collaboration, some formal partnerships and others in which assistance was episodic or informal as needed. Several FBCOs studied connected with local, state, or federal agencies. These relationships were based more on social and professional networks than on support from formal hierarchical affiliations. These relationships created access to restricted areas, access to rebuilding assistance, sharing of facilities or resources, and access to financial help or professional expertise.

Accountability and Equity

- Accountability for handling funds, distributing other resources, identifying needed services, and ensuring that they are delivered to those in need can be problematic in an emergency. There is clearly a trade-off between accountability and flexibility in the context of an emergency. Oversight of the emergency response sometimes took a back seat because of the magnitude of need and to allow for more flexibility in the delivery of assistance. Only two organizations studied were held explicitly accountable for the populations they were serving. In three sites, the principal reason for working outside formal long-term recovery structures was the ability to help more people without the burden of red tape and bureaucracy.
- The lack of guidelines and specificity for designated use of funds, populations served, standards about what constituted need, or service units raises questions about equitable treatment among service recipients. While income and other assistance received was typically a part of the review in a long-term recovery committee structure, some in the field complained about the lack of transparency in needs assessments. In cases that were not part of a formal case management framework, chance and informal contacts often determined allocation of assistance. How evacuees sorted themselves or were triaged to different congregations for assistance is unknown.

Life Cycles and Sustainability

- As time passes, funding diminishes, and the needs of those served before the storm come back into focus, many FBCOs return to their original mission despite continuing needs related to the 2005 hurricanes. Three FBCOs studied that did not previously have a disaster response mission have returned to their original functions, but each is likely to retain the internal capacity to respond to future disasters.

Connections to Traditional Disaster Relief and Human Services Systems

- Except for the two FBCOs that were part of the formal response system, connections to traditional response or human service systems were rare or nonexistent among the studied sites. Two sites declined invitations to participate in long-term recovery structures or resigned after a short time, viewing these structures as too slow and burdened by red tape, or potentially inequitable. Some officials interviewed who were responsible for the area's emergency response plans were focusing on how to incorporate local FBCOs into their plans, though the specifics were not always clear.

- Among those FBCOs that provided emergency assistance, cross-communication was often minimal, especially for coordinating volunteers and distributing donations. This lack of communication could create duplication of services and oversupplies of certain types of donations.
- The Red Cross and FEMA were perceived as overwhelmed by the magnitude of the storm, the duration of needed assistance, and the nature of need. FEMA was criticized for its slow, rigid bureaucracy and the absence of a strategy to provide needed social services as a part of the provision of emergency housing. The use of rotating teams of those unfamiliar with the local area and unable to make meaningful referrals was also criticized.
- Despite the massive need for health and social services, FBCOs that did not typically provide social services did not usually connect to the larger human services system. FBCOs post-hurricane contacts were more likely to be the result of efforts connected to long-term recovery structures, chance, or the doggedness of individual staff to locate services. Vulnerable populations often have an array of preexisting challenges, which are exacerbated by the trauma of evacuation and dislocation and the breaking of essential family and social networks that are difficult, if not impossible, to reestablish. Without attention to the full dimensions of psychological trauma, there was greater potential for persistent dysfunction and inability to resettle successfully.

Lessons Learned

Many organizations that are not traditional disaster responders, including small community-based social service providers and local congregations, played important roles in the aftermath of hurricanes Katrina and Rita. Several lessons can be drawn from the telephone survey and the case studies about what roles such organizations might play in future disasters.

- **Those preparing emergency preparedness plans need to better understand the availability and capability of FBCOs.** Recent federal recommendations[1] recognize the importance of including FBCOs in emergency planning and delivery of human services. Simply being able to identify who is left after a disaster, what their needs are, and who might provide assistance is critical to a response effort. The majority of survey respondents provided assistance; how many other organizations were unavailable because they were wiped out by the storm is unknown. Incorporating an inventory of local FBCOs and their contact information into disaster plans would be helpful. Ideally, the nature of their facilities, their capabilities, and prior experience would be included in the plan.
- **Recovery services after a disaster of this magnitude extend far beyond the traditional boundaries of emergency relief.** Longer-term recovery activities in a traditional disaster response model are largely focused on physical rebuilding and dependent on a limited circle of organizations providing aid. These traditional models are not well equipped to deal with deep and sustained injuries of disaster victims, both physical and psychological, and they are not well connected to the broader universe of expertise and service delivery that might provide appropriate and

sustained interventions. Lists of potential governmental and private providers, as well as regional and national experts who specialize in trauma and vulnerable populations, could help local areas tap into that expertise after a disaster.

- **Many FBCOs involved in long-term recovery appreciate the need to coordinate activities, as evidenced by new attention to data-sharing mechanisms among some traditional responders.** The case studies suggest the critical need for coordination among a wider array of providers, including federal, state, and local agencies; experts in various specialized interventions; and private donors whose contributions may be critical to success.

- **Major disasters generate major humanitarian responses, which sometimes include those with the best intentions but uneven capabilities.** The case studies suggest the importance of seeking out the best performers—those with proven track records in addressing complex or challenging needs, the ability to work with the populations affected, and the ability to integrate their work with others. Those who are not sufficiently experienced, not culturally competent, or cannot recognize appropriate ways to coordinate their services with others are likely to be less successful in their relief efforts or create problems for others trying to give assistance.

- **Soliciting and managing cash and material donations as well as volunteers is a key to effective disaster response.** Some FBCOs studied learned to use the Internet to disseminate real-time information, reach out for help, solicit and vet volunteers, share databases, and establish 211 directories to identify resources. Government and FBCOs might devise ways to work together to set up web sites to serve as clearinghouses, manage solicitations, and allocate resources, including donations, volunteers, and emergency services.

- **How FBCOs will respond in the future will likely depend on the magnitude of the disaster and the extent of damage they sustain to their own operations.** Many that were new to disaster response learned how to perform effectively after the 2005 hurricanes. It would be valuable to incorporate those experiences into disaster preparedness planning, including how to increase flexibility for traditional disaster responders. The fact that social and professional connections were so important to case study organizations reinforces the need to nurture connections, perhaps through strategic conferencing and other methods, to create awareness of how to tap connections before disaster strikes.

The Gulf Coast hurricanes of 2005 have put a new lens on the limits of understanding among researchers and policymakers of the breadth and depth of a major disaster's effects. More work remains to understand the effects of the disaster and the most effective ways to provide immediate and long-term assistance. Collecting and reexamining data on the effects of the storms, particularly on the most vulnerable populations, and incorporating these lessons into planning for future disaster responses is clearly important. Data sharing among organizations, such as FEMA, that have detailed information on hurricane victims could be used to provide follow-up services for people who still need help. These data could also be used to support needed evidence-based research on the effects of the storms and outcomes of sustained treatment, particularly mental health services, for individuals who are the victims of major disasters. The data could also provide needed evidence for proposed changes in disaster response planning.

INTRODUCTION

By almost any measure—geographic reach of the storm, population displaced, destruction of property and infrastructure, costs of disaster relief, and the prospective costs of rebuilding—the effects of hurricanes Katrina and Rita in 2005 represent the largest single natural disaster on U.S. soil in the past 100 years. Because the storm and the breaking of the levees devastated a major population center and totally obliterated large swaths of coastal areas, their effects were extraordinary. By one account, more than 100,000 square miles of land were affected[2]—roughly the size of Great Britain—and about 160,000 homes and apartments were destroyed or suffered major damage.[3] The Federal Emergency Management Agency (FEMA) estimated damage at $37.1 billion—or four times higher than the costs associated with the World Trade Center attack in 2001.[4]

The events surrounding the storms also produced one of the largest disaster response efforts by nongovernmental, charitable organizations. These included faith-based and secular groups, religious congregations both locally based and from other states, national umbrella organizations with substantial experience in human services delivery, and groups with specific disaster response expertise. By some accounts, the response of charitable groups was regarded as more effective than that of federal, state, or local governmental agencies.[5]

For many faith-based and community organizations (FBCOs), the outpouring of services and generosity after the hurricanes was consistent with their missions and traditions of helping people in need.[6] Yet, there have been few systematic studies on how these organizations function during emergency situations, what they do, who they serve, and with whom they collaborate.

Purpose of the Study

This report, prepared by the Urban Institute for the Office of the Assistant Secretary for Planning and Evaluation, U.S. Department of Health and Human Services, presents findings from a large-scale study of FBCOs in the Gulf Coast region that provided relief and recovery services after hurricanes Katrina and Rita. The purpose of the study was to document the resources, networks, and collaborations used to provide relief and recovery services after the storms, and to assess the experiences, successes, and challenges that these organizations had in providing assistance. The study was particularly interested in FBCOs that are not characteristically considered traditional emergency responders.[7] It addressed the kinds of services given in the immediate and long-term aftermath of the disasters, the extent of coordination and collaboration among charitable service systems, and how such services were or can be integrated with governmental responses to help the nation's disaster preparedness agencies better prepare for the next emergency whether from natural or other causes.

Research Questions

The study addressed five research questions:

1. What are the characteristics of FBCOs that provided disaster-related human services?
2. What services were provided, and to whom?
3. What resources (monetary, material, and human) were used to deliver services?
4. What networks facilitated the ability of FBCOs to deliver services?
5. What lessons can be learned from these relief efforts?

Overview of Methodology

To understand both the depth and breadth of response, the study used two research approaches to collect data: (1) a telephone survey of FBCOs in the Gulf Coast region that provided relief and recovery services, and (2) in-depth, field-based case studies of eight organizations that provided disaster-related services. Each method is described briefly below.

Telephone Survey

The telephone survey was designed to provide quantitative information on the FBCOs that participated in the relief and recovery efforts, the services provided, individuals served, monetary and human resources used to deliver services, the networks and collaborations used to provide relief and recovery services, and the lessons learned from the Katrina and Rita experience that can inform responses to future disasters. Information was collected through a telephone survey conducted between November 2007 and February 2008 of a stratified random sample of FBCOs in the Gulf Coast region. Telephone interviewers successfully contacted 271 FBCOs. Of these, 202 FBCOs indicated that they provided relief and recovery services and completed the survey. The overall response rate for the survey was 55.0 percent—42.7 percent for churches and religious congregations and 71.8 percent for nonprofit organizations.

Case Studies

The case studies were designed to provide qualitative information using in-depth, field-based exploration to understand what motivated the responses of the organizations under study, how they related to the larger web of disaster response, and whether the efforts of these generally smaller or nontraditional responders will be sustainable over time or replicated in future disasters. Six of the eight cases were in Louisiana (two in New Orleans, two in Baton Rouge, and two in southwestern Louisiana), and two were in Mississippi in the areas on the Gulf Coast directly hit by Hurricane Katrina.

The cases were selected for their variation in location and organizational type and the types of assistance provided, and because they might have important stories to tell about collaborations crafted, the uniqueness of the response, or the relationships developed to larger disaster relief networks. As such, the findings raise important issues about what types of responses are likely, under what conditions, from smaller and nontraditional responders, and when and how to connect these organizations with the larger system of disaster response and human service delivery in planning for future disasters.

General Structure of the Report

The report is organized into three main sections, followed by technical appendices:

- Part I presents the findings of the telephone survey of FBCOs that provided relief and recovery services in the Gulf Coast region after the hurricanes. The analysis includes
  - types and characteristics of FBCOs that participated in the survey;
  - types of services provided;
  - number and types of clients served;
  - use of paid staff and volunteers in the relief and recovery efforts;
  - types of networks and collaborations formed;
  - monetary costs of providing relief and recovery services and the sources of this financial support; and
  - a summary of key findings.
- Part II presents the findings of the in-depth case studies. The analysis includes
  - general characteristics of the eight cases;
  - snapshot portraits of each case and how the stories unfolded;
  - the mechanics of response (that is, services provided, staffing, funding, communications, individual and organizational expertise, networks and collaborations);
  - major issues, including catalysts for response, accountability, equity, life cycles and sustainability of the response, and relation to the traditional disaster relief networks and other human service providers; and

  - a summary of key findings.
- Part III presents overall conclusions and lessons learned from the study. In particular, the discussion identifies catalysts for response, promising avenues for strengthening collaboration and coordination among local FBCOs and government relief agencies, and the challenges and limitations likely to be encountered in these arrangements.
- Two appendices provide additional technical information. Appendix A details the telephone survey methodology, and Appendix B reproduces the telephone survey questionnaire.

PART I. TELEPHONE SURVEY FINDINGS

Although anecdotal stories suggest the important role that FBCOs played in the aftermath of the storm, little systematic information is available to measure their capacity to engage in relief and recovery activities and the scope of their activities. The purpose of the telephone survey was to obtain quantitative measures on the types of FBCOs that participated in relief and recovery efforts; the individuals served; and the resources, networks, and collaborations used to facilitate service delivery.

The survey was conducted between November 2007 and February 2008, using a stratified random sample of FBCOs in the Gulf Coast region. Telephone interviewers successfully contacted 271 FBCOs. Of these, 202 FBCOs indicated that they provided relief and recovery services and completed the survey.

This section describes the methods used to design and conduct the telephone survey and the survey's findings.

Methodology

The survey methodology had four main tasks: (1) to prepare an interview protocol to address the research questions, (2) to develop a sampling design, (3) to calculate response rates, and (4) to identify faith-based organizations. Each task is discussed briefly below. Additional information is provided in Appendix A.

Interview Protocol and Research Questions

The telephone survey of FBCOs in the Gulf Coast region was designed to assess the scope and complexity of relief and recovery efforts undertaken by FBCOs after hurricanes Katrina and Rita. The study's five main research questions helped guide the formulation of specific survey questions:

1. What are the characteristics of FBCOs that provided disaster-related human services after the storms?
2. What services were provided, and to whom?
3. What resources (monetary, material, and human) were used to deliver services?
4. What networks facilitated the ability of FBCOs to deliver services?
5. What lessons can be learned from these relief and recovery efforts?

Sample Design

The goal of the sampling design was to select sufficient numbers of organizations to complete 200 telephone interviews, while maximizing the response rate. A sample of this size is large enough to investigate what services were delivered after hurricanes Katrina and Rita and the collaborations used.[8]

The telephone survey was conducted in three geographic areas: the states of Louisiana and Mississippi and an area 50 miles in radius around the Houston Astrodome where many evacuees from New Orleans were sheltered.

Because there are no existing lists of FBCOs in the region or nationally, we used two independent sources to identify organizations of interest and create a master list from which to draw the sample. The American Church List (ACL), a database of religious congregations, is regarded as the most complete and current information on congregations in the United States. The ACL contains contact information, such as address and telephone number for congregations, and, for some entries, demographic information about the congregation. The list, purchased in July 2007, had 14,213 religious organizations in Louisiana, Mississippi, and a 50-mile radius around the Houston Astrodome. The National Center for Charitable Statistics (NCCS) database contains information on 501(c)(3) organizations that have revenues of $25,000 or more and file annual Forms 990 with the U.S. Internal Revenue Service. The latest NCCS data available (2005) identified 2,957 human service nonprofits in the geographic areas of study.[9]

Two considerations shaped the sample design. First, it was assumed that the intensity of the storms' impact affected the ability of FBCOs to provide relief and recovery services. FBCOs closest to the heavily damaged areas might be less able to respond than those farther away. To adjust for this likelihood, the sample was divided into three strata: (1) areas directly impacted by the storm,[10] (2) those partially impacted or adjacent to directly impacted areas, and (3) the remainder of the state. All FBCOs selected from Houston were regarded as part of the third (or distant) stratum.

Second, prior research suggested that congregations would be more difficult to reach by telephone than nonprofit groups. So, the sampling plan called for oversampling congregations to achieve an adequate number of them in the final sample.

Proportional random samples of congregations and nonprofits, stratified by state and impact area, were drawn from the master list derived from the ACL and NCCS databases.

This selection process produced a sample of 615 organizations. This pool of potential respondents contained both large and small congregations and nonprofits.

Response Rates

From the sample of 615 organizations, 100 were deemed ineligible because no valid contact information could be found during the survey period. Of the remaining 515 organizations, we were unable to contact 111 of them. In these cases, no one answered the telephone or responded to messages left on answering machines. An additional 133 organizations either declined to participate or could not find a convenient time to participate. Ultimately, 271 organizations participated in the study.

To calculate the response rate, the 271 organizations that participated in the survey were divided by the total number of organizations operating during the survey period. Because the operational status of 111 organizations was unknown, we needed to estimate the denominator for the response rate.[11] Based on this estimate, the overall response rate was 55.0 percent—more specifically, 42.7 percent for congregations and 71.8 percent for nonprofits. Response rates at this level are typical of surveys of congregations and community-based organizations (see Appendix A for further detail).

Identifying Faith-Based Organizations

The term "faith-based organization" is a term that emerged in the public lexicon during the welfare reform debates of the mid-1990s, but there is no consensus on what constitutes a faith-based organization. It can include organizations with historic ties to a religious entity but minimal or no current connections, such as the YMCA; organizations with extant religious ties that deliver secular services, such as Catholic Charities; small community-based organizations with links to a religious body whose services may or may not have religious content; local houses of worship; or any combination of the above characteristics. The term "faith-based organization" has no consistent or predictive meaning about the organization's connection to religion, and some organizations with religious roots or religious ties do not self-identify as faith based. In conducting research on faith-based organizations, a major challenge is determining how to define the term "faith based."

As is common in many studies involving organizations with origins or current connections to religion, we asked survey respondents to self-identify as faith based. All 106 respondents that originally were drawn from the American Church List indicated that they were either a church or faith based, while 14 of the 96 respondents drawn from the NCCS database of 501(c)(3) organizations indicated that they were faith based. For purposes of analysis when comparing faith-based organizations and community-based (secular) nonprofits, we included the 14 self-identified faith-based organizations with the 106 congregations, resulting in a sample composed of 59 percent faith-based organizations and 41 percent secular nonprofits. Throughout the remainder of the report, we will use the term faith-based and community organizations (FBCOs) when referring to all respondents and call the comparison groups "faith-based organizations" and "secular nonprofits."

By allowing respondents to self-identify as faith based, the analysis reflects the broadest definition of the term. The survey does not, however, measure the extent to which faith or religion plays a role in the delivery of services. The findings of this survey cannot be generalized to all faith-based groups because, given definitional and identification problems, there is no comprehensive list of faith-based organizations from which to draw a representative sample.

The Survey Findings

The findings of this telephone survey of FBCOs provide important insights into the ways that locally based FBCOs responded to the needs of people affected by hurricanes Katrina and Rita and the number and types of collaborations that assisted these organizations in delivering services.

Characteristics of FBCOs Providing Services

In general, the survey respondents reflect a wide range of faith-based and secular organizations in the region—large, small, relatively new, and others that have been in their communities for decades.

Geographically, about half (52 percent) of the FBCOs in the survey are located in Louisiana, 41 percent in Mississippi, and 7 percent in the vicinity around the Houston Astrodome. Almost two in five respondents (38 percent) are in the areas hit hardest by the hurricanes; one in three (36 percent) is in an area of secondary impact (that is, partially impacted by the storms or adjacent to areas of direct impact) and one in four (26 percent) is in a tertiary or distant area (that is, all other parishes or counties in Louisiana and Mississippi and around the Houston Astrodome). These distributions mirror the proportional distribution of organizations sampled for the study.

The survey respondents were from both large and small FBCOs. Although many respondents (35 percent) were unable or declined to indicate the size of their operating budgets, of those that answered, the smallest operated on less than $500 annually, while the largest reported budgets of more than $1 million. Faith-based providers in the survey tended to be smaller than their secular counterparts. The median annual budget for faith- based groups was $259,000, while for secular nonprofits, it was $452,000. As seen in Table 1, about

10 percent of the faith-based organizations had operating budgets of more than $1 million, compared with 34 percent of the nonprofits. FBCOs from the primary impact areas had higher median operating budgets ($343,000) than those in the secondary ($275,000) and distant ($317,000) areas.

Table 1. Size of FBCOs by Type, State, and Distance to Impact Area

| Characteristic | N | Percent of Organizations with Operating Budgets of: | | | | | | | Median budget |
		Less than $5,000	$5,000 to $10,000	$10,000 to $50,000	$50,000 to $100,000	$100,000 to $500,000	$500,000 to $1 million	More than $1 million	
All respondents	132	3.0	0.8	7.6	12.9	45.5	9.8	20.5	$326,667
Faith-based organization	73	4.1	0.0	6.8	17.8	53.4	8.2	9.6	$258,974
Secular nonprofit	59	1.7	1.7	8.5	6.8	35.6	11.9	33.9	$452,381
Louisiana	69	4.3	0.0	10.1	14.5	44.9	11.6	14.5	$287,097
Mississippi	53	1.9	1.9	0.0	11.3	50.9	9.4	24.5	$374,074
Houston, Texas	10	0.0	0.0	30.0	10.0	20.0	0.0	40.0	$300,000
Primary impact area	50	2.0	0.0	2.0	12.0	56.0	12.0	16.0	$342,857
Adjacent to impact area	49	6.1	2.0	10.2	10.2	40.8	6.1	24.5	$275,000
Farthest from impact area	33	0.0	0.0	12.1	18.2	36.4	12.1	21.2	$316,667

Source: Urban Institute 2007–08 Survey of FBCOs in Louisiana, Mississippi, and Houston.
Note: Data are missing for 70 respondents.

The median age of FBCOs in the survey is 37 years, but this measure varies widely (Table 2). For example, FBCOs in the vicinity of the Houston Astrodome have the youngest median age (15 years), and no organization in the Houston sample is older than 100 years. In contrast, the median ages of FBCOs in Louisiana and Mississippi are 37 and 42 years, respectively, and about 14 percent of FBCOs in these two states are older than 100. The younger age of Houston's FBCOs may partly reflect the dynamics of demographic and economic growth and change in the Houston region. The sharpest contrast in age is seen between faith-based organizations and secular nonprofits. The median age of faith-based organizations is more than twice that of their secular counterparts—55 years versus 25 years. Roughly 20 percent of faith-based organizations in the survey are more than 100 years old. These data suggest the deep roots that religious congregations have in the Gulf Coast region.[12]

Types of Services Provided

In the aftermath of a hurricane, there are at least two phases to recovery that necessitate different types of services. First are the immediate rescue and relief activities to help victims of the storm. Later, recovery activities help individuals and families reconstruct their lives and cope with loss. The survey asked questions to learn what types of services were provided by FBCOs and how long groups provided these services.

Although hurricanes are common in the Gulf Coast region, hurricanes Katrina and Rita were so powerful and damage so extensive that the response of organizations in the region and around the country was unprecedented. Indeed, two-thirds of the FBCOs in the survey said that this was the first time that they provided disaster relief services after a hurricane. The share of first-time providers was slightly higher for secular nonprofits (71 percent), perhaps reflecting the fact that congregations commonly provide emergency services as distinct from ongoing social services. Seventy-five percent of FBCOs in the distant (tertiary) areas of the region also were first-time providers.

Table 2. Age of FBCOs by Type, State, and Distance to Impact Area

| Characteristic | N | Percent of Organizations with Age of: | | | | | Mean age | Median age |
		Less than 10 years	10 to 25 years	26 to 50 years	51 to 100 years	More than 100 years		
All respondents	200	12.0	23.0	27.5	25.0	12.5	51	37
Faith-based organization	118	6.8	16.9	22.9	33.1	20.3	65	55
Secular nonprofit	82	19.5	31.7	34.1	13.4	1.2	30	25
Louisiana	104	12.5	23.1	25.0	26.9	12.5	51	37
Mississippi	82	8.5	20.7	31.7	24.4	14.6	55	42
Houston, TX	14	28.6	35.7	21.4	14.3	0.0	25	15
Primary impact area	76	13.2	25.0	27.6	22.4	11.8	48	36
Adjacent to impact area	73	11.0	17.8	31.5	27.4	12.3	54	40
Farthest from impact area	51	11.8	27.5	21.6	25.5	13.7	51	31

Source: Urban Institute 2007–08 Survey of FBCOs in Louisiana, Mississippi, and Houston.
Note: Data are missing for two respondents.

Immediate Relief Services

The most common services provided immediately after the storm by FBCOs in the survey were provision of clothing, food, water, monetary or in-kind assistance, and temporary housing. Roughly 70 percent of respondents indicated that they had engaged in at least one of these activities (Table 3). To a much lesser extent, FBCOs provided first aid or medical care (25 percent), transportation out of the impacted areas (21 percent), and search and rescue activities (8 percent). These patterns of service provision were similar regardless of the FBCO's location. Providing clothing and food were generally the most common activities, while engaging in medical care, transportation away from the disaster area, and search and rescue missions were far less common.

A larger proportion of faith-based organizations in the survey provided immediate relief services than did their secular counterparts. For example, between 70 and 85 percent of faith-based organizations provided clothing, food, water, and in-kind assistance compared with roughly 40 to 55 percent of the secular nonprofits—a statistically significant difference. Also, higher percentages of faith-based organizations provided temporary housing, transportation out of the affected areas, and search and rescue activities than did secular nonprofits in the survey, but the differences in percentages between these two types of providers are relatively small and not statistically significant.

Table 3. Services Most Commonly Provided Immediately after the Hurricanes

Characteristic	N	Percent of Organizations That Provided the Following Immediate Services:							
		Clothing/ household goods	Food	Water & emergency supplies	Money or in-kind donations	Temp housing & shelter	First aid/ medical services	Transportation out of affected areas	Search & rescue activities
All respondents	202	71.8	69.3	63.4	58.4	53.0	24.8	21.3	8.4
Faith-based organization	120	84.2**	78.3**	72.5**	70.8**	59.2	30.8*	25.8	10.0
Secular Nonprofit	82	53.7**	56.1**	50.0**	40.2**	43.9	15.9*	14.6	6.1
Louisiana	105	66.7	66.7	59.0	56.2	55.2	21.9	24.8	10.5
Mississippi	83	75.9	69.9	67.5	60.2	51.8	25.3	16.9	7.2
Houston, TX	14	85.7	85.7	71.4	64.3	42.9	42.9	21.4	0.0
Primary impact area	77	67.5	67.5	62.3	59.7	53.2	19.5	20.8	7.8
Adjacent to impact area	73	74.0	67.1	63.0	53.4	54.8	26.0	23.3	12.3

Source: Urban Institute 2007–08 Survey of FBCOs in Louisiana, Mississippi, and Houston.
* Difference significant at 0.05 level.
** Difference significant at 0.01 level.

Two-thirds of the respondents said they began providing immediate relief services during the storm or within the first week after the storm (Table 4). Distance from the hurricanes' direct impact was a significant factor in determining when services began. FBCOs located in the adjacent parishes and counties outside the immediate impact areas were quickest to respond. Three-quarters of them started providing services during or just after the storm, and 90 percent were assisting within the first month. Similarly, in the areas farthest from the impact, 90 percent of the FBCOs were taking action within the first month after the storm. The devastation that occurred in the hardest hit areas undoubtedly slowed the response of many FBCOs in those locations. Just over half (52 percent) in the hardest hit areas started providing services within the first week after the storm, but a quarter did not begin until after the first month. Distance from the storms' impact appears to be the key factor in the quickness of response. No other factor was statistically significant.

About one in three FBCOs was continuing to provide immediate relief services, such as temporary housing, two years after the storms. The highest share of these services (35 percent) was located in the primary impact areas, reflecting the rebuilding that continues there. Also, a somewhat greater share of secular nonprofits (33 percent) than faith-based organizations (28 percent) continued to provide such services, perhaps reflecting the short-term, emergency services that congregations often provide. For the most part, immediate relief services were offered for a relatively short duration. Of those that no longer delivered services, most FBCOs in the survey (53 percent) stopped within three months of the storm.

Fewer than one in five (17 percent) provided immediate relief services for more than one year (Table 5). FBCOs in the primary impact areas and secular nonprofits were mostly likely to provide these services for the longest time. In each case, slightly more than a quarter (27 percent) of these organizations provided immediate relief services for more than a year before ending the services.

Table 4. Inception of Immediate Relief Services

Characteristic	Number	When Did You Begin Providing Immediate Services?		
		During or right after storm (first week)	Not in first week but in first month	Sometime after first month
All respondents	186	65.6	19.9	14.5
Faith-based organization	117	65.8	19.7	14.5
Secular nonprofit	69	65.2	20.3	14.5
Louisiana	98	63.3	21.4	15.3
Mississippi	74	68.9	17.6	13.5
Houston, TX	14	64.3	21.4	14.3
Primary impact area*	69	52.2	23.2	24.6
Adjacent to impact area*	67	76.1	16.4	7.5
Farthest from impact area*	50	70.0	20.0	10.0

Source: Urban Institute 2007–08 Survey of FBCOs in Louisiana, Mississippi, and Houston.
Note: Data are missing for 16 respondents.
* Difference significant at 0.05 level.

Table 5. Duration of Immediate Relief Services

Characteristic	Still Providing Service?		When Did You Stop Providing Immediate Services?					
	Yes (N)	% of total	All (N)	Do not know	After one month	After three months	After one year	Sometime later than one year
All respondents	56	30.1	128	4.7	27.3	25.8	25.0	17.2
Faith-based organization	33	28.2	83	4.8	28.9	30.1	24.1	12.0
Secular nonprofit	23	33.3	45	4.4	24.4	17.8	26.7	26.7
Louisiana	27	27.6	71	5.6	29.6	32.4	18.3	14.1
Mississippi	24	32.4	49	2.0	22.4	16.3	36.7	22.4
Houston, TX	5	35.7	8	12.5	37.5	25.0	12.5	12.5
Primary impact area	24	34.8	45	4.4	15.6	24.4	28.9	26.7
Adjacent to impact area	18	26.9	48	4.2	37.5	29.2	18.8	10.4
Farthest from impact area	14	28.0	35	5.7	28.6	22.9	28.6	14.3

Source: Urban Institute 2007–08 Survey of FBCOs in Louisiana, Mississippi, and Houston.
Note: Data are missing for 18 respondents.

Long-Term Recovery Services

In the aftermath of hurricanes, many types of services are needed to help individuals and families recover from the devastation of the storms. These services often include counseling to address the mental and emotional traumas suffered because of the storm, repair and reconstruction of damaged property, finding new jobs, and addressing educational and child care needs of children.

After hurricanes Katrina and Rita, the most common types of long-term recovery services offered by FBCOs were spiritual counseling (53 percent), housing rehabilitation (42 percent), and mental health counseling (36 percent). Much less common were services addressing child care and school needs, job training, and family reunification (Table 6).

Not surprisingly, the faith-based organizations in the survey were most likely to engage in spiritual counseling. Three-quarters of them indicated that they provided this service, and about one-tenth provided only spiritual counseling. One-fifth of secular nonprofits also addressed spiritual needs. About equal proportions of faith-based and secular nonprofits offered mental health counseling (roughly 35 percent), although it is difficult to know what distinctions respondents made between, for example, pastoral counseling and mental health counseling.

Long-term housing services—that is, cleanup, repairs, and rebuilding (as distinct from emergency shelter)—are also prominent among services provided by faith-based groups. Nearly three in five faith-based respondents (58 percent) reported providing long-term housing services, compared with one in five nonprofit respondents (20 percent). Further, as Table 6 also shows, more than half of all respondents in the directly impacted areas engaged in housing services. Understandably, FBCOs farther away from the primary impact area were less likely to offer long-term housing assistance. Also, a significantly larger share of FBCOs in Mississippi (57 percent) than in Louisiana (34 percent) was active in long-term housing assistance. The number of respondents in Texas is too small to have reliable estimates.

Although fewer than one in four FBCOs in the survey reported offering child care, job training, and family reunification services in the wake of the hurricanes, these types of services tended to be more prevalent among FBCOs located far away from the heavily impacted areas. In the vicinity of the Houston Astrodome, for example, half the FBCOs in the survey offered child care or school services, and 57 percent offered job training programs. In contrast, the percentage of FBCOs in Louisiana and Mississippi that offered these services was roughly half as large. The data suggest that the farther from the directly impacted areas, the more likely it is that a FBCO will engage in services such as child care and job training, which might be associated with resettlement activities.

Similar to immediate relief services, some long-term recovery services began within days of the hurricanes. Sixty-four percent of FBCOs offered long-term recovery services within the first week of the storm. An additional 22 percent were providing these services within the first month (Table 7). Distance from the storms' impact significantly affected when these services began. FBCOs in the sample were slower to begin services if they were in the heavily impacted areas compared with those in the secondary and tertiary areas, no doubt partly reflecting quarantines that remained in areas of impact, including all of New Orleans. There were no significant differences between faith-based and secular nonprofits or among the three states in the survey. Almost half of FBCOs (47 percent) were continuing to provide long-term recovery services at the time of the survey. A higher proportion of FBCOs in the primary impact areas than organizations located farther away reported that they were continuing to provide recovery services, although the differences are not statistically significant (Table 8).

Table 6. Most Common Long-Term Recovery Services

	N	Percent of Organizations That Provided the Following Long-Term Recovery Services:					
		Spiritual counseling	Housing Rehab	Mental health	Child care	Job training	Family reunification
All respondents	202	53.0	42.1	35.6	25.7	20.8	19.8
Faith-based organization	120	75.0**	57.5**	35.8	23.3	17.5	20.0
Secular nonprofit	82	20.7**	19.5**	35.4	29.3	25.6	19.5
Louisiana	105	49.5	34.3**	33.3	25.7	21.0**	21.0
Mississippi	83	56.6	56.6**	38.6	21.7	14.5**	16.9
Houston, TX	14	57.1	14.3**	35.7	50.0	57.1**	28.6
Primary impact area	77	57.1	53.2*	44.2	22.1	14.3*	18.2
Adjacent to impact area	73	49.3	38.4*	34.2	27.4	19.2*	17.8
Farthest from impact area	52	51.9	30.88*	25.0	28.8	32.7*	25.0

Source: Urban Institute 2007–08 Survey of FBCOs in Louisiana, Mississippi, and Houston.
*Difference significant at 0.05 level.
** Difference significant at 0.01 level.

Table 7. Inception of Long-Term Recovery Services

Characteristic	N	When Did You Begin Providing Long-Term Recovery Services?			
		Do not know	right after storm (first week)	Not in first week but in first month	Sometime after first month
All respondents	167	1.2	63.5	22.2	13.2
Faith-based organization	103	1.9	64.1	22.3	11.7
Secular nonprofit	64	0.0	62.5	21.9	15.6
Louisiana	82	1.2	63.4	20.7	14.6
Mississippi	73	1.4	61.6	26.0	11.0
Houston, TX	12	.	75.0	8.3	16.7
Primary impact area*	68	1.5	50.0	26.5	22.1
Adjacent to impact area*	57	1.8	77.2	17.5	3.5
Farthest from impact area*	42	0.0	66.7	21.4	11.9

Source: Urban Institute 2007–08 Survey of FBCOs in Louisiana, Mississippi, and Houston.
Note: Data are missing for 35 respondents.
* Difference significant at 0.05 level.
** Difference significant at 0.01 level.

Table 8. Duration of Long-Term Recovery Services

Characteristic	Still Providing Service?		When Did You Stop Providing Immediate Services?					
	Yes (N)	% of total	All (N)	Do not know	After one month	After three months	After one year	Sometime later than one year
All respondents	79	47.3	87	6.9	14.9	28.7	32.2	17.2
Faith-based organization	51	49.5	51	7.8	17.6	35.3		23.5
Secular nonprofit	28	43.8	36	5.6	11.1	19.4	44.4	19.4
Louisiana**	38	46.3	44	11.4	13.6	40.9	25.0	9.1
Mississippi**	34	46.6	38	2.6	10.5	15.8	42.1	28.9
Houston, TX**	7	58.3	5	0.0	60.0	20.0	20.0	0.0
Primary impact area	38	55.9	30	13.3	3.3	26.7	40.0	16.7
Adjacent to impact area	26	45.6	30	3.3	20.0	30.0	23.3	23.3
Farthest from impact area	15	35.7	27	3.7	22.2	29.6	33.3	11.1

Source: Urban Institute 2007–08 Survey of FBCOs in Louisiana, Mississippi, and Houston.
Note: Data are missing for 36 respondents.
** Difference significant at 0.01 level.

Among the FBCOs that stopped providing long-term recovery services, nearly half (49 percent) continued their programs for one year or longer. FBCOs in Mississippi and secular nonprofits were particularly likely to offer recovery services for an extended period. In Mississippi, about 70 percent of FBCOs that discontinued providing recovery services had provided the service for at least a year, as did 64 percent of the secular nonprofits. In contrast, 34 percent of FBCOs in Louisiana and 39 percent of faith-based providers in the survey continued their recovery services for at least one year.

Help with Paperwork and Claim Forms

The survey data suggest that helping individuals and families file damage claims or complete applications for other types of assistance was an uncommon activity for FBCOs (Table 9). Roughly 60 percent of FBCOs in the survey, regardless of the type of organization, state, or distance from the storm, reported that they did not provide assistance with claims forms and other types of paperwork.

The most common type of assistance was helping people with claims to FEMA. About one in three FBCOs that responded to the survey provided this service. The second most common assistance was helping people complete welfare applications—about one in five FBCOs gave this type of assistance. Much smaller proportions of FBCOs helped with private insurance claims (15 percent) and applications for legal assistance (12 percent). Differences by type of provider and location were generally not statistically significant.

Because a relatively small number of FBCOs in the survey provided assistance with paperwork and given the difficulty of recalling details about these activities, the survey provides only rough estimates of when these services started and stopped. The data suggest, however, that most (57 percent) FBCOs that provided assistance with paperwork and insurance claims forms began helping within the first week of the storm (Table 10). About 21 of the 70 FBCOs that could recall details about this service were still providing help at the time of the survey. Of those that reported discontinuing the service, the majority stopped within three months after the storms (Table 11). Compared with FBCOs in other locations, those in the primary impact areas were more likely to still provide assistance with claims (41 percent) and to have offered the services for a longer time. Fifteen percent stopped providing assistance with paperwork more than a year later.

Table 9. Help with Paperwork

	N	Percent of Organizations That Provided the Following Paperwork Services:				
		None	Apply to FEMA	Apply for welfare	Apply for private insurance	Apply for legal aid
All respondents	202	59.9	32.7	22.3	15.3	12.4
Faith-based organization	120	60.8	33.3	24.2	16.7	10.0
Secular nonprofit	82	58.5	31.7	19.5	13.4	15.9
Louisiana	105	61.9	31.4	21.9	12.4	7.6*
Mississippi	83	57.8	33.7	20.5	18.1	15.7*
Houston, TX	14	57.1	35.7	35.7	21.4	28.6*
Primary impact area	77	63.6	32.5	24.7	18.2	18.2
Adjacent to impact area	73	50.7	35.6	19.2	15.1	8.2
Farthest from impact area	52	67.3	28.8	23.1	11.5	9.6

Source: Urban Institute 2007–08 Survey of FBCOs in Louisiana, Mississippi, and Houston.
* Difference significant at 0.05 level.

Table 10. Inception of Services to File Claims

Characteristic	N	When Did You Begin Providing Paperwork Assistance?			
		Do not know	During or right after storm (first week)	Not in first week but in first month	Sometime after first month
All respondents	70	12.9	57.1	17.1	12.9
Faith-based organization	41	9.8	65.9	12.2	12.2
Secular nonprofit	29	17.2	44.8	24.1	13.8
Louisiana	31	16.1	58.1	16.1	9.7
Mississippi	33	9.1	57.6	18.2	15.2
Houston, TX	6	16.7	50.0	16.7	16.7
Primary impact area	27	14.8	48.1	18.5	18.5
Adjacent to impact area	26	11.5	61.5	15.4	11.5
Farthest from impact area	17	11.8	64.7	17.6	5.9

Source: Urban Institute 2007–08 Survey of FBCOs in Louisiana, Mississippi, and Houston.
Note: Analysis based on 70 respondents providing the service.

Table 11. Duration of Assistance with Paperwork

Characteristic	Still Providing Services?		When Did You Stop Providing Paperwork Assistance?					
	N	% of total	All	Do not know	After one month	After three months	After one year	Sometime later than one year
All respondents	21	30.0	45	8.9	24.4	33.3	24.4	8.9
Faith-based organization	8	19.5	30	3.3	26.7	33.3	26.7	10.0
Secular nonprofit	13	44.8	15	20.0	20.0	33.3	20.0	6.7
Louisiana	9	29.0	19	10.5	26.3	36.8	21.1	5.3
Mississippi	10	30.3	22	9.1	22.7	27.3	27.3	13.6
Houston, TX	2	33.3	4	0.0	25.0	50.0	25.0	0.0
Primary impact area	11	40.7	13	7.7	23.1	15.4	38.5	15.4
Adjacent to impact area	7	26.9	18	11.1	22.2	44.4	22.2	0.0
Farthest from impact area	3	17.6	14	7.1	28.6	35.7	14.3	14.3

Source: Urban Institute 2007–08 Survey of FBCOs in Louisiana, Mississippi, and Houston.
Note: Data are based on 21 organizations providing service.

Individuals Who Received Services

Records were not always kept on the number or types of individuals served, but 90 percent of respondents provided an estimate of the individuals they helped (Table 12). Of those who did provide an estimate, about a quarter of the respondents (28 percent) served fewer than 50 individuals, while almost one in five (18 percent) reported that they served more than 1,000. The median number of individuals helped was 112. These numbers do not distinguish between individuals served once and those served multiple times.

Along this continuum, faith-based organizations reported a higher median number of people served (134) than did secular nonprofits (93), perhaps reflecting the typical role of congregations to provide immediate relief services such as food, water, and temporary shelter compared with secular social service providers. Median numbers also declined away from the heavily impacted areas—162 for the prime impact areas, 88 for secondary areas, and 89 for tertiary areas. FBCOs in Texas reported a very high median (200), but this is probably because of the concentrated response to the evacuees who were housed in the Astrodome.

Although most FBCOs could provide a rough estimate of the number of people served, about a third of the respondents could not give demographic information (Table 13). Based on those who responded, the most common types of recipients were low-income and families with children.[13] Half the organizations estimated that at least 75 percent of the people they served were low income, and half said that at least 50 percent of those served were families with children. Also, half the FBCOs that responded to questions on client demographics indicated that at least 20 percent of the service recipients were elderly. Likewise, half the FBCOs said that the majority of recipients (88 percent) came from outside the community in which the FBCO is located.

Statistically significant differences were found between faith-based organizations and secular nonprofits in the median percentage of elderly, low-income, and families with children served. Secular nonprofits served a higher (median) percentage of low-income people than faith-based organizations (90 versus 60 percent, respectively), and families with children (70 versus 50 percent, respectively). On the other hand, faith-based groups reported higher median proportions of elderly served (25 percent) than did secular nonprofits (10 percent).

As might be expected, FBCOs in the primary impact areas reported that most of their service recipients were local people, whereas FBCOs in secondary and tertiary impact areas served mostly people from outside their communities. Other differences were either not statistically significant or based on a very small number of respondents.

Paid Staff and Volunteers

Delivering services to people in need is a labor-intensive activity. In the first few months after the storms, both paid staff and volunteers were called upon to deliver relief and recovery services.

Paid Staff

Over half (53 percent) of the survey respondents used paid staff to deliver their post-hurricane services. Secular nonprofits were significantly more likely to use paid staff than faith-based organizations (Table 14). Nearly 80 percent of the nonprofits in the survey reported using paid staff, compared with 35 percent of faith-based groups. There was no significant difference, however, in the use of paid staff by state or distance from the impacted areas.

When FBCOs used paid staff, the actual number of employees was small. Half the FBCOs with paid staff reported five or fewer employees. For faith-based organizations, the median number of paid staff was four; for secular nonprofits, it was seven. About 14 percent of FBCOs that responded to the survey had more than 20 paid staff delivering hurricane-related services.

Table 12. Number of People Served

Characteristic	N	Percent of Organizations Serving # of People between:						Median # of People served
		< 50	50–100	101–250	251–500	501–1,000	>1,000	
All respondents	180	27.8	21.1	15.6	10.6	6.7	18.3	112
Faith-based organization	106	24.5	21.7	17.0	8.5	8.5	19.8	134
Secular nonprofit	74	32.4	20.3	13.5	13.5	4.1	16.2	93
Louisiana	96	30.2	17.7	15.6	13.5	8.3	14.6	121
Mississippi	72	26.4	26.4	13.9	6.9	4.2	22.2	60
Houston, TX	12	16.7	16.7	25.0	8.3	8.3	25.0	200
Primary impact area	70	15.7	24.3	11.4	12.9	8.6	27.1	162
Adjacent to impact area	70	37.1	17.1	17.1	10.0	7.1	11.4	88
Farthest from impact area	40	32.5	22.5	20.0	7.5	2.5	15.0	89

Source: Urban Institute 2007–08 Survey of FBCOs in Louisiana, Mississippi, and Houston.
Note: Data are missing for 22 respondents.

Table 13. Types of People Served

Characteristic	Median Percentage of Types of People Served						
	Elderly n=145	Low- income n=147	Families with children n=152	Immigrants n=145	Members of the church n=93	Usual clients n=67	People from outside community n=168
All respondents.	20	75	50	0	0	15	88
Faith-based organization	25**	60**	50**	0	0	0	90
Secular nonprofit	10**	90**	70**	0	0	20	75
Louisiana	15	75	50	0	0	20	83
Mississippi	25	70	55	1	5	10	80
Houston, TX	25	95	73	0	0	1	100
Primary impact area	30	78	53	1	33**	65	25**
Adjacent to impact area	20	73	50	0	0**	13	97**
Farthest from impact area	10	75	68	0	0**	0	100**

Source: Urban Institute 2007–08 Survey of FBCOs in Louisiana, Mississippi, and Houston.
Note: Data are missing for 34 respondents.
* Difference significant at 0.05 level.
** Difference significant at 0.01 level.

Table 14. Number of Paid Staff

Characteristic	Used paid staff		Percent of Organizations with Paid Staff between:					Median number of paid staff
	N	%	Do not know	1–5	6–10	11–20	More than 20	
All respondents	107	53.0	2.8	52.3	19.6	11.2	14.0	5
Faith-based organization	42	35.0**	0.0	66.7	16.7	4.8	11.9	4
Secular nonprofit	65	79.3**	4.6	43.1	21.5	15.4	15.4	7
Louisiana	55	52.4	1.8	47.3	23.6	16.4	10.9	6
Mississippi	46	55.4	2.2	58.7	15.2	6.5	17.4	4
Houston, TX	6	42.9	16.7	50.0	16.7	0.0	16.7	4
Primary impact area	42	54.5	2.4	64.3	14.3	4.8	14.3	4
Adjacent to impact area	39	53.4	0.0	43.6	17.9	17.9	20.5	7
Farthest from impact area	26	50.0	7.7	46.2	30.8	11.5	3.8	14

Source: Urban Institute 2007–08 Survey of FBCOs in Louisiana, Mississippi, and Houston.
** Difference significant at 0.01 level.

Except for the areas directly impacted by the storms, the number of paid staff did not change significantly after the hurricanes (Table 15). About two-thirds (67 percent) of the FBCOs surveyed said that they had about the same number of paid employees after the storm as before. Another 11 percent reported a modest increase (10 percent or less), and 9 percent said they had a substantial increase of more than 10 percent.

Table 15. Change in Number of Paid Staff after the Hurricane

Characteristic	N	Compared with before the Storm, Percent of Organizations with:					
		Do not know	Substantial increase (>10%)	Modest increase (≤10%)	About the same	Modest decrease (≤10%)	Substantial decrease (>10%)
All respondents	107	1.9	9.3	11.2	67.3	6.5	3.7
Faith-based organization	42	.	11.9	11.9	73.8	.	2.4
Secular nonprofit	65	3.1	7.7	10.8	63.1	10.8	4.6
Louisiana	55	1.8	9.1	14.5	60	9.1	5.5
Mississippi	46	2.2	8.7	8.7	73.9	4.3	2.2
Houston, TX	6	0.0	16.7	0.0	83.3	0.0	0.0
Adjacent to impact area*	39	2.6	2.6	20.5	71.8	2.6	0.0
Farthest from impact area*	26	3.8	11.5	3.8	76.9	0.0	3.8

Source: Urban Institute 2007–08 Survey of FBCOs in Louisiana, Mississippi, and Houston.
Note: Analysis based on respondents with paid staff.
* Difference significant at 0.05 level.

The only statistically significant differences were found in the distance from the impacted areas. FBCOs closest to the devastation reported the most fluctuation in numbers of paid staff. About 57 percent of respondents in the primary impact area said they experienced no appreciable change, while equal proportions of FBCOs (21 percent each) reported increases or decreases in size of their paid staff. In the areas adjacent to or more distant from the impacted areas, respondents said that the number of paid staff either stayed about the same or increased. Twenty percent of FBCOs in the areas adjacent to the direct impact reported modest increases, while about 12 percent of FBCOs in the most distant places had substantial increases in paid staff. These data reflect the hurricane's disruption of service delivery by providers located in the most affected areas and the increase in demand for services in the areas away from the storm.

Volunteers

Volunteers were an important part of the service delivery process. As Table 16 shows, about three-quarters (77 percent) of FBCOs in the survey reported using volunteers in the first three months after the storms, and faith-based organizations were much more likely than secular nonprofits to work with volunteers (86 percent versus 63 percent, respectively). For those that used volunteers, the median number of volunteers that worked in a typical week was fairly similar—21 for faith-based organizations and 18 for nonprofits. No significant differences were found by state or distance from the impacted areas.

As Table 17 shows, nearly half (48 percent) of the survey respondents said they had more than a 10 percent increase in their volunteer workforce, and another 13 percent said they experienced a modest increase (up to 10 percent). Only 5 percent of FBCOs reported a decrease in volunteers. These patterns were fairly consistent for all types and locations of FBCOs and showed no statistical differences.

Table 16. Number of Volunteers

Characteristic	Used volunteers		Percent of Organizations Reporting Number of Volunteers between:					Median # of volunteers
	N	%	Don't know	1–25	26–50	51–100	>100	
All respondents	155	76.7	3.8	60.6	14.2	11.6	9.7	20
Faith-based organization	103	85.8**	3.8	56.3	15.5	13.6	10.7	21
Secular nonprofit	52	63.4**	3.8	69.2	11.5	7.7	7.7	18
Louisiana	78	74.3	3.9	70.5	12.8	9.0	3.8	17
Mississippi	65	78.3	4.5	49.2	15.4	16.9	13.8	24
Houston, TX	12	85.7	0.0	58.3	16.7	0.0	25.0	22
Primary impact area	60	77.9	1.7	55.0	15	16.7	11.7	22
Adjacent to impact area	60	82.2	6.7	65.0	13.3	8.3	6.7	18
Farthest from impact area	35	67.3	2.9	62.9	14.3	8.6	11.4	20

Source: Urban Institute 2007–08 Survey of FBCOs in Louisiana, Mississippi, and Houston.
Note: Analysis based on organizations that used volunteers.
** Difference significant at 0.01 level.

Table 17. Change in Number of Volunteers after the Hurricane

Characteristic	N	Compared with Before the Storm, Percent of Organizations with:					
		Do not know	Substantial increase (>10%)	Modest increase (≤10%)	About the same	Modest decrease (≤10%)	Substantial decrease (>10%)
All respondents	155	1.3	48.4	12.9	32.3	2.6	2.6
Faith-based organization	103	1.0	51.5	10.7	32.0	2.9	1.9
Secular nonprofit	52	1.9	42.3	17.3	32.7	1.9	3.8
Louisiana	78	1.3	41.0	17.9	33.3	2.6	3.8
Mississippi	65	1.5	53.8	9.2	30.8	3.1	1.5
Houston, TX	12	0.0	66.7	0.0	33.3	0.0	0.0
Primary impact area	60	0.0	56.7	6.7	28.3	3.3	5.0
Adjacent to impact area	60	3.3	35.0	20.0	36.7	3.3	1.7
Farthest from impact area	35	0.0	57.1	11.4	31.4	0.0	0.0

Source: Urban Institute 2007–08 Survey of FBCOs in Louisiana, Mississippi, and Houston.

Among the FBCOs that used volunteers, the two most common ways of recruiting them were word of mouth (used by nearly half of respondents) and encouraging volunteerism through the FBCO's own membership (38 percent of respondents). Other forms of recruitment included drawing from other organizations or congregations in the local area (13 percent), using existing rosters of volunteers (12 percent), receiving volunteers from national organizations or other affiliates (6 percent), conducting outreach efforts such as distributing posters or flyers (6 percent), using web sites (6 percent), and media coverage (5 percent).

Both faith-based organizations and secular nonprofits relied on word-of-mouth referrals to attract volunteers, but they drew from different pools of potential volunteers. Faith- based groups turned to their congregational members, whereas secular nonprofits used existing lists of volunteers to find help (Table 18). These differences in recruitment methods are statistically significant and may reflect organizational structure and past experience in providing services to people in need.

When asked about managing this volunteer workforce, most respondents (68 percent) said that they had about the right number of volunteers, although about a quarter said they had too few (Table 19). These responses were fairly uniform by type of organization and location.

For the most part, FBCOs were very satisfied with their experience working with volunteers. Only a handful of respondents reported any difficulties. The most common challenge was having insurance to cover the volunteers (reported by eight respondents). Other challenges mentioned were transporting volunteers to the work site (six respondents), managing or supervising volunteers (five respondents), and providing housing or food for volunteers (four respondents).

Table 18. Methods for Recruiting Volunteers

Characteristic	N	Percent of Organizations That Used:								
		Word of mouth	Their congregation	Local nonprofits & congregations	Roster of volunteers	Outreach	National groups	Web sites	Media	Other
All respondents	155	48.0	38.1	12.9	12.4	6.4	6.4	5.9	4.5	13.4
Faith-based organization	103	57.5**	60.0**	13.3	6.7**	7.5	7.5	5.8	4.2	10.0
Secular nonprofit	52	34.1**	6.1**	12.2	20.7**	4.9	4.9	6.1	4.9	18.3
Louisiana	78	40.0	34.3	9.5	11.4	4.8	3.8	2.9	2.9	14.3
Mississippi	65	56.6	42.2	16.9	13.3	8.4	9.6	9.6	7.2	9.6
Houston, TX	12	57.1	42.9	14.3	14.3	7.1	7.1	7.1	.	28.6
Primary impact area	60	48.1	33.8	13.0	10.4	6.5	7.8	7.8	6.5	15.6
Adjacent to impact area	60	49.3	42.5	15.1	13.7	8.2	4.1	6.8	0.0	12.3
Farthest from impact area	35	46.2	38.5	9.6	13.5	3.8	7.7	1.9	7.7	11.5

Source: Urban Institute 2007–08 Survey of FBCOs in Louisiana, Mississippi, and Houston.
Note: Analysis based on respondents with volunteers.
** Difference significant at 0.01 level.

Table 19. Sufficient Levels of Volunteers

Characteristic	N	Did You Recruit Too Many/Right Amount/Not Enough Volunteers? (percent)			
		Do not know	Too many	About right	Not enough
All respondents	155	2.6	2.6	68.4	26.5
Faith-based organization	103	1.9	2.9	68.0	27.2
Secular nonprofit	52	3.8	1.9	69.2	25.0
Louisiana	78	2.6	0.0	65.4	32.1
Mississippi	65	1.5	6.2	70.8	21.5
Houston, TX	12	8.3	0.0	75.0	16.7
Primary impact area	60	3.3	5.0	66.7	25.0
Adjacent to impact area	60	1.7	0.0	68.3	30.0
Farthest from impact area	35	2.9	2.9	71.4	22.9

Source: Urban Institute 2007–08 Survey of FBCOs in Louisiana, Mississippi, and Houston.
Note: Analysis based on respondents who used volunteers.

Networks and Collaborations

Anecdotal stories tell of the important role that FBCOs have played in the relief and recovery efforts in the Gulf Coast region. Less well documented are the networks and collaborations used to accomplish this work. The survey explored the prevalence of affiliations with other organizations, collaborations that were formed, and the experiences FBCOs had working with other organizations.

Types of Arrangements

About half (53 percent) of respondents indicated that they were formally affiliated with a larger entity (such as a Catholic diocese, the Southern Baptist Convention, YMCA, Boys and Girls Clubs of America, or Child Welfare League of America). Such affiliation was much more likely among faith-based organizations (63 percent) than secular nonprofits (38 percent).

However, being affiliated with a larger entity did not affect the likelihood that a FBCO worked with other organizations. In fact, two of every three respondents (68 percent) indicated that they worked with one or more other groups as part of their relief and recovery efforts. Further, for those that worked collaboratively, respondents were fairly evenly divided between affiliated and unaffiliated FBCOs. There was no significant distinction between faith-based and secular organizations or among geographic locales.

Collaborations were most commonly formed with secular nonprofits and churches rather than governmental or business entities (Table 20). Between 35 and 40 percent of the respondents indicated that they had worked with secular nonprofits and churches to provide their relief and recovery services. A much smaller proportion worked with state and local government (15 percent) and businesses (11 percent). Only a handful of FBCOs collaborated with the federal government, schools, universities, and hospitals (about 7 percent in each category).

Table 20. Types of Organizations in the Collaboration

Characteristic	N	Percent of Organizations That Worked with:							
		Secular nonprofits	Churches	State/local gov't	Business	Federal gov't	K-12 schools	Colleges	Hospitals
All respondents	138	39.1	35.6	15.3	11.4	6.9	6.9	6.9	6.4
Faith-based organization	81	38.3	40.8	10.0*	12.5	6.7	5.8	6.7	6.7
Secular nonprofit	57	40.2	28.0	23.2*	9.8	7.3	8.5	7.3	6.1
Louisiana	68	34.3	31.4	14.3	11.4	7.6	6.7	7.6	4.8**
Mississippi	59	43.4	38.6	16.9	8.4	7.2	4.8	7.2	4.8**
Houston, TX	11	50.0	50.0	14.3	28.6	0.0	21.4	0.0	28.6**
Primary impact area	52	39.0	37.7	20.8	9.1	10.4	2.6	10.4	5.2
Adjacent to impact	48	37.0	30.1	9.6	9.6	6.8	8.2	2.7	5.5
Farthest from impact	38	42.3	40.4	15.4	17.3	1.9	11.5	7.7	9.6

Source: Urban Institute 2007–08 Survey of FBCOs in Louisiana, Mississippi, and Houston.
Note: Analysis based on 138 respondents that reported collaborations.
* Difference significant at 0.05 level.
** Difference significant at 0.01 level.

As Table 20 also shows, faith-based organizations in the survey worked almost equally with churches (41 percent) and nonprofits (38 percent), while secular nonprofits were more likely to work with other nonprofits (40 percent) than churches (28 percent). These patterns are not statistically significant, however.

Two significant patterns emerged from the survey data. First, a much higher proportion of secular nonprofits (23 percent) than faith-based groups (10 percent) worked with state and local governments. Because many congregations and other faith-based organizations do not typically partner with government, they may have been less familiar with how to work with government or lacked the capacity to do so. Second, the proportion of FBCOs working with hospitals was roughly six times greater in the Houston area (29 percent) than in either Louisiana or Mississippi (5 percent each). Although the number of FBCOs that worked with hospitals is small (about three respondents in each location), the finding is statistically significant and may partly reflect the disruption of the health care system in the areas of impact after the hurricanes.

Many of these collaborations were new arrangements (Table 21). Nearly half (47 percent) of the FBCOs that worked with others said their collaborations did not exist before the storms. Almost a third (31 percent) of the respondents said the arrangements were a continuation of prior relationships that existed before the storms, and about 20 percent described their collaborations as a combination of new and existing relationships. There was no significant difference in these proportions by type of organization or locale.

Experiences with Collaboration

Collaborations and partnerships can encompass many activities. After Katrina and Rita, the most common way that groups in the survey collaborated was to share resources (Table 22). Three- quarters of the FBCOs that worked with other groups indicated that they shared physical resources such as space, equipment, and supplies. Faith-based organizations more often than secular nonprofits shared physical resources (82 percent versus 63 percent). This is consistent with the fact that most faith-based respondents in this survey are congregations, and congregations frequently have shelter and feeding facilities that they enlist during a disaster. Also, the farther away from the impacted areas, the less resource sharing occurred. About 85 percent of FBCOs in the primary areas shared resources, compared with 75 percent in the secondary areas and 58 percent in the tertiary areas. These differences were statistically significant.

After resource sharing, the next most common collaborative activity was referrals or information exchange. More than half of FBCOs that worked with other groups referred individuals or families *to* other organizations for assistance (56 percent) and received referrals *from* other organizations (53 percent), and about half received advice or instructions from other organizations (49 percent). A smaller proportion of FBCOs gave advice or instructions to the other groups with which they collaborated (33 percent).

There were statistically significant differences between faith-based and secular nonprofit organizations in collaboration that involved referrals. A larger proportion of secular nonprofits than faith-based groups referred clients to other providers (67 percent versus 48 percent) and received referrals from other organizations (68 percent versus 42 percent). These differences may reflect that secular nonprofits are often professional service providers and by extension recognized as part of a social service delivery system. Also, a larger proportion of FBCOs in the primary impact areas (71 percent) referred individuals to other providers than did those in the secondary or tertiary areas (46 and 47 percent, respectively). Because many service providers in the heavily impacted areas may have been damaged and not open for business after the storms, the circumstance may have necessitated greater use of referrals in the most damaged areas.

Table 21. History of the Collaboration

Characteristic	N	Were These Relationships New or Continuing from before the Storm?			
		Do not know	New	Continuing	Both
All respondents	138	2.2	47.1	31.2	19.6
Faith-based organization	81	3.7	50.6	25.9	19.8
Secular nonprofit	57	0.0	42.1	38.6	19.3
Louisiana	68	2.9	41.2	32.4	23.5
Mississippi	59	0.0	57.6	27.1	15.3
Houston, TX	11	9.1	27.3	45.5	18.2
Primary impact area	52	0.0	50.0	28.8	21.2
Adjacent to impact area	48	4.2	54.2	27.1	14.6
Farthest from impact area	38	2.6	34.2	39.5	23.7

Source: Urban Institute 2007–08 Survey of FBCOs in Louisiana, Mississippi, and Houston.
Note: Analysis based on 138 respondents that reported history of collaboration.

Table 22. Activities within the Collaboration

Characteristic	N	Shared resources	Referred individuals to others	Received referrals	Received advice	Gave advice	Received financial support
		Percent of Organizations That:					
All respondents	138	73.9	55.8	52.9	48.6	32.6	28.3
Faith-based organization	81	81.5*	48.1*	42.0**	40.7**	27.2	19.8**
Secular nonprofit	57	63.2*	66.7*	68.4**	59.6**	40.4	40.4**
Louisiana	68	76.5	52.9	48.5	45.6	35.3	27.9
Mississippi	59	72.9	62.7	61.0	55.9	33.9	30.5
Houston, TX	11	63.6	36.4	36.4	27.3	9.1	18.2
Primary impact area	52	84.6*	71.2*	57.7	53.8	42.3	46.2**
Adjacent to impact area	48	75.0*	45.8*	56.3	52.1	29.2	22.9**
Farthest from impact area	38	57.9*	47.4*	42.1	36.8	23.7	10.5**

Source: Urban Institute 2007–08 Survey of FBCOs in Louisiana, Mississippi, and Houston.
Note: Analysis based on 138 respondents that reported on collaboration.
* Difference significant at 0.05 level.
** Difference significant at 0.01 level.

The least common collaborative activity was sharing financial resources. Overall, 28 percent of the FBCOs that worked with other organizations said that they received financial support from groups they worked with. However, there are at least two significant differences in this pattern. First, more than twice the proportion of secular nonprofits received financial support from their partners than did faith-based organizations—40 percent versus 20 percent. And, second, a larger proportion of respondents in the hardest hit areas (46 percent) received financial support from their partners than did those in the secondary (23 percent) and tertiary areas (11 percent). This may reflect a greater level of financial need in the hardest-hit areas.

When asked how well these collaborative arrangements worked, 70 percent of respondents replied "very smoothly." Another 27 percent said "somewhat smoothly" and "reasonably well." Less than 2 percent indicated that they had a "mixed" experience of good and not-so-good experiences. FBCO respondents in Mississippi and those in the areas adjacent to the direct impact were slightly less positive about their collaborative experiences than other FBCOs, but the differences are not statistically significant.

Only a handful of respondents (nine faith-based organizations and eight secular nonprofits) said they had tried to work with other organizations but were unsuccessful. These respondents primarily identified secular nonprofits and government organizations as the ones that they were unable to work with. Poor communication among groups and difficult protocols were frequently mentioned as barriers that prevented collaborations from taking place.

Cost of Providing Services

Obtaining information from survey respondents on the cost of providing services was difficult. More than a third of respondents (36 percent) did not know how much was spent, did not keep records, or refused to indicate an amount. Of those that provided information, the median expenditure was about $6,700 (Table 23). Secular nonprofits spent somewhat more than faith- based groups ($7,500 versus $6,100, respectively), and FBCOs in the directly hit areas reported the largest median expenditure ($10,000). About 10 percent of secular nonprofits in the survey reported spending more than $1 million.

When asked about the sources of financial support for their relief and recovery efforts, many respondents (about 38 percent) were unable to answer these questions. However, based on those who did respond, most (72 percent) received donations from individuals (Table 24). The next most common source of financial support was from faith-based organizations (45 percent) and nonprofit organizations such as the United Way and Red Cross (39 percent).

As Table 24 also illustrates, there were statistically significant differences in the sources of financial support for faith-based and secular nonprofits. A greater percentage of faith-based groups than secular nonprofits received donations from individuals and other faith-based organizations, while a larger share of secular nonprofits got financial support from other nonprofits, private foundations, and government. Secular nonprofits were about four times more likely than faith-based groups to have received financial support from the federal government and about 3.5 times more likely to have received support from state and local governments. These data suggest that secular nonprofits may have more capacity to work with government and meet requirements that accompany the receipt of public dollars. Survey respondents in the directly impacted areas were more likely than those in other areas to receive support from faith- based groups and nonprofit groups. There were no statistically significant differences in the sources of financial support when the data were controlled for state.

Table 23. Amount Spent on Relief Services

Characteristic	N	Percent of Organizations with Relief Budgets of:									Median budget
		Less than $500	$500 to $2,500	$2,500 to $5,000	$5k to $10k	$10k to $50k	$50k to $100k	$100k to $500k	$500k to $1m	More than $1m	
All respondents	130	13.8	14.6	18.5	9.2	22.3	5.4	9.2	2.3	4.6	$6,667
Faith-based organization*	75	10.7	14.7	22.7	9.3	24.0	8.0	6.7	4.0	0.0	$6,071
Secular nonprofit*	55	18.2	14.5	12.7	9.1	20.0	1.8	12.7	0.0	10.9	$7,500
Louisiana	72	15.3	12.5	19.4	6.9	27.8	4.2	8.3	1.4	4.2	$7,000
Mississippi	50	14.0	16.0	18.0	10.0	14.0	6.0	12.0	4.0	6.0	$6,000
Houston, TX	8	0.0	25.0	12.5	25.0	25.0	12.5	0.0	0.0	0.0	$7,500
Primary impact area	48	16.7	8.3	14.6	10.4	20.8	4.2	14.6	6.3	4.2	$10,000
Adjacent to impact	47	19.1	12.8	17.0	6.4	27.7	4.3	6.4	0.0	6.4	$5,833
Farthest from impact	35	2.9	25.7	25.7	11.4	17.1	8.6	5.7	0.0	2.9	$4,583

Source: Urban Institute 2007–08 Survey of FBCOs in Louisiana, Mississippi, and Houston.
Note: Data are missing 72 respondents.
* Difference significant at 0.05 level.

Table 24. Sources of Financial Support for Relief Services

Characteristic	N	Percent of Organizations That Received Financial Support from:							
		Individuals	Faith-based organization	Secular nonprofit	Business	Private foundation	Federal gov't	State/local gov't	Other
All respondents	125	72.0	44.8	39.2	31.2	19.2	15.2	14.4	8.0
Faith-based organization	74	82.4**	55.4**	24.3**	25.7	10.8**	6.8**	6.8**	5.4
Secular nonprofit	51	56.9**	29.4**	60.8**	39.2	31.4**	27.5**	25.5**	11.8
Louisiana	57	70.2	38.6	36.8	33.3	17.5	15.8	15.8	10.5
Mississippi	58	70.7	50.0	44.8	27.6	20.7	15.5	13.8	6.9
Houston, TX	10	90.0	50.0	20.0	40.0	20.0	10.0	10.0	0.0
Primary impact area	56	71.4	62.5**	57.1**	26.8	25.0	21.4	17.9	5.4
Adjacent to impact	41	68.3	24.4**	26.8**	39.0	17.1	9.8	14.6	14.6
Farthest from impact	28	78.6	39.3**	21.4**	28.6	10.7	10.7	7.1	3.6

Source: Urban Institute 2007–08 Survey of FBCOs in Louisiana, Mississippi, and Houston.
Note: Analysis based on respondents that reported amount spent and sources of support.
** Difference significant at 0.01 level.

Most FBCOs in the survey delivered relief services without direct financial support from government. Only 18 respondents said that they applied for reimbursement from the federal or state government, and most of these (11) were larger organizations with budgets over $500,000. The reimbursement requests were primarily directed at FEMA or other federal agencies (11 of 18 respondents).

Of the 18 FBCOs that applied for public funds, most said that the application process was very difficult (nine) or somewhat difficult (four). Only four respondents described the process as "very easy" or "somewhat easy." When asked why the process was difficult, typical responses included "the application process was unclear"; "takes a lot of paperwork and time to get it done"; "we lost all of the records [in the storm] … so not able to collect because [the records were] not recovered"; and "a lot of things they asked for weren't told to [us] in advance, but after it had already been done." Eleven of the 18 applicants received some reimbursement for their services. The others had been waiting two or more years to receive payment. It is unknown how many FBCOs chose not to apply for reimbursement because of the presumed difficulties of the process or because they were able to use other resources.

Lessons Learned

Hurricanes Katrina and Rita were extraordinary events. When asked to reflect on the lessons learned, survey respondents expressed a wide range of views and opinions.

Steps Taken to Address Future Emergencies

In the aftermath of the hurricanes, some FBCOs in the survey had taken steps to prepare for future emergencies (Table 25). One in four respondents said that since the hurricanes, they have created an emergency action plan to help direct their relief and recovery efforts. One in six cited collaborations as an important outcome of the storms. Less common actions included creating lists of volunteers to use in the future (9 percent) and developing directories of services such as 211 or 311 systems that can serve as information centers (5 percent). Still, more than one in three FBCOs in the survey (36 percent) reported that they have not taken *any* steps that might prepare them for future emergencies.

The steps taken by faith-based and secular nonprofit organizations differed significantly in some cases. For example, faith-based organizations were much more likely than secular nonprofits to report that they have taken no steps since the storm to prepare for future emergencies—45 percent versus 22 percent. In contrast, proportionately twice as many secular nonprofits (35 percent) have created emergency action plans than faith-based providers (18 percent), and a greater share of secular nonprofits (22 percent) reported that they have created collaborations and partnerships than faith-based organizations (13 percent), although the difference is not statistically significant. The different steps taken by faith-based and secular respondents to plan for future emergencies may reflect the types of services faith-based organizations, predominantly congregations, provided in response to the storm—that is, short-term, emergency relief services. These organizations may see their mission as helping during emergency situations, and they may have less interest in building the infrastructure critical to providing other, long-term human services.

Distance from the storms' direct impact also appears to be a factor in the likelihood of planning for the next emergency. The farther from the hurricanes' impact, the less likely FBCOs reported any emergency planning activities. For example, half the FBCOs in the most distant areas reported that they have taken no action since the hurricanes to prepare for future emergencies, whereas in the primary and secondary areas, only a third of the FBCOs have taken no action.

FBCO Perceptions of What Went Well

In general, FBCOs in the survey reported that their experiences in providing relief and recovery services were positive. When asked what went well, the most frequent response was "we were able to help people in need," followed by "we brought people together and worked as a team," and then "we formed collaborations and shared information."

As Table 26 shows, faith-based and secular nonprofit organizations emphasized different aspects of their service delivery experiences when asked what worked well. The most common answer for faith-based organizations was their ability to help people in need (20 percent), while for secular nonprofits, it was forming collaborations and sharing information (23 percent). Faith- based groups tended to emphasize working together as a team (14 percent), providing volunteers (11 percent), and providing supplies (8 percent). Secular nonprofits cited their ability to help people (11 percent), provide counseling (10 percent), and connect people with services (9 percent). Faith-based organizations were twice as likely as secular nonprofits (10 percent versus 5 percent) to say that everything went well.

The distance from the impacted areas also significantly shaped FBCOs' perceptions of what went well. In the primary impact areas, for example, the most common response referred to the collaborations formed and information shared. FBCOs in the primary impact areas named collaborations more than twice as often (19 percent) as those in the secondary (8 percent) or distant areas (7 percent). In contrast, FBCOs in the secondary areas were much more likely to cite their ability to provide counseling (14 percent) and housing assistance (10 percent) than FBCOs in either the primary or distant areas.

Table 25. Steps Taken to Prepare for Future Emergencies

| Characteristic | N | Percent of Organizations with the Following in Place for Future Storms: | | | | | |
		Nothing	Emergency Action plans	Partnerships/ collaborations	List of volunteers	Directories of services	Other
All respondents	202	35.6	25.2	16.3	9.4	4.5	37.6
Faith-based organization	120	45.0**	18.3**	12.5	9.2	4.2	36.7
Secular nonprofit	82	22.0**	35.4**	22.0	9.8	4.9	39.0
Louisiana	105	38.1	27.6	16.2	9.5	4.8	37.1
Mississippi	83	32.5	22.9	18.1	8.4	4.8	39.8
Houston, TX	14	35.7	21.4	7.1	14.3	0.0	28.6
Primary impact area	77	31.2*	31.2	20.8	6.5	5.2	39.0
Adjacent to impact area	73	30.1*	24.7	17.8	11.0	5.5	43.8
Farthest from impact area	52	50.0*	17.3	7.7	11.5	1.9	26.9

Source: Urban Institute 2007–08 Survey of FBCOs in Louisiana, Mississippi, and Houston.

* Difference significant at 0.05 level.

** Difference significant at 0.01 level.

Table 26. What Went Well in Providing Relief/Recovery Services

Characteristic	N	Percent of Organizations That Had the Following Successes:											
		Helped people in need	Brought people together/ worked as team	Collaborated & shared information	Provided volunteers	Provided counseling	Everything went well	Efficiency/timeliness of service delivery/ well organized	Provided supplies	Provided housing	Connected people with services	Do not know/no response/nothing	Other
All respondents	221	16.3	12.2	11.8	10.0	8.1	7.7	6.3	5.4	5.0	4.5	3.6	9.0
Faith-based organization**	132	19.7	14.4	4.5	10.6	6.8	9.8	4.5	7.6	6.1	1.5	3.8	10.6
Secular nonprofit**	89	11.2	9.0	22.5	9.0	10.1	4.5	9.0	2.2	3.4	9.0	3.4	6.7
Louisiana	117	15.4	12.0	9.4	7.7	6.8	7.7	6.0	6.8	6.8	6.0	4.3	11.1
Mississippi	90	16.7	13.3	16.7	10.0	10.0	7.8	5.6	4.4	3.3	2.2	2.2	7.8
Houston, TX	14	21.4	7.1	0.0	28.6	7.1	7.1	14.3	0.0	0.0	7.1	7.1	0.0
Primary impact area*	85	15.3	12.9	18.8	14.1	3.5	4.7	5.9	8.2	3.5	4.7	2.4	5.9
Adjacent to impact*	79	16.5	12.7	7.6	3.8	13.9	8.9	3.8	3.8	10.1	3.8	2.5	12.7
Farthest from impact*	57	17.5	10.5	7.0	12.3	7.0	10.5	10.5	3.5	0.0	5.3	7.0	8.8

Source: Urban Institute 2007–08 Survey of FBCOs in Louisiana, Mississippi, and Houston. Note: The "N" reflects the number of answers given, not the number of respondents.

** Difference significant at 0.01 level. * Difference significant at 0.05 level.

Table 27. What Did Not Go Well or Could Have Gone Better in Providing Relief/Recovery Services

Characteristic	N	Percent of Organizations That Had the Following Problems:											
		Don't know/no response/nothing	Insufficient service delivery/supplies	Poor communication	Poor coordination	Insufficient preparation	Not enough volunteers/staff	Not enough funding	Problems with FEMA	Problems with government	Problems with Red Cross	Did not get reimbursed	Other
All respondents	213	33.3	20.7	8.5	8.0	5.6	5.2	5.2	3.3	3.3	1.9	0.5	4.7
Faith-based organization**	126	40.5	20.6	7.1	8.7	7.1	2.4	2.4	4.0	0.8	3.2	0.0	3.2
Secular Nonprofit**	87	23.0	20.7	10.3	6.9	3.4	9.2	9.2	2.3	6.9	0.0	1.1	6.9
Louisiana	107	37.4	17.8	7.5	6.5	2.8	6.5	7.5	3.7	3.7	0.0	0.9	5.6
Mississippi	90	26.7	22.2	10.0	10.0	10.0	3.3	3.3	3.3	3.3	4.4	0.0	3.3
Houston, TX	16	43.8	31.3	6.3	6.3	0.0	6.3	0.0	0.0	0.0	0.0	0.0	6.3
Primary impact area	80	33.8	17.5	10.0	11.3	3.8	6.3	5.0	3.8	3.8	1.3	0.0	3.8
Adjacent to impact area	78	28.2	21.8	7.7	9.0	9.0	3.8	3.8	1.3	5.1	2.6	1.3	6.4
Farthest from impact area	55	40.0	23.6	7.3	1.8	3.6	5.5	7.3	5.5	0.0	1.8	0.0	3.6

Source: Urban Institute 2007–08 Survey of FBCOs in Louisiana, Mississippi, and Houston. Note: The "N" reflects the number of answers given, not the number of respondents.

** Difference significant at 0.01 level. * Difference significant at 0.05 level.

FBCO Perceptions of What Could Have Gone Better

Respondents had a much more difficult time answering "what did not go well or could have gone better." One-third of respondents indicated they did not know or could think of nothing to report (Table 27). Faith-based organizations (40 percent) were more likely than secular nonprofits (23 percent) to express this opinion.

The most frequently mentioned challenge was insufficient supplies or other services. One in five FBCOs in the survey named this as something that could have been improved. Other common challenges were poor communication (named by 9 percent of the FBCOs) and poor coordination of services (cited by 8 percent).

Again, secular nonprofits and faith-based organizations had different perceptions of what could have been done better. For example, four times more secular nonprofits than faith-based groups (9 percent versus 2 percent) said there were not enough volunteers and not enough funding. A greater share of faith-based organizations than secular nonprofits indicated problems working with FEMA and the Red Cross, while secular nonprofits named "government" as a challenge for them. A larger share of faith-based organizations than secular nonprofits (7 percent versus 3 percent) indicated that they had insufficient preparation to respond to the aftermath of the hurricane.

Summary of Key Survey Findings

The telephone survey findings document FBCOs' involvement in delivering hurricane relief and recovery services, and the networks created to assist people. The findings can serve as an important basis for understanding the work of FBCOs after disasters and for improving the coordination of relief efforts by public and private entities. Key findings include:

Faith-based and secular nonprofit organizations tend to play slightly different roles in the relief and recovery efforts. Faith-based organizations were particularly active in providing immediate relief services such as food, clothing, water, and temporary shelter, and are now active in housing repair and rebuilding programs. The role of congregations in providing emergency services is well documented in the research literature, so their involvement in immediate relief activities after hurricanes Katrina and Rita is not surprising. Secular nonprofits, on the other hand, also provided many immediate relief services but have a larger presence in providing longer-term recovery services such as child care and job training services, which serve longer-term needs and may require more professionally trained staff. Another distinction between faith-based and secular providers is that the secular nonprofits in the survey continued their services for a longer time.

Distance from the immediate impact of the disaster is a significant factor in determining when services began. FBCOs outside the immediate impact areas were more likely to begin relief and recovery services sooner than those in the primary impact areas. The evacuation ordered by governmental authorities for some areas of impact remained in effect for over a month, and the damage and destruction of many FBCOs in the impact areas undoubtedly contributed to the slow start. Once back on their feet, however, FBCOs in the immediate impact areas were more likely to sustain services for a longer period. This is consistent with the logical progression of services after an emergency—that is, emergency services provided to evacuees outside the impact areas diminish as evacuees return to their homes or resettle in other areas; long-term recovery services, however, are needed and sustained in the impacted areas.

Both paid staff and volunteers formed the backbone of relief and recovery efforts. Half the FBCOs in the survey, particularly the secular nonprofits, reported using paid staff to deliver their relief and recovery services, although the number of paid staff reported by survey respondents (median of five) was relatively small. More than three-quarters of FBCOs, particularly faith- based organizations, used volunteers. For most FBCOs in the survey, this was a substantial increase in their volunteer workforce. Although the vast majority of respondents indicated that their experiences with volunteers went smoothly, areas that might be improved included finding insurance to cover the volunteers, housing and transporting them, and managing their work.

FBCOs' relief efforts were enhanced by the collaborations that were formed, but few of these arrangements included government entities. Two of every three respondents indicated that they worked with other groups as part of their relief and recovery work, and at least half these collaborations were formed as a result of the storms. Faith-based organizations worked almost equally with other faith-based groups and with secular nonprofits. In contrast, a larger share of secular nonprofits tended to work with other secular nonprofits than with faith-based groups. A statistically significant finding is that more than twice as many secular nonprofits as faith-based organizations reported working with all levels of government.

Perceptions of what went well in the relief and recovery effort appear influenced by distance from the storms' impact and type of organization. For example, FBCOs in the primary impact areas identified the collaborations formed and information shared as positive parts of the relief and recovery efforts, while those in the secondary and distant areas cited their ability to provide counseling and housing. Faith-based organizations frequently cited the people who were helped, and secular nonprofits pointed to the collaborations made.

Survey respondents noted several areas that could have gone better in the relief and recovery efforts. Among the most common challenges mentioned were insufficient supplies and services, poor communication, and poor coordination of services.

Many FBCOs lack preparation for a future emergency. More than one in three FBCOs in the survey reported that they have not taken any steps to prepare for future emergencies. This was especially true of faith-based groups and FBCOs located farthest from the primary impact areas.

These findings underscore the important role that local faith-based and secular nonprofits play in disaster relief and recovery efforts and the need for continued planning and coordination between these groups and government responders. The stories of FBCOs in the Gulf Coast area that emerge from these findings offer important lessons for preparing for future disaster relief efforts. Findings from the in-depth case studies, which are presented in the next section, provide detailed analysis of FBCOs' experiences providing services to people in need after the 2005 hurricanes.

PART II. CASE STUDIES OF EIGHT RESPONSES

The findings from the telephone survey, presented in the previous section, provide a profile of the faith-based and community organization response to the 2005 hurricanes. The case studies, discussed in this section, focus on an individual organization as a means to better understand what took place in a single community affected by Hurricane Katrina, or Rita, or both, and to map connections and disconnections that suggest how FBCOs might be used effectively in future disasters. These organizations operated in a complex environment that affected what they did and how they did it. The case studies look in depth at what was happening on the ground in different communities that motivated the response of these eight organizations; how their different purposes and goals created different responses; who else (both governmental and nongovernmental) was providing relief; and how the larger context may have influenced why and how organizations did what they did and, in some cases, why others may have been unable to respond.

To put their efforts in that context, these organizations operated sometimes alongside, but often independently of, a massive humanitarian response. This large network of responders included such organizations such as the American Red Cross, FEMA, local offices of emergency preparedness and designated first responders, other military and law enforcement agencies, and national and international religious and secular organizations with dedicated arms for disaster services (e.g., United Methodist Committee on Relief, Episcopal Relief and Development, and Mennonite Disaster Services). Regardless of whether these responders interacted directly with the FBCOs under study, they helped shape the environment in which the smaller FBCOs operated.

Similarly, while the general perception is that government at all levels failed to respond effectively, many public entities were providing services quickly, and human service providers— public and private—were rapidly working to get themselves back into operation to serve those who needed help. Understanding how this complex web of public and private organizations functioned, and how they can work in tandem with FBCOs to get individuals and families back on their feet, is critical to making the process work better the next time a disaster occurs.

Finally, the massive crisis caused by hurricanes Katrina and Rita generated an unprecedented outpouring of cash, material donations, and volunteers from domestic and international sources, all of which had to be managed on the ground. How that assistance was managed, and whether it helped or hindered the response of the FBCOs under study, is important to understand for future disasters.

The case studies are a way to understand where organizations fit in the larger web of disaster response, if and how interactions with this web produced an enhanced service response, and whether the efforts of these generally smaller or nontraditional responders will be sustainable over time or replicable in future disasters. More typically than not, these organizations did interact with other parts of the disaster relief system; in three cases, they were part of the larger formalized response structure.

The process for selecting case studies was designed to identify organizations that had important stories to tell, as measured by the variety of collaborations, the uniqueness of the response, or by other experiences that might directly inform issues of interest. The study aimed to discover relationships that might help explain the nature, duration, intensity, and success of responses. Relationships might be vertical (e.g., an umbrella organization within a denominational hierarchy or type of affiliation) or horizontal (e.g., pre-existing or new collaborations to coordinate response across organizations with similar or varied functions and expertise). The case studies also include organizations with narrow missions and those with multipurpose missions, and relief efforts of limited duration, as well as those that evolved or were sustained over time.

The selection was also intended to capture many variations, resulting in cases that differ greatly from each other. While this makes cross-site comparisons difficult and generalizing largely inappropriate, the material provides a basis for developing hypotheses about what responses under what conditions are likely in the future, what networks might form, and when and how these sorts of organizations could connect with the larger system for disaster response and human service delivery.

The analysis is framed around four research questions to draw out key aspects of the eight case studies:

1. What was the catalyst for the initial disaster response?
   - Was it mandated, preplanned, and/or part of a larger emergency response?
   - Was it driven by organizational or individual mission or competence (in emergency services or other expertise)?
2. How did these FBCOs do what they did?
   - What was their expertise? With whom did they work? How did they connect, and when did they not?
   - Where did they fit into larger disaster relief efforts, both governmental and nongovernmental?
   - To whom were they accountable, and for what services, populations, outcomes, and resource utilization?
3. Why did these FBCOs continue, fold, or change course?
   - How did they define their mission initially?
   - Was their effort intended to be sustainable over time?
   - Is their disaster response likely to reemerge in a future disaster?
4. What are reasonable expectations about FBCOs' roles in future disasters?
   - How dependent is their engagement on the magnitude of the disaster?
   - How can successes be replicated and challenges be overcome?
   - How can FBCO activities be integrated with, or supportive of, other governmental or nongovernmental relief functions?

The following sections present the methodology for site selection and data collection for the case studies, general characteristics of the eight cases, snapshots of each of these very different stories, and major findings.

Methodology

The unit of analysis for each case study is the FBCO, and the focus is on services provided in response to the disaster and interactions with others to provide those services. In some cases, the disaster response differed vastly from the organization's usual role; in other cases, the organization was created in response to the disaster. In still other cases, the disaster response of the organization hinged on broader relationships with other entities and can only be understood as part of a larger whole.

The case study organizations represented different organizational types and prior experiences with disasters. Candidates for case study were also chosen to reflect variation in size, geographic location (e.g., distribution across states affected by the storms, and representation of both rural and urban areas), proximity to the disaster (whether they were operating in an area directly impacted by the storms or were not directly affected but hosted evacuees), and types of services provided and interorganizational relationships, both governmental and nongovernmental. The cases are a mix of faith-based and community-based organizations, although the web of affiliations and networks made those distinctions less meaningful.

Two sources were used to identify cases for possible in-depth field study: the knowledge of local partners, the Louisiana Association of Nonprofit Organizations (LANO) and the Mississippi Center on Nonprofits (MCN), about ongoing relief and recovery work; and the survey findings. In October 2007, before the telephone survey was completed, the partners were asked to suggest individuals or organizations that had been especially active in relief work and might address the issues of interest. Informants in LANO and MCN were encouraged to consider the dimensions of interest, including in particular interorganizational or complex collaborations and connections to public agencies.

Exploratory calls to potential sites were conducted in October and November 2007 to determine when and how the responses emerged, what the organizations' or their collaborators' functions were (e.g., providing physical facilities, particular skill sets, leadership, or community connections), the mechanics of the relief effort (e.g., staffing, funding, communication, leadership structure), and how and why they appeared to succeed or what challenges they faced. Informants were reminded that this study was focused on a mix of faith- and community-based organizations, emergency and long-term recovery assistance, organizations with prior disaster experience and those that were new to such services, and organizations whose responses had changed over time.

The second source for case study nominations, the findings from the telephone survey, was used when those data became available in March 2008. Responses were analyzed by state and impact zone, to determine the breadth and complexity of the networking and collaboration undertaken, and then sorted to select a range of faith-based and nonprofit organizations (self-identified, as described in Part I) that had collaborated with a range of other organizations. Exploratory telephone conversations with approximately 55 of those organizations were conducted in March and April 2008, using the same conversational protocol used in earlier calls.

Calls to approximately 75 FBCOs identified through these two sources were used to determine when the organizations became involved in disaster services, whether they had prior disaster experience, what kinds of services they provided, whether that had changed over time, and whether their efforts were continuing. Organizations were asked about successes or failures to draw out experiences that might be emblematic and worth in-depth study. The FBCOs provided information on where the services were provided, and an idea of the magnitude, either in people served or dollars expended, and funding sources. These calls also helped to determine the nature of collaboration, if any (e.g., ad hoc, deliberate, preplanned), and whether the organizations had interacted with public agencies. Finally, the respondents confirmed that they would be willing to participate in a longer, field-based study. The telephone conversations generally lasted less than an hour but were sufficient to identify a small number of candidates for potential study.

Fourteen organizations were identified for Department of Health and Human Services approval, from which eight were selected for study. In planning the fieldwork, the research team mapped the network with which the organizations interacted, as well as others identified as critical to the work of the organization (e.g., public officials who played a critical role in the organization's disaster response but may not have been a direct collaborator). As noted earlier, the selection is dominated by cases that illustrated some complexity—perhaps in the number of other organizations with whom they interacted, the complexity of services, or changes in mission over time. The organizations or collaborations are all exemplary; while they may illustrate challenges and frustrations, none are examples of broad failures.

Site visits were conducted between May and July 2008 and typically extended over two days per site and consisted of semistructured interviews with key informants using discussion guides approved by the Office of Management and Budget, and collection of secondary documentation such as budgets, presentations, brochures, meeting notes, videos, or web site materials. Focus groups were conducted in two sites with individuals who were served by the organization and who remained in the area and in contact with the organization. In the other six sites, the recipients of services could not be contacted.

Each site visit entailed interviews with the principals in the organization under study and others with whom important relationships were formed in the process of the disaster response. This meant that, in some cases, interviews were conducted with individuals representing perhaps a dozen other organizations, including other local and national faith-based and secular nonprofits, foundations, FEMA officials, American Red Cross representatives, and state government officials overseeing the recovery effort or related social services.

General Characteristics of the Eight Cases

The eight cases selected for study include faith-based organizations, secular community-based organizations, and those that represent a combined effort of faith-based and community organizations in a formal collaboration. Table 28 describes the type and location of each organization, its origin and purpose, and the reach of each response.

Six of the eight cases were in Louisiana, two in Mississippi. The six in Louisiana were Common Ground Health Clinic (CGHC), Community Initiatives Foundation (CIF), Greater New Orleans Disaster Recovery Partnership (GNODRP), Partners in Prayer (PIPS), St. Luke's Episcopal Church, and Vermilion Faith Community of Care (VFCC). The two in Mississippi were Community Care Network (CCN) and Hope Haven (HH). Four were based in urban areas—two in New Orleans (CGHC, GNODRP) and two in Baton Rouge (St. Luke's and CIF). CIF served evacuees from New Orleans. St. Luke's served evacuees from New Orleans, but also worked directly in New Orleans in the immediate cleanup after the storm. GNODRP is based in New Orleans but is a regional consortium serving nine parishes in the southeastern part of Louisiana that were directly impacted by Katrina. Four cases serve areas that are less densely populated, a mix of small cities and rural areas—VFCC in Vermilion Parish, PIPS/United Way in the City of Lake Charles (but serving five southwestern Louisiana parishes), and CCN and Hope Haven in small communities on the Mississippi Gulf Coast.

Six of the eight cases served areas immediately impacted by either Hurricane Katrina or Rita. The two impacted directly by Rita—PIPS and VFCC—had two stories. First, they housed Katrina evacuees, principally from New Orleans, as they made their way west on Interstate Highway 10. Then, three weeks later, PIPS and VFCC were forced to displace those evacuees to serve their own residents when Hurricane Rita headed directly toward their communities.

Table 28. General Characteristics of the Cases

Case	Faith-based or secular	Location	Relation to Hurricane Impact (Katrina or Rita)		Organizational mission	Created in response to storm	Disaster Response Operations	
			Area of direct impact	Outside area of impact			Highest number of staff in disaster response	Over $1 million for disaster response
Louisiana								
Common Ground Health Clinic	Secular	New Orleans	✓		Emergency and primary health care to the predominantly low-income African American community of Algiers	✓	7	✓
Community Initiatives Foundation	Secular	Baton Rouge		✓	Advocacy and provision of services to children displaced by Hurricane Katrina	✓	2	✓
Greater New Orleans Disaster Relief Partnership	Secular	New Orleans	✓		Regional coordination of long-term recovery and preparedness services following Hurricane Katrina	✓	3	✓
Partners in Prayer for Schools	Faith-based	Lake Charles	✓ (Rita)	✓ (Katrina)	Reduction of violence and promotion of parental involvement in schools through prayer and volunteerism		2	
St. Luke's Episcopal Church	Faith-based	Baton Rouge		✓	Church and day school		7–8	
Vermilion Faith Community of Care	Faith-based	Abbeville	✓ (Rita)	✓ (Katrina)	Unification of the faith community of Vermilion Parish to assist families and communities in preparation for and recovery from disasters, and support and expansion of other programs that meet critical human need		2	
Mississippi								
Community Care Network	Faith-based	Ocean Springs	✓		Reintegration of homeless women from adult detention centers or substance abuse programs		2	
Hope Haven	Secular	Waveland	✓		Licensed shelter for abused and neglected children		2	

The types of organizations were varied. St. Luke's was a place of worship. CCN and Hope Haven were direct social service providers: CCN provided services to female prisoners reentering the community, and Hope Haven was a shelter for abused and neglected children. CGHC provided health care services. Three cases were collaborations focused specifically on disaster response—GNODRP for long-term recovery of the southeastern Louisiana region, VFCC for uniting the faith-based community to respond to disasters generally, and CIF for helping children affected by the 2005 hurricanes. PIPS was founded as a faith-based organization in Lake Charles to address school violence. Only one case was formally part of a larger governing structure: St. Luke's is overseen by the Episcopal Diocese of Louisiana.

Of the three organizations created as a result of the storm, CIF and GNODRP as of this writing remain focused on the needs of Hurricane Katrina victims, while CGHC, created as a response to the collapse of the health care system in the wake of the hurricane, remains broadly focused on health care for low-income residents of the Algiers community in New Orleans.

Three of the four organizations that were faith based (PIPS, CCN, and St. Luke's) provided faith- infused services in their pre-hurricane missions. However, because of the nature of collaborations, all but one of the eight cases represent a mix of faith-based and secular organizations in their disaster response. The melding of faith and community-based organizations is significant. While religious conviction may have been the basis for personal motivation to respond, the general humanitarian response and specific catalyst for involvement is often indistinguishable between religious and secular organizations. Whether or how faith was infused in disaster assistance is unclear in several cases.

In order to understand these very different and complex stories, and as a preface to the analysis that follows, snapshots of the eight cases studied are provided. The snapshots tell how the disaster response emerged, and key attributes that help explain why the organizations responded as they did and where they were as of summer 2008.

Snapshots

Common Ground Health Clinic, New Orleans, LA

Common Ground Health Clinic (CGHC) was the product of a grassroots effort to provide medical services to the many largely low-income and African American individuals who remained in the Algiers community on the west bank of the Mississippi River in New Orleans. Algiers did not flood, and, contrary to public perception, many in the community did not evacuate. The principal catalyst, a community organizer living in Algiers, saw a critical need for health services because low-income African Americans, who had been poorly served before the storm, were now largely abandoned as the city's health services collapsed.

The call for assistance used personal connections, e-mail, and the Internet, including a web site with a live camcorder set up within days. The call also linked the post-storm emergency with the history of racism and poor health services. The aggressive outreach generated a groundswell of response from a mix of anti-establishment youth, including street medics trained in providing medical assistance at political demonstrations; licensed physicians and nurses; and nontraditional health practitioners. An interview on a national public radio program generated further response. The mix offered a range of expertise, from primary care to psychiatric services. In the first week, Common Ground had two or three trained emergency medical technicians, one physician, two herbalists, a physician's assistant, and an acupuncturist. To date, about 1,000 trained and licensed medical volunteers, plus about 150 others, have provided services.

The first volunteers spray-painted a scrap of plywood as a first aid sign and set up a street- corner clinic in a donated neighborhood mosque. They also conducted a door-to-door campaign with the help of local women to learn who remained and needed assistance. Early clinic organizers expected to find a high level of trauma resulting from the storm, but instead found a range of other maladies, including hypertension, old gunshot wounds that had never been treated, and a population that had used emergency rooms for basic primary care and now had none. Chronic health issues such as hypertension and diabetes required vigilant monitoring and medication. The nearest pharmacy was reportedly in Jefferson Parish, and those who had not evacuated, overwhelmingly people of color, were reportedly not allowed through police checkpoints. In the first month and a half after the storm, the street medics visited about 200 households and took phone calls from caretakers followed by home visits to evaluate patients. FEMA and the Red Cross reimbursed pharmacies for patients who were deemed "shelter eligible." By the end of October 2005, CGHC had seen about 4,000 at the clinic—100 to 200 a week at its peak.

KEY FEATURES OF COMMON GROUND HEALTH CLINIC

- Grassroots community activism as a catalyst, and aggressive outreach for help.
- Clear mission, professional and organizational expertise, and cultural competence.
- Formal collaborations with other professional providers to augment services, informal relationships with FEMA, National Guard, and American Red Cross.

Organizers also learned that immigrant laborers brought in to the city to do much of the "de- mucking" were housed in hotels with no access to health care and inadequate protections from health hazards (e.g., no gloves or vaccinations, one gallon of water for two workers working 10- to 12-hour shifts). They went to hotels to vaccinate laborers for hepatitis A and B and tetanus. Emblematic of the magnitude of the response to Katrina, the clinic, like several other sites, was inundated with donations, sometimes creating major challenges for storage, use, or redistribution. They used the door-to-door effort to distribute donations as well (e.g., two tons of clothing, food that would otherwise spoil).

By November 2005, the clinic organized formally as a 501(c)(3), with a governing board and bylaws, and created relationships with several providers in the larger public health system to procure specialized medical services. By early 2006, about five months after the storm, a landlord from the mosque offered a storefront facility across the street at a nominal rent, and the clinic was able to create a more standard clinic space and regularize and expand services. The facility observed in 2008 was a modest but attractive storefront on the exterior, and a spotless and orderly waiting room and examining rooms on the interior.

CGHC maintains a pronounced allegiance to its philosophic roots of independence, eschewing subservience to the medical establishment and attempting to controvert the underlying racism that it believes has limited access to health care for low-income blacks. But it has reorganized several times and matured over three years, to increase professionalization and quality of care, reportedly earning the respect of members of the medical establishment with whom it partners for providing high-quality services.

While committed to governing through open participation, CGHC has created internal organizing structures to address financial management, clinical services, community outreach, and management of volunteers. It administers nearly $1 million from public and foundation sources and serves 100 patients during a three-day clinic week. It still provides alternative medicine services, including herbal remedies and acupuncture, remaining close to the culture of the community it serves.

Community Initiatives Foundation, Baton Rouge, LA

The effort that was to become the Community Initiatives Foundation (CIF) about a year after the storm, began the morning after the storm in the River Center, the public arena that was the largest receiving venue in Baton Rouge for Katrina evacuees. Recognizing the catastrophic nature of the storm and the expertise of a retired high school principal who was heading an effort to promote systems change in the public schools, the Baton Rouge Area Foundation (BRAF) president asked her to become an advocate for the displaced children. Additional funds from another foundation enabled the retired principal to hire an assistant and focus entirely on the evacuee children.

Over the course of about six weeks in the Center, the CIF director helped organize services for both the children and their traumatized parents. She worked with a colleague from the charter school system and the state department of education to create a modular charter school—a small school for the younger children and one for the older children. The intention was to use displaced teachers from New Orleans, try to hire the best, and give the schools back to New Orleans when neighborhoods had been restored. The model was never implemented because of other rivalries between New Orleans and Baton Rouge.

When the River Center was closed, many of those remaining were bused to Renaissance Village in Baker, north of Baton Rouge, the largest FEMA trailer park in Louisiana. At its height, the park housed 595 families. As many as 2,000 people quickly overwhelmed FEMA, and the need for a complex combination of services that would have to be provided by others was obvious. CIF became a facilitator to receive services from the authorities, including FEMA; a collaborator with other professionals, including foundations and university- based efforts to develop or leverage funding and health, mental health, housing, and case management services; and a direct provider, in effect a case manager and trusted confidante, for individual children and families.

KEY FEATURES OF COMMUNITY INITIATIVES FOUNDATION

- Clear mission combined with insight, creativity, and adaptability to address changing needs.
- Ability to connect with highest levels of government, professionals, and individuals and families served.
- Social and professional connections granted access to facilities, facilitators, and funding.

In Renaissance Village, CIF worked with several large donors and local and national nonprofit organizations to set up a range of services and access assistance from public agencies. As time went on, some of the most distressed children and families were understood to be "near homeless" as resettlement became increasingly elusive.

Signs of trauma in the children persisted. In the second year, only about a third attended regular school, some not resilient enough to get on the bus each day. About 120 children came intermittently to on-site service providers. As families remained, dysfunction amplified, and many were increasingly unable to find new housing or return to their homes, find jobs, or otherwise reclaim their lives and families. CIF formed a consortium with the Coalition for the Homeless and Family Road of Greater Baton Rouge to resettle evacuees, using $1.2 million of Community Development Block Grant (CDBG) funds that the Coalition was administering. The consortium would provide continuing services for more than 200 households that faced severe challenges to successful resettlement as they relocated to precarious or temporary situations. At the time of the site visit, the Coalition had hired two housing specialists who were working to locate affordable housing options in the Baton Rouge area for these individuals.

CIF was the consistent presence, at times the critical source of information and order among disparate players, and often the linchpin among public authorities and a mix of national and local experts who came to provide assistance, among them the efforts of Rosie O'Donnell's foundation to build a service center for children, which ultimately housed a Head Start and Early Head Start program operated by the YWCA; teams of art therapists from Los Angeles funded initially by the O'Donnell foundation who came every 6–7 weeks for a total of nine times and worked with the children for a week to 10 days; Paul Newman's Hole in the Wall Gang, which ran camps over holidays and school vacations; scholars in child trauma from Yale University who trained clinicians and advised BRAF and others providing services; Big Buddy, which provided after-school services; Catholic Charities case manager teams funded by the Louisiana Family Recovery Corps and Katrina Aid Today (KAT); and outside clinicians providing psychological assessments and other services to support children's school attendance.

Initial funding to work in the River Center came from BRAF. BRAF did not typically focus on direct services, so in September 2006, it provided $100,000 in seed money to set up CIF, and that money permitted absorption of a $1 million grant from another foundation— CIF's largest single source of direct funds. The creation of CIF became the means for its director to expand her sphere of influence within the park and with individuals whom she has continued to assist directly.

As of July 2008, CIF staff and partners were continuing to work directly with families, providing funds for rent or to reach a potential job opportunity, access to furniture and other household provisions, scoping out transitional and permanent housing, and following these individuals and families through the exigencies of resettlement.

Community Care Network, Ocean Springs, MS

The Community Care Network (CCN) has operated a transitional program in Ocean Springs, Mississippi, since 1993, for women reentering the community from the county detention center or residential substance abuse treatment. The organization was formalized as a 501(c)(3) in 2003, and opened a transitional housing facility that could serve up to nine residents in 2005, offering a general educational development diploma, job skills assistance, and religiously based services. It had four clients at the time of the storm.

Because of the magnitude of the storm, the director's local church began receiving both volunteers and hurricane victims; the pastor asked the director, a congregant, to coordinate the influx. She put the transitional program on hold and took on volunteer coordination two weeks after the storm. Using web sites, including Katrina Recovery Mississippi and Volunteer Mississippi, which were linked to the governor's web site, the director posted information on the housing facility and asked for volunteers. People began "pouring in; there were at times 250 people in the [church] gym." The YMCA down the street offered the use of its showers.

Volunteer teams were sent into the community to repair houses, targeting populations deemed particularly needy—the elderly, single mothers, and individuals who were defrauded by contractors. By October 2005, the director hired a former employee with whom she had worked at a substance abuse program, using funding provided by a church in Olympia, Washington.

KEY FEATURES OF COMMUNITY CARE NETWORK

- Response to local pastor's request to coordinate influx of volunteers and evacuees in director's church.
- Close connection to church created access to facilities, volunteers, and funding.
- Targeted services to populations of perceived need.

CCN and the church also became an informal distribution point for the extensive donations coming into the area, including military vehicles with water and Meals Ready to Eat, and other donations arriving on tractor-trailers. Volunteer teams were used to assess individual needs in the community and distribute goods. Official points of distribution were set up by the military four months later, and CCN scaled back its efforts. But individuals and organizations in the immediate community continued to arrive with donations and set tables up on their own, distributing materials from the church parking lot. According to one, the donation effort "took on a life of its own."

After 11 months, Volunteers of America (VOA) donated a mobile home and two VOA case managers, permitting CCN to relocate to the church parking lot, use teams to identify families in the community who needed assistance, and refer them to VOA to take their cases to the county's long-term recovery structure[14] for funding.

Volunteer teams continued for two and a half years, at first mostly "demucking" and gutting houses; distributing clothes, water, and food; and assessing needs. As rebuilding needs changed, CCN posted requests for skilled teams competent to provide specific housing repairs, matching teams to the work required. Teams in the field often inquired about residents on the same street and forwarded those requests to CCN. The program reportedly filled over 500 work orders on over 300 homes and ultimately fielded more than 5,500 volunteers. CCN received two $50,000 grants from the Maryland Crime Victim Resource Center (under an overall grant from the U.S. Department of Justice Office of Victims and Crime), with which it repaired 35 houses.

At this writing, CCN's recovery efforts are expected to end as outside support for the rebuilding activities has waned and volunteer flows have ebbed. CCN has returned to its original mission, reopened the transitional home for women, and teaches Bible-based self-esteem and life skills classes in collaboration with a six-month program at the county detention facility. That program has 30 to 40 female participants (with a waiting list) and around 120 men.

Greater New Orleans Disaster Recovery Partnership, New Orleans, LA

The Greater New Orleans Disaster Recovery Partnership (GNODRP) was founded in November 2005 by leaders of United Way of Greater New Orleans Area member organizations to coordinate efforts, pool financial and material resources, stem duplicative efforts, and advocate for effective policies among eight long-term recovery structures in nine parishes of southeastern Louisiana.[15]

The long-term recovery structures have been advocated by the National Voluntary Organizations Active in Disaster and now by FEMA, as the principal vehicle for assessing needs and allocating assistance after basic disaster relief has been exhausted. The structures generally involve roundtable meetings in which case managers present the cases of individuals with "unmet needs" to providers of social services and other assistance, and assistance is negotiated among grantors (e.g., Salvation Army, American Red Cross). GNODRP at this writing has approximately 90 partners from the nonprofit, nongovernmental organization, and faith-based communities that share resources, services, and information to address long-term recovery.

By early 2006, GNODRP had constituted a board of directors (the Partnership Council), and seven standing committees: advocacy, case management, donations management, emotional and spiritual care, preparedness, rebuilding, and volunteer coordination. The eight unmet needs structures of Plaquemines, Jefferson, St. Bernard, Orleans, Tangipahoa, Washington, St. Tammany parishes, and St. John the Baptist and St. Charles parishes (combined) are represented on the Partnership Council. Several national organizations, including the Coordinated Assistance Network (a shared database among seven national disaster relief organizations), Church World Service, FEMA, and Katrina Aid Today, are also heavily involved in the region's recovery efforts and have nonvoting membership on the council.

KEY FEATURES OF GREATER NEW ORLEANS DISASTER RECOVERY PARTNERSHIP

- Using traditional disaster recovery structure for coordinated regional collaborative to respond to Hurricane Katrina and prepare for the next disaster.
- A creation of lead social service providers in New Orleans and partnership among 90 partner agencies.
- Support and oversight of eight parish long-term recovery structures.

GNODRP created several mechanisms to facilitate more efficient processing of unmet needs cases. A November 2007 report by a George Washington University researcher found many remaining challenges, including cases tabled because of missing information, no guidance for case managers to obtain needed information, and social service systems still in disarray and unable to provide direct services and financial assistance. In response, GNODRP created a single presentation package for funders; as a result, the long-term recovery structures funded and closed as many cases in six months as they had in the two previous years. The standing committees continue to meet and streamline policies and practices.

In addition to helping develop the eight unmet needs structures, GNODRP created a warehouse for donated household goods and rebuilding materials. GNODRP leaders also recognized the frustrations felt by case managers who have their own traumas to cope with as a result of Hurricane Katrina and created access to spiritual and mental health counseling.

Most funding for unmet needs from the American Red Cross and the Salvation Army will end by 2009. GNODRP leaders are aware that recovery from Katrina is likely to take 10 to 20 years, and they are now concerned with developing resources to continue operation and sustain the momentum of the early recovery efforts, and have adjusted their model to respond to current needs. Holding the attention of policymakers and funders is increasingly challenging as other disasters occur and the public seeks to move on from Katrina.

Hope Haven, Waveland, MS

Hope Haven for Children in Waveland, Mississippi, had been Hancock County's only shelter for neglected and abused children since 1996. In anticipation of Hurricane Katrina, the children were evacuated by the county child welfare authorities. Staff also relocated, and the storm surge and flooding severely damaged the facility. Once restored but without proper staff, Hope Haven was unable to reopen as a licensed shelter. Over the course of two and a half years of recovery, because of the director's determination, social and professional connections, and some serendipity, Hope Haven played several roles in relief efforts.

The shelter was rebuilt during the immediate aftermath of the storm through a confluence of social and professional connections. The director returned to demuck and rebuild, using program funds to purchase equipment and hire local help. A police officer happened upon him, offered water in the oppressive heat, and later came into contact with a group of 200 Navy Seabees that had been ordered from their home base in Gulfport, Mississippi, to report to the Hancock County Emergency Operations Center to help clear roads. The chief of battalion, hearing the story of Hope Haven's director who was a retired Navy chief, redirected the Seabees to assist, and over a period of two months two teams of Seabees rebuilt the shelter.

Knowing Hope Haven would not reopen as a licensed children's shelter, the director used the program's resources for several post-storm services. When he voiced his concerns about the availability of social services to a state social worker, he learned that the entire county Division of Family and Children's Services had lost its facility in the storm. He offered the use of Hope Haven, and within three days the entire Division of Family and Children's Services moved in. After the Division moved out, the facility was used through July 2008 to house 10–12 volunteers a week who came to rebuild. The director used a web-posting to amass material donations, largely toys and furniture, but also appliances and clothing, and used the children's recreation building as a warehouse and distribution center. A furniture company in Wisconsin donated 800 pieces of furniture, mostly bedroom sets, and those were distributed to target groups viewed as particularly needy or deserving, including police, fire fighters, and teachers, the Salvation Army's homeless shelters in Jackson County and Mobile, and another shelter in Louisiana. In the first year, Hope Haven also distributed over $40,000 in gift cards and cash. When the city pressed to close free food distributions to stimulate local restaurants and businesses, the warehouse served as a distribution point for the local food bank.

KEY FEATURES OF HOPE HAVEN

- Social and professional connections shaped relief efforts.
- Highly motivated and respected director used organization funds and donations to fill perceived gaps in human services, specifically child services.
- Conscious effort to document and segregate disaster-related expenditures.

The massive donation distributions made it clear that the organization, unlike some others, needed to formalize its relief efforts and extensive records. By March 2006, Hope Haven created a separate accounting structure, the Helping Hands Fund, to manage Katrina relief donations, and the mission statement was changed to include Helping Hands and disaster relief. The program has detailed records on funds disbursement (e.g., purchase of school uniforms, paying for utilities, food, respite care).

By early 2008 volunteers had begun to leave, and on July 21 Hope Haven reopened as a children's facility, but reconfigured as a small foster home with a live-in foster parent structure for six to seven children. Because insurance rates have nearly doubled, Hope Haven plans to sell the building and move to another facility further inland.

Partners in Prayer for Schools, Lake Charles, LA

Partners in Prayer (PIPS), unlike other cases studied, played an instrumental role early in relief efforts, but only a small part in a complex disaster response in five southwestern Louisiana parishes largely led by the mayor of Lake Charles. Established in 1999 in reaction to the Columbine school shootings, PIPS was a largely informal two-person volunteer recruitment organization based in Calcasieu Parish in southwestern Louisiana that aimed to reduce school violence by promoting parental involvement in school, volunteerism, and prayer. In its advocacy for prayer and voluntarism, PIPS had created a unique database of local congregations that became a key part of hurricane relief efforts.

KEY FEATURES OF PARTNERS IN PRAYER FOR SCHOOLS

- A conduit to local congregations for larger public relief efforts.
- Use of public funding and previous experience with volunteer coordination.
- Disaster response work ended and principal now part of United Way

---

Immediately after Katrina's landfall, 15,000 to 20,000 evacuees began showing up in southwestern Louisiana parishes needing shelter. In response, a group of about 26 churches, government agencies, and businesses, calling themselves Moss Bluff Disaster Relief (MBDR), met in a church in Moss Bluff; PIPS provided its church list and offered to send out an invitation to house evacuees. PIPS used the MBDR web site as a clearinghouse to match evacuees with emergency housing, reportedly referring about 10 Katrina evacuees a day to a distribution site and linking them with housing. It used another web site, Share Your Home, to match evacuees with potential hosts around the country, with small success.

Within three weeks, Rita forced the Lake Charles area to evacuate both Katrina evacuees and local residents. On return within days, the PIPS director was invited to attend the twice-weekly meetings of the Human Services Resource Initiative (HSRI), a group of government, faith-based and nonprofit organizations convened by the mayor's office and a precursor to the Calcasieu Parish Long-Term Recovery Group. The United Way, a member of the HSRI, had begun looking for housing for the many volunteers coming to Lake Charles to assist in recovery work and PIPS helped identify an abandoned middle school building in Moss Bluff large enough to house over 200 volunteers. The United Way received permission from the school district to use the building in exchange for repairs and upkeep, the Salvation Army donated 200 beds, a local culinary school helped renovate the kitchen, and volunteers made repairs.

While PIPS was an early presence in the Lake Charles disaster response, it had a relatively short role as a separate entity. It assisted in the collaboration between the local school board and the United Way to renovate the school building, and through the local Workforce Investment Board received a U.S. Department of Labor National Emergency Grant in November 2005, to use 30 Katrina victims to conduct basic needs assessments for the United Methodist Committee on Relief (UMCOR) and the Disaster Recovery Center on referrals from the HSRI. By May 2006, PIPS had conducted more than 4,000 assessments for residents of the five southwestern parishes (Calcasieu, Cameron, Jeff Davis, Allen, and Beauregard). By the next year the director was hired by the United Way to manage the Volunteer Housing Center, which houses AmeriCorps volunteers and others who help in the rebuilding process. The Center also serves as an emergency housing location for first responders.

St. Luke's Episcopal Church, Baton Rouge, LA

St. Luke's Episcopal Church is a large, wealthy congregation in Baton Rouge, Louisiana, on a campus of several buildings including the church, an elementary school, a gymnasium, and a large kitchen. Its parking lot borders Woman's Hospital. The physical plant, proximity to the hospital, and the special abilities of its associate rectors were the springboard for several innovative relief efforts.

The first was related to the hospital next door. Immediately after the storm, the hospital became a principal receiving facility for late- term maternity patients and premature infants evacuated from New Orleans. According to respondents, the American Red Cross could not serve women with advanced pregnancies, the hospital systems in New Orleans were collapsing, and seriously ill patients and those needing intensive care, including premature infants, were being air evacuated to Woman's Hospital and other facilities able to serve them. The hospital approached the church, among eight others in the area, for emergency shelter space so mothers might be near their infants. The church sheltered up to eight families at a time over a six-week period, while church staff and volunteers cooked meals, laundered clothes, and helped them find remaining family, often fathers and older children who were evacuated to other cities across the country.

KEY FEATURES OF ST. LUKE'S EPISCOPAL CHURCH

- Innovative, multipronged relief effort based on expertise and creativity of church leaders.
- Resources for relief efforts drawn from social and professional connections.
- Short-term emergency relief effort, not long-term recovery.

The church facility could shelter up to 80 people. At the request of the federal Environmental Protection Agency (EPA), St. Luke's also housed 20 to 30 EPA investigators who were returning to New Orleans each day to address water and other pollution issues. An associate rector coordinated more than 120 volunteers from the congregation to staff the shelter, buy and cook food, answer phones, and do laundry. Kitchen volunteers prepared food both for the St. Luke's shelter operations and for other shelters. For a short time, the church operated a day care center in its gym for its staff and for hospital employees so the parents could continue their relief work.

St. Luke's other major relief effort was the creation of a mobile van unit, the product of the particular skills and forethought of an associate rector who was also a lawyer and retired military officer with logistical experience. The rector suspected that there would be need for food, water, cleaning supplies, and communications equipment because there were no utilities in New Orleans, as well as spiritual counseling as evacuees were allowed back into the city to survey the damage and begin the cleanup process.

In early September 2005, the associate rector purchased and, with the help of another associate rector, outfitted a mobile van with laptop computers and Internet access so it could serve just- opened impact areas in New Orleans and other areas that might need assistance. Church staff and volunteers began taking donations of food, clothes, and other supplies to towns such as Slidell, which had not yet been reached with any emergency assistance. They then traveled daily to other devastated areas to bring food, clothes, and cleaning supplies and to provide pastoral counseling to those who needed it.

One of the first areas in New Orleans to open for so-called "look and leave" visits was the Lakeview area on the south shore of Lake Pontchartrain. About a month and a half after the storm, St. Luke's sent the mobile unit, staffed by a driver, a priest, and other volunteers, to Lakeview and established operations on the grounds of an Episcopal church. When the Red Cross arrived approximately 10 days later, the mobile van unit moved to the Ninth Ward, which had also sustained massive damage.

St. Luke's recruited 30–40 volunteers to look for individuals returning to the neighborhood and hand out materials. Everyone who came to the mobile unit received a case of water, bottle of bleach, other cleaning supplies, personal hygiene kits, canned food, a bucket, and baby products if needed. It also offered an air-conditioned place to cool off, and counseling for those who were traumatized by seeing the devastation of their homes and for first responders. Interviewees estimate that there were 300–400 visits every day, with many people returning multiple times for replenishment of water and cleaning supplies. They suggest that there were perhaps 80,000–90,000 units of service delivered by the time they sold the van to the Episcopal Diocese of Louisiana in December 2005. These estimates represent both multiple visits by the same individuals and multiple types of service.

The relief work was supported mainly by donations from Episcopal churches and congregants across the country and from the military and seminary network of the associate rector. Neither state nor national Episcopal affiliates provided financial or other support, although they were in communication. The state diocese, located in New Orleans, was hit directly by Hurricane Katrina; it held meetings with its entire clergy in the first week after the storm but was not available to assist directly in relief efforts. Episcopal Relief and Development, which provides domestic and international disaster assistance, was connected with the state diocese rather than local churches, so it too was not a part of St. Luke's response.

According to interviewees, the church did not and would not in the future wish to be a part of the larger emergency response structure, such as become a certified American Red Cross shelter, or be involved with government disaster activities. At the end of four months of intense work and after exhausting donations and resources, church leaders felt it was time to return to some normalcy rather than participate in the long-term recovery process.

Vermilion Faith Community of Care, Abbeville, LA

Vermilion Faith Community of Care (VFCC) is located in Abbeville, Louisiana, the parish seat and a largely rural area two hours west of New Orleans on Interstate 10. The organization was created in February 2003, after a meeting between a community leader (now VFCC's executive director), two local pastors representing local ministerial alliances, and a representative from Church World Service, to unite local faith-based organizations' response to Hurricane Lili, which hit the area in 2002. VFCC formed broad connections with local churches, secular nonprofits, and government offices—most notably the Vermilion Office of Emergency Preparedness (OEP). Its activities focused on coordinating the distribution of goods and volunteers to repair houses and the dissemination of information for a long-term relief effort. After a year and a half, the organization ended regular meetings but maintained personal correspondence and semiannual board meetings.

The maintenance of communication enabled VFCC to become a critical source of coordination and distribution when Katrina evacuees arrived in Vermilion Parish in 2005. Two or three days after landfall, VFCC organized local nonprofits to provide 400 hot meals a day and distributed donated goods and funds. Working with the Clerk of Court, it helped distribute donated goods throughout the parish and from a distribution center set up in a local church. When Rita forced parish residents and Katrina evacuees to evacuate, VFCC, working with local shelters, distributed $4,350 (in $20 to $50 increments) to Katrina families for travel expenses.

KEY FEATURES OF VERMILION FAITH COMMUNITY OF CARE

- Disaster mandate, part of the local Office of Emergency Preparedness emergency response plan.
- Expertise and relationships in place from previous disaster relief efforts.
- Ability to go dormant between disasters and reconstitute itself when need arises.

Two or three weeks after Rita's landfall, VFCC again took the lead in distributing donated goods through the distribution center and a newly acquired warehouse used to store building materials and tools. Because of its prior work in Lili, VFCC had gained the confidence of the OEP, which began referring all incoming private donations to VFCC for distribution. Within three months of Katrina, VFCC had received over $100,000 in donations, which were used over the next year to assist local families in recovery efforts and to pay modest overhead costs.

In early October 2005, VFCC set up a Volunteer Reception Center, first in a local recreation center, then in VFCC's own facility, using two Louisiana Department of Labor volunteers provided by the United Way of Acadiana. All volunteers coming into Abbeville were directed to the center, registered, and assigned to areas of need. By mid-December 2005, VFCC had processed more than 220 volunteers and, according to its report, supported 5,200 hours of work on 61 houses. During the first few months after Hurricane Rita, VFCC took the lead in organizing over 20 other organizations into a long-term recovery committee, the director was elected chair, and VFCC largely refocused its relief services on home repairs and distribution of building supplies, appliances, and furniture through the committee. By early 2008, despite the director's efforts to keep VFCC active, the organization ended its relief services and became dormant until needed again.

Major Findings

Findings are presented on key issues that illustrate why and how the FBCOs studied responded, and how they connected to the larger context of disaster response and human service delivery.

Catalysts for Response

FBCOs studied responded as they did because it was their personal or professional mission to do so, or because of individual or organizational competencies, or as a result of an explicit mandate—either preplanned or dictated by the moment. Based on field observations, what appears nearly universal was that the magnitude of the disaster propelled those in the case studies into action, and serendipity explained the direction that the responses often took.

Magnitude

Everything about this disaster was bigger than anyone had experienced in previous storms. Katrina (and then Rita) was unprecedented, both in the damage from flooding or wind and in the response from around the country and around the world. For the principal actors in case study organizations, the breadth of the disaster moved them to respond; they "had to do something." According to respondents, the small communities on the Mississippi Gulf Coast had lived through many severe storms, so many residents misjudged the potential of Hurricane Katrina and were complacent about planning for its arrival or had little means to make a timely evacuation. The storm surge from the Gulf had never come so far inland.

In the city of Waveland, Mississippi, 95 percent of residential structures, all commercial structures, and every emergency vehicle were destroyed. When the storm surge receded, respondents described that residents, regardless of color, age, or economic means, were just wandering in the streets in shock. For those who had housing and were able to help, the motivation to provide some assistance was overwhelmingly compelling. Much of the devastation, well documented in the press, was still obvious during field investigation nearly three years later. City government remained in temporary trailers, and the community consisted mostly of vacant land or construction sites where residences had been before.

As portrayed prominently in the media, the utter devastation of much of New Orleans and surrounding areas was unimaginable. Social services that typically assisted the neediest residents were limited once the city reopened more than a month later. Few would have the resources or other capabilities to rebuild their homes without help.

Baton Rouge, which was little damaged by Katrina, reportedly doubled in population as it absorbed the human flood, mostly from New Orleans. In both case study organizations based in Baton Rouge, one aspect of their relief efforts was in response to the area's new role as a host community to the evacuees.

The communities studied in southwestern Louisiana were forced to deal with two storms in quick succession, propelled into action by the inundation of Katrina evacuees, and then forced to regroup to take care of their own when Hurricane Rita arrived three weeks later. There was urgent need to deal with Katrina evacuees who quickly overwhelmed small communities.

Compared with other disasters that are more geographically bounded and affect fewer people, the helpers and those seeking help were all victims, creating even larger service needs. Several respondents retold the psychological trauma that helpers and evacuees alike experienced. One described that the din of medical evacuation helicopters bringing New Orleans hospital patients to Woman's Hospital in Baton Rouge continued day and night for weeks, creating unrelenting reminders of the trauma around them. They turned off the television to give both volunteers and evacuees some respite.

Depth and Duration of Need

The depth of trauma in the children of evacuees motivated the array of interventions used by CIF and those with whom it associated in Renaissance Village. The extent of psychological trauma evident in wide portions of the population would require a degree of sensitivity on the part of volunteers and their ability to access trained mental health professionals. As one observer noted, "Extreme trauma calls for an extreme level of care." Some stayed in trailers for nearly three years—at the time of the site visit in June 2008, 109 families were still in trailers in that park. But the notion that the housing was temporary resulted in a failure to recognize, according to informants, the need for medical and mental health screening, which would have created baseline measures to facilitate better receipt of services from many experts who came to help.

According to respondents, the storms and resultant flooding also created a vacuum in the human service delivery system and a serious challenge to serving the swelling numbers who needed assistance with resources that were already strained before the storm. For a subset of the population, psychological effects would worsen over time, with nowhere to return and no means to relocate. A participant in a focus group conducted three years after the storm, for example, continued to relive an encounter with a corpse in the New Orleans floodwaters that he and his child experienced. The multiple strategies to deal with mental health services for children were in response to the lingering effects of the trauma and the need to change approaches as issues changed over time.

Limitations of Traditional Models

Traditional models for disaster response were severely challenged, overwhelmed, and dysfunctional, motivating newcomers to disaster response to try to help and spawning new approaches to both relief and recovery. Disaster response has typically been conceived in two phases: immediate relief within the context of an emergency and long-term recovery.

With regard to the first phase, few were prepared for the duration of need for emergency shelter. According to informants, neither the American Red Cross in emergency shelters nor FEMA in the trailer parks had the trained staff, resources, or protocols to provide more than limited assistance. Some respondents believed that FEMA had the authority to provide more services than they did. There was apparently little thought given when the parks were set up to the unprecedented length of time that the trailers would be occupied, or to connecting with schools, jobs, and other services to facilitate resettlement.

Bus service from Renaissance Village, for example, was limited to hours that did not support commuting to most jobs for park residents, the vast majority of whom were without cars. Children were stigmatized in the local schools and many refused to go, creating truancy and behavior problems in the park. The temporary housing model did not include spaces within the park to facilitate social interaction. Seemingly simple solutions, such as erecting a tent for a common space and as a venue for some services, raised alleged liability issues and demanded creative approaches to overcome bureaucratic obstacles. It took a year to put up the Children's Center because of bureaucratic issues that no one understood, and despite the availability of funding and materials from donor sources. In these examples, CIF became the connective tissue for the multiple interventions brought into the park by outsiders.

In addition, many reported that both FEMA and the Red Cross relied on rotating teams of volunteers. Because of the duration of the crisis, new responders were constantly arriving and were unfamiliar with conditions on the ground, such as the people and organizations that made up the local service delivery systems with which they might interact or to whom they could refer for further help. By other accounts, FEMA was criticized for massive confusion, either imposing unclear or inappropriate rules, changing them constantly, referring to headquarters for every decision, or being insensitive to local practices.

With regard to the second phase, many respondents criticized the long-term recovery structures, which most typically provide assistance, such as for housing repair or furnishings, when all other assistance is exhausted. Several respondents in the case study communities rejected the local long-term recovery structures. Some cited the time it took to bring cases before them and get results. Others cited the lack of training of the case managers who reportedly were hired quickly and trained inadequately in order to use a massive infusion of case management funds—the Katrina Aid Today (KAT) funds, about $66 million received from foreign governments and contracted by FEMA to the United Methodist Committee on Relief to provide case management to Katrina evacuees across the country. In one instance cited as more successful, the supervision was consistent and remained for a long time, and case managers got to know the clients and establish relationships. One informant noted that the International Rescue Committee, which has provided emergency relief for more than 75 years, used a much higher case manager–to–client ratio for this sort of work, facilitating greater attention to client needs. Another informant noted the importance of sustained leadership, citing other experiences with disaster assistance in which outside leaders were brought in, paid well, and actually moved into the community for long periods to supervise the relief and recovery work.

In addition, case management must be followed by services sufficient to address the needs presented, such as a range of behavioral health issues (e.g., depression, substance abuse, domestic violence, adolescent truancy) likely to result from or be aggravated by the trauma of a major disaster. An expert in the field who came to help noted that those who have dealt with earthquake victims have understood the need to get to know the population—as might be gained from sustained case management by trained personnel, and the provision of adequate services to treat the sustained trauma. Some respondents characterized their efforts as trying to fill the void in services needed for long-term recovery.

Need to Manage Donations

The magnitude of donations also became a driver of the FBCO response. According to respondents, the magnitude of donations from around the country and the world was not comparable to anything anyone had seen before. Donations were not centrally vetted, there was often no way to distribute what came in, no way to "turn off the spigot," and no way to scale back the donations even when the initial crisis had subsided. As one respondent stated, "…it [the onslaught of donations] took on a life of its own." Media stories piqued the national interest in helping victims, and those stories resulted in assistance far beyond the ability of some FBCOs to absorb it. As an example, the stories of the airlifted babies to Baton Rouge produced 1,500 maternity outfits. One program director posted a request on the Internet for toys and received, unannounced, 10,000 toys from a group in one Midwestern city and an 18-wheel tractor-trailer filled with toys from another city. One respondent recounted the arrival of a truck full of donations from Ohio, with a driver proclaiming, "God sent me," but he did not have the gas money to return home. By another account, some donations simply got dumped by the warehouse-full and some were sent to Africa when they could not be used in local efforts.

On the other hand, the support could be energizing, and many attributed their ability to persevere to that support. Items "would just magically appear," such as bedroom sets to outfit newly repaired homes or to help the homeless still in shelters. As another explained, "We kept doing it [housing volunteers who came to help rebuild] because we had all these people who would come and keep coming." Others foresaw the long road to recovery and the extensive needs that it would generate over many years and beyond the life of volunteer efforts.

Specific Mandates

Two of the organizations studied had an explicit mandate to respond to disasters. Both VFCC and GNODRP are formally part of local disaster response plans, though only VFCC was formally involved with the local Office of Emergency Preparedness at the time of the hurricanes. GNODRP was formed after the 2005 hurricanes as a result of meetings among the major social service providers in the Greater New Orleans area, which identified a need for coordination of the region's long-term recovery efforts. GNODRP was asked by the City of New Orleans to serve as a Community Organization Active in Disasters (COAD); it is the only COAD in the southeast region of the state. It has created its own mandate to plan for and participate in responses to new disasters. While not based on a formalized agreement, city and community leaders asked Hope Haven's director to participate in post-disaster coordination efforts.

Two other case study organizations were asked to respond to specific needs—CIF to become an advocate for children affected by Katrina, and St. Luke's to shelter families of the premature babies evacuated to Woman's Hospital from New Orleans. St. Luke's other disaster responses were self-initiated.

Chance characterizes many of the details of the responses. The sequence of events in Hope Haven, from the director encountering the police officer, who connected to the Navy Seabees, who reconstructed the children's shelter, which enabled its use by the Department of Human Services, can only be described as serendipity. In the case of St. Luke's, the New Orleans rector had a fleeting acquaintance with the rector of St. Luke's, which prompted him to evacuate to St. Luke's while he located his flock. It was because of that connection that he was available to staff the mobile unit and bring it down to New Orleans for its daily cleanup operation. PIPS's role in the Lake Charles disaster relief effort was born out of its church database and knowledge of the abandoned school in Moss Bluff, which facilitated the collaboration between the United Way and the school board to create the Volunteer Housing Center. The many approaches to treating the trauma of the children in Renaissance Village were described as a "learning laboratory," which changed over time and as new players came in to help; while they had the help of some of the nation's experts in art therapy, child psychology, and children's mental health services, the concentrated population of traumatized children and their caretakers and the persistent uncertainty of the fate of the families made each intervention a step into the unknown.

Interviews confirmed that the leaders of the organizations studied were motivated out of compassion for their fellow human beings who were struggling to survive after the disaster, whether spiritually based or not. These individuals also brought personal or organizational competencies that would lend themselves to recognizing what was needed, applying their own skills, or finding others to lend to the efforts.

Mechanics of Response

How each organization did what it did reveals much about what might facilitate effective responses in the future. It is often difficult to make meaningful comparisons among the sites because the organizations and the work that they did were substantially different. Still, while each case must be considered on its own terms, some similarities offer lessons for FBCOs' potential role in disaster response.

Services

Broadly speaking, the eight cases studied provided many of the same services, as Table 29 indicates, though some service provision was a function of timing (immediate relief or long-term recovery) and location in relation to areas of impact. Five service typologies emerge from the experiences of these eight FBCOs:

1) *emergency aid*, in which FBCOs provide immediate needs such as food and water, temporary shelter, and medical care to hurricane victims;
2) *donations management*, in which FBCOs manage warehouses or points of distribution or otherwise receive and distribute donated goods;
3) *volunteer coordination, volunteer housing*, and rebuilding projects;
4) *case management* of the unmet needs of hurricane victims; and

5) *direct human services*, such as health and mental health services, welfare assistance, housing, and employment services.

Several cases—St. Luke's, VFCC, and PIPS—provided emergency supplies, water, food, and shelter. These emergency relief services occurred mostly in the first months after the hurricanes. CGHC provided emergency medical care. CIF filled in the gaps in emergency care in the Baton Rouge River Center.

As the need for immediate relief services ebbed, other needs arose. Most cases distributed cash, gift cards, and other donations such as clothing and household goods, and some served as formal points of distribution or operated a warehouse for donations. Almost all these cases provided some volunteer coordination for rebuilding, distribution of goods, staffing shelters, or other relief activities. Some provided housing for volunteers. Several provided or coordinated some case management services for hurricane victims, including conducting unmet needs assessments in their communities, and sometimes outside a long-term recovery structure.

It is notable that only two organizations provided human service assistance, such as applying for welfare or FEMA assistance that would connect people to the social welfare system. This is consistent with the survey findings in which about one-third of FBCOs surveyed reported assisting with FEMA claims and about one-fifth with welfare applications. Some used their own expertise and capabilities to deliver more professionalized human services. Two cases (CGHC and CIF) provided professional health or mental health counseling to hurricane victims. Two cases (CCN and St. Luke's) provided spiritual or religious counseling, and others may have provided religious services. GNODRP created access to counseling for its own staff. CIF, through its collaborators, provided child care and education services, and St. Luke's briefly provided child care for neighboring hospital workers' children. CCN, PIPS and VFCC provided access to employment services.

Table 29. Services Provided by FBCO

Services	Common Ground Health Clinic	Community Care Network	Community Initiatives Foundation	Greater New Orleans Disaster Relief Partnership	Hope Haven	Partners in Prayer for Schools	St. Luke's Episcopal Church	Vermilion Faith Community of Care
Emergency Relief	✓	✓	✓		✓	✓	✓	✓
Donations Management	✓	✓	✓	✓	✓		✓	✓
Volunteer Coordination and Housing	✓	✓	✓	✓	✓	✓	✓	✓
Case Management			✓	✓				✓
Direct Human Services	✓	✓	✓	✓		✓	✓	✓

Staffing

All the FBCOs studied used both paid staff and volunteers. Much of the actual relief and recovery work was heavily reliant on volunteers, some who applied their professional skills to the disaster work and some who simply were part of the great numbers who descended upon the area to help in whatever way they could. For some cases, the staffing capabilities must be measured as the combined expertise of the larger whole that was created through a collaboration, described below.

Finding and maintaining staff in the context of the extreme devastation created by the storms has been a challenge for some organizations studied. One public official interviewed noted that the order for total evacuation meant that all public employees who were not exempt would be unavailable in the critical first days after the storms. These employees were often in other states and out of contact, making it impossible to anticipate their return to jobs or to help in other ways in relief and recovery efforts. Problems with communication attest to the discontinuities. One expert noted that first responders are likely to be unavailable in future disasters if their own families have not been provided for, and this would likely require prearranged plans. CCN lost staff halfway through its relief work. Several of GNODRP's partners, which are major social service organizations in New Orleans, reported losing most of their staff because of lack of housing and basic infrastructure in the city, and some were still trying to get back to full staffing capacity.

As reported by respondents in this study, the support and interest of volunteers often from outside the community to help the affected areas recover was remarkable. For those cases primarily focused on rebuilding homes, volunteers were the primary vehicle for accomplishing the work. Some volunteers were also involved in warehousing and sorting in-kind donations as well as surveying neighborhoods for recovery needs. For organizations that provided professional services such as health care and teaching, many of these services were also provided by volunteer professionals. Individual volunteers and volunteer groups found the FBCOs through web sites and word of mouth. For example, the State of Mississippi sponsored a web site for FBCOs and volunteer groups to connect, which Community Care Network used to post volunteer needs. Based on the reported influx of volunteers to the affected areas, it is not surprising that all the FBCOs in this study used many volunteers from outside the community.

However, problems arose with the types and numbers of volunteer groups coming to help. As occurred in one FBCO, some volunteers came with truckloads of goods but had no place to stay and little money. According to several respondents, as the "demucking" was completed, more skilled labor was needed, and it became harder to fill work orders for rebuilding tasks.

Volunteers who were medical or education professionals also provided much-needed help. They also could cause liability concerns. While Common Ground Health Clinic now has a paid staff of seven, the clinic began with all-volunteer staff that included professional doctors, nurses, and emergency medical technicians, and continues to attract volunteer professionals. The State of Louisiana instituted emergency medical credentialing, which relieved the clinic of its responsibility for ensuring proper licensing so the clinic was able to organize and begin operating quickly. But as one informant noted, beyond basic licensing, they had no way of evaluating the quality or competence of medical volunteers. Community Initiatives Foundation was careful to connect with volunteers who were professionals licensed in art therapy, mental health counseling, and education, and it stressed the importance of connecting with the best. Licensing did not ensure that professionals were well suited to deal with the unique circumstances of this disaster, and some of those who lent their services in Renaissance Village did not succeed or stay long to create the consistent care that children and adults suffering extreme psychological trauma need to recover.

The FBCOs in this study have reported that the numbers of volunteers and volunteer groups coming to help with the disaster response has been diminishing even though there is still much work to do. However, some respondents reported that they now have a cadre of reliable volunteers either in the community or through groups that return to the area to help.

Funding

All the FBCOs studied received donations, both cash and in kind, and grants from more than one source. The funding used for the disaster response by these eight organizations ranged from $42,000 to over $1 million. As in the survey, establishing the cost of the disaster assistance was difficult, in part because cash and in-kind donations that were distributed early in the relief efforts were not well documented, relief activities were often a cooperative effort among several organizations, and many staff were themselves volunteering services apart from their regular functions so the real cost of those services is not separated from their other functions.

Seven of the eight cases, as shown in Table 30, received some public funding, but most of the funding came from private sources. One, the Community Initiatives Foundation, was begun with seed money from a local foundation and received the core of its funding a year after the start of relief work from a foundation source. Much of the work with which it was associated in Renaissance Village was foundation funded. The CIF, the Coalition for the Homeless, and Family Road consortium is using $1.2 million in CDBG funds that the Coalition is charged with administering. As discussed later under sustainability, available funding and donations have diminished as new disasters and priorities gain the spotlight.

All cases received and distributed some type of in-kind donations such as clothes, nonperishable food, building supplies, household goods, and gift cards. Storage was a problem for several sites. Some (e.g., VFCC, GNODRP, Hope Haven) already had or created warehouse space to handle the influx. Others (e.g., Community Care Network) became official points of distribution, and others just distributed the goods as they came. How the beneficiaries of cash and in-kind donations were selected and how organizations were accountable for managing the funds and targeting deserved recipients is addressed in the section on accountability.

Communications

While it is only part of the story in the immediate aftermath of the storms, the inability to communicate readily created a major challenge to responding with expediency. For the leaders of the FBCOs that evacuated, locating their staff, members, congregants, and partners who had also evacuated was a necessary precondition to sort out when and how to restart operations.

The FBCOs studied dealt with the communications blackout in several ways. The larger FBCO collaborators often had disaster communications plans in place as a part of their evacuation plans. For example, the United Way of Greater New Orleans Area was able to set up a 211 information number outside the impact area to help hurricane victims find the social services they had used in New Orleans. The United Way convened the leaders of its member organizations in Hammond, Louisiana, by the end of September to begin planning the city's human services response. St. Luke's Episcopal Church equipped its recreational vehicle with satellite communications and computer equipment in order to operate in affected areas, and hurricane victims and first responders could use the equipment to call and e-mail to let people know that they were safe and to try to find relatives.

Many used the Internet, including other organizations' web sites, to list volunteer opportunities for people across the country looking to help. Some, such as St. Luke's, were able to set up their own web sites quickly to reach out for assistance. CGHC used a live camcorder to broadcast local conditions and attract support. As the affected areas' communications came back online, many respondents said that they began to tap their own networks of social and professional contacts to help with relief and recovery. They used their mailing and membership lists, e-mail address books, web sites, and phones to obtain resources—mainly donations and volunteers. They also began to hold meetings with other FBCOs, national affiliates, and government in the months following the storms.

Table 30. Funding and In-Kind Donations by Type of Source

Cases	Individual Giving Local	Individual Giving National	Organizational/ Religious Affiliates Local	Organizational/ Religious Affiliates National	Congregations Local	Congregations National	Nonprofit Organizations/ Foundations Local/State	Nonprofit Organizations/ Foundations National	Government Local	Government State	Government Federal	Business Local	Business National
Common Ground Health Clinic		✓		✓			✓	✓		✓	✓		
Community Care Network	✓	✓		✓		✓		✓			✓		
Community Initiatives Foundation	✓	✓					✓	✓		✓	✓		
Greater New Orleans Disaster Relief Partnership				✓			✓	✓			✓		✓
Hope Haven	✓	✓			✓	✓	✓	✓	✓	✓		✓	
Partners in Prayer and Service							✓				✓		
St. Luke's Episcopal Church	✓	✓			✓	✓						✓	✓
Vermilion Faith Community of Care	✓	✓	✓	✓	✓	✓	✓	✓	✓	✓		✓	✓

Individual and Organizational Capabilities

The specific skill sets of the leaders of the organizations help explain why particular FBCOs responded as they did. The question of expertise needs to be addressed on two dimensions. The expertise and professional experience of the leaders provided the means to implement their efforts directly; it also explained their ability to recognize their limitations and find others with whom they could join forces.

With regard to the first, the leader of the St. Luke's effort was an expert in military operations, casualty recovery, and logistics, and he understood the stress of emergencies. That experience helped him recognize the need for the mobile unit equipped with satellite communications to deliver assistance from Baton Rouge to New Orleans. Hope Haven and CCN were shelters for vulnerable individuals before the storm. Both directors knew how to run group homes, which helped each set up housing for volunteers. PIPS had experience in volunteer coordination. St. Luke's as an institution had the know-how, as they put it, to "take care of people," which included shelter, feeding, day care, and spiritual counseling. One of the principals in St. Luke's had experience counseling in a psychiatric hospital before becoming a rector and could use that experience in working with people who were severely traumatized. Both Hope Haven and CCN had social service experience and knowledge of the local social service system. Hope Haven's director offered to house the county social services unit as a result of that connection. In a large collaborative like GNODRP, the members were the leadership of charitable and social service providers in New Orleans.

In many cases, the leaders were visionary, high energy, and able to donate large amounts of time, sometimes pro bono, even after the initial emergency had subsided. In addition, the world around them really did not return to normal for a long time, and they remained focused on the continuing magnitude of need.

Leaders at CIF and CGHC also brought unique and broad perspectives to their relief efforts, which included an understanding of the complexity of the problems of hurricane victims and the skills needed to address that complexity. CIF's efforts were grounded in the director's professional training and her ability to recognize that individuals and families lived in precarious circumstances before the storm and over time would be unable to resettle because of the combined effect of those circumstances, the depth of the trauma experienced, and the lack of affordable housing and job opportunities to enable them to get back on their feet again. Her training, drive, continued attention, and sense of mission facilitated her ability to look for creative solutions for the long-term dislocated. Her connections to community and political institutions enabled her to leverage funding, and to recraft services as populations and needs changed over time.

Informants noted the importance of perceived legitimacy in overcoming distrust of individuals who have been traumatized and are difficult to reach. The CIF director became intimately familiar with the circumstances of children and families in Renaissance Village, stayed with them over their years in the park, and continues to follow several hundred children since their transition out of the park. That familiarity was also developed by the art therapists who came repeatedly to treat the children. As one child reportedly remarked, "we know you love us because you keep coming back." Other interventions, which were more limited or delivered by those less familiar with the populations in the park, were reportedly less successful. Similarly, one informant noted that donations that were well intended but ill informed (e.g., WalMart gift cards used to buy bicycles that had no place to be stored) failed.

Another expert on victims of trauma noted that a major predictor of poor outcomes for children is the physical disruption of daily routine. The first efforts to assist children in the River Center, establishing playgroups and some sense of calm, were in response to the chaos that confronted traumatized children and parents.

CGHC brought together unique training of so-called street medics—emergency medical technicians and others trained in delivering emergency first aid, with expertise in administering medical care under various stressful circumstances and avoiding legal and credentialing entanglements. They also were grounded in an understanding of and desire to change how discrimination and cultural competence affect access to medical care. The clinic required all staff to take formal racism and discrimination training, which has been adopted by at least one other long-standing community clinic.

In other case study organizations, staff also appears to have had the requisite knowledge of local areas and omnipresence to be able to offer meaningful help. One observation repeated by several focus group participants was that the FBCO staff member helping them rebuild their houses always seemed to be able to anticipate what they needed and know how to get it.

As noted at the outset, the case study organizations are exemplars, not chosen to be representative of the universe of responding organizations. Several leaders seemed to understand the limits of their expertise by connecting with experts in other areas. CGHC connected with other community health clinics for specialized services and professional advice, and it created an active board to provide continuing advice and oversight. CIF made a point of connecting to the best performers, those with highly developed professional skills, proven track records, and competency to work with the particular populations that they were trying to serve. Collaborators, whether local or national, were selected with those standards as a guide.

Organizational capacity was less striking than the characteristics of the leadership in the FBCOs studied. Although VFCC's past experience in disaster response also gave it the imprimatur of legitimacy to become the repository of donations coming through the local emergency response office, past experience with disasters was not a necessary component in defining other case study organizations' approach to assistance. VFCC and PIPS staff had current databases of local organizations and resources that assisted the local area response. Certainly, St. Luke's physical plant, including multiple facilities, accommodated its shelter operations. But the responses of Community Care Network, Hope Haven, Community Initiatives Foundation, and Common Ground Clinic were creations of the moment and the product of the skills and insights of their leaders.

On the other hand, several informants referred to other FBCOs that came to help and were in "over their heads"—for example, taking on shelters or feeding responsibilities with inadequate experience or resources. Organizations that were less competent to address the specific problems of the populations that needed help, or less experienced in working in collaborative settings and integrating their efforts with others, were not as successful. In one example, an individual was highly committed to offering his professional skills and worked tirelessly to help, but at a certain point his inability to connect with the larger assistance efforts became problematic. Working alone, he could neither fold his effort into that larger whole nor appreciate when to allow the larger organizational efforts to overtake his own.

Networks and Collaborations

In one way or another, all the relief efforts studied were the product of multiple organizational collaborations, some representing formal partnerships and others using episodic or informal assistance as needed. As noted in the methodology, cases were selected for study that had important stories to tell; those stories tended to be associated with multiple organizational or institutional connections. The findings from the telephone survey of a larger group of FBCO responders indicated that hierarchical or formal affiliates did not increase the likelihood of working with others. Consistent with those findings, the case study collaborations appear to be based more on social and professional networks than on support from formal hierarchical affiliations. For some cases, however, horizontal affiliations, such as the Interfaith Disaster Task Force on the Mississippi Gulf Coast, were instrumental in making connections between organizations that were used in the 2005 hurricane response. Vermilion Faith Community of Care and GNODRP represent the formalization of horizontal networks.

Especially in the immediate aftermath of Hurricanes Katrina and Rita, the FBCOs in existence before the storms tapped into their social and professional networks for resources, information, and coordination. Reliance on these networks in St. Luke's and Hope Haven's response was described earlier. Hope Haven was put on the mayor's top ten targets for rebuilding.

Social and professional networks were also used as long-term recovery activities began. Community Care Network's director went to her pastor to ask what she could do to help. Her church lent CCN office space and put her in charge of housing and coordinating the volunteers who descended on the Gulf Coast and on the church to help rebuild. The connection to the local YMCA, which was down the street from the church, was the result not of proximity but of networking at Interfaith Disaster Task Force meetings. GNODRP was formed by social service organization leaders in the New Orleans area who had known each other professionally and who together recognized a lack of regional coordination for long-term recovery.

Respondents reiterated that they called whomever they could in a broad social and professional network, and they reached beyond their immediate circle to create new relationships to meet the needs of hurricane victims and their communities. For the most part, they cited high levels of cooperation and a willingness to set aside turf issues or concerns for rules and protocols in order to respond to the disaster. These working relationships with old and new associates continued when the disaster response moved from emergency relief into long-term recovery.

Several FBCOs studied connected with local, state, or federal agencies. GNODRP leaders worked closely with the FEMA Voluntary Agency Liaison (VAL), who helped develop the structure and activities of GNODRP and the parish-level long-term recovery structures in the region. In contrast, some respondents in Mississippi reported that turnover in the FEMA VALs assigned to the area made it difficult to create partnerships with them. Hope Haven, PIPS, and VFCC had existing relationships with local government officials that supported their response. In several other FBCOs, connections to government were remote, usually through receipt of funding or grants, or nonexistent.

Accountability

Accountability for handling funds, distributing other resources, identifying needed services, and ensuring that they are delivered to those in need can be problematic in the context of an emergency. In that context, there is clearly a trade-off between accountability and flexibility. The issue relates both to the ability of responders to document their efforts and the proclivity of oversight bodies to require it. But if FBCOs beyond the traditional providers are to play a prominent role in future disaster relief, particularly in the direct distribution of goods and services to disaster victims, mechanisms for increasing accountability are of particular importance.

During the initial emergency, when the interest was in getting funds and donations distributed and services available as quickly as possible, detailed records on whom organizations were serving or how much cash or other units of service were being distributed may not have been kept. Some in the field noted that oversight took a back seat in the emergency response because of the magnitude of need. For those FBCOs that had oversight structures, many of those bodies took a step back specifically to allow for more flexibility in the delivery of assistance after the storms. In the words of one respondent: "We had guidelines that our agencies have to adhere to.

Our board has established these policies....When it came to Katrina, though, all bets were off." As another remarked, "it was so easy to help people in the days after the storm" because there were so few restrictions on funds. As time went on, he noted, helping people became harder because of an increasing number of rules.

Most sites that provided services beyond emergency relief had some oversight structure in place, though the level of oversight varied widely. In three sites, interviewees noted that they reported funding and expenditures and major service decisions (e.g., setting up a shelter or a point of distribution) to an oversight body. However, only two of the eight organizations studied were held explicitly accountable for the populations they were serving. One problem may be that the development of new and untried approaches to relief, as the magnitude of the disaster demanded, made it challenging to define service units or desired outcomes. One site was given broad discretion by funders and the board, and though it meticulously documented its efforts, it could not get more guidance on whether it was using funds in ways desired by the funders, for example in identifying needs or choice of services.

As the disaster response transitioned to longer-term recovery activities, accounting for those activities was more common. Long-term recovery structures generally maintained oversight on funding and eligibility criteria as prescribed by the board or membership organizations on these committees. Two interviewees who worked in long-term recovery structures, however, complained that committees lacked transparency because of low member participation and confidentiality strictures on resource allocations among individual cases that came before them.

The massive influx of donations created its own challenges, including competition and turf battles. In one case, a local faith-based organization accused another of hoarding donations and not distributing resources equitably among other faith-based organizations in the area, though the accusation may have been more a result of envy than mismanagement of funds.

In three sites, the principal reason for working outside formal long-term recovery structures was the ability to help more people without the burden of red tape and bureaucracy. One government official attributed his success to putting a high premium on flexibility, remarking, "Don't ask questions; ask forgiveness." Another echoed the sentiment, saying there was a need for "flex rules" when dealing with a crisis, and that both FEMA and the Red

Cross lacked the ability to move quickly because of their more rigid and rule-bound structures.

Equity

The lack of guidelines and specificity for designated use of funds, populations served, standards about what constituted need, or service units raises questions about equitable treatment among recipients. For example, the storms were indiscriminate with respect to who endured major housing damage; some respondents viewed all victims as equally deserving, regardless of personal income or prospects for insurance reimbursement, and made no formal inquiries into clients' financial circumstances. As one staff member who assigned rebuilding teams noted about a house on the beach, "Just because you have a big home doesn't mean you have a lot of money."

Other respondents, understanding that funds were limited, required that the neediest, by their definition, be given priority and therefore that income and access to other resources, including insurance coverage, be considered in distributing assistance. In the sites that used long-term recovery structures, assessments included formal attempts to establish need and assistance received, either using FEMA or Coordinated Assistance Network databases, required documentation, or case management assessments regarding the extent of damage, resource levels, and other funding sources accessed.

In cases that were not part of a formal case management framework, chance and informal contacts determined the allocation of assistance. Some simply claimed that they knew the area, knew where the needs of the community were, and could appropriately bypass tedious paperwork that others could not. In their experience, those asking for services needed it most, and the greater problem was getting people to accept help. Some public funding was distributed without income eligibility criteria, as in one federal emergency grant that was used to hire local residents regardless of their level of victimization from the storm, and in another without regard to evacuee status.

In sites providing assistance through a congregation network or simply to those who appeared at their doors, questions naturally occur about how individuals who are not congregation members or who are not aggressive advocates on their own behalf are served. One church-based group that partnered with the case study organization attempted to serve its members first: "We established a clear tracking system ...we were trying to identify [our members]...Once I didn't need to focus on [them], I just focused on the mental health stuff." With regard to the same issue, a public agency that became a conduit for donations routed significant private donations to a local faith- based organization because the director believed that pastors were best suited to identify where services were needed. At least one case studied established networks based almost entirely on relationships the staff and board had with the members. Another case study organization alleged that no one was given religious services unless requested; a staff member in the same organization reported praying with everyone receiving assistance.

Similarly, the case studies leave open the question of how evacuees sorted themselves or were triaged to different congregations to obtain shelter. Evacuees are by definition strangers to host communities. A number of case study organizations made specific attempts to serve those that were outside their immediate networks. One faith-based organization with which PIPS and United Way worked as part of the Lake Charles disaster response structure set up a network of secular providers specifically because it recognized that many people were not involved in the church system. Another interviewee recalled an African American woman breaking down in tears saying she never expected the level of generosity that she received from white people. On the other hand, news of civil unrest in New Orleans and at Baton Rouge's River Center was a sobering backdrop to those attempting to host evacuees, which could have influenced the response of FBCOs providing assistance. When reports surfaced of unrest at the Baton Rouge center, one shelter hired temporary security guards.

The government also had control over assistance by setting the rules by which public funds were allocated. Some on the Mississippi Gulf Coast were angered by the governor's decision to allocate CDBG funds for flood damage but not wind damage. In so doing, according to some, thousand of homes of low-income individuals that were farther inland from the storm surge but severely damaged by wind were denied assistance from these funds.

Life Cycles and Sustainability

As seen in the FBCOs under study, the temporary shift to disaster response was often driven by the compelling circumstances of the storms, the expertise and initiative of their leadership, and the rush of funding and materials flowing to the region. However, as time passes, funding diminishes, and the needs of those served by these organizations before the storm come back into focus, many return to their original mission despite continuing needs related to the 2005 hurricanes.

Three of the FBCOs studied that did not have a disaster response mission have returned or are in the process of returning to their original functions and activities. Each of these FBCOs is likely to retain the internal capacity to respond to future disasters. Thus, Community Care Network maintains a strong relationship with the local church that hosted the disaster relief efforts, and its director is experienced in operating a shelter and in coordinating volunteers. Whether another disaster would generate the same level of volunteer and material donations is unknowable. Hope Haven, similarly, is now positioned to distribute monetary donations through its Helping Hands Fund and knows how to operate a housing facility. However, by the time of the site visit the organization was attempting to sell its facility because of skyrocketing housing insurance prices, its large debt resulting from its relief efforts, and funding sources that had dried up.

St. Luke's retains its large campus, solid funding, and congregant base, and it has updated a disaster relief plan for the church. The leadership sees a similar role in future disasters as it played in 2005, as a provider of shelter, materials, and spiritual support and counseling. It stocks up on essential items such as nonperishable food, water, and baby supplies to be prepared for the next event. But the church saw its role in 2005 as only immediate relief, terminated those services after four months, and sold the mobile unit to the Archdiocese. Partners in Prayer has not resumed its pre-storm mission; its director is staff to United Way, which is itself part of Lake Charles' strong mayoral-led disaster response apparatus that has built expertise from its several hurricane experiences and from collaboration among a broad range of governmental and nongovernmental components. Several respondents credited the leadership of the mayor as being critical to the strength of the collaboration among faith-based, secular, and public organizations.

Those organizations whose missions are related to case management within a long-term recovery or unmet needs committee structure have continued to provide services as long as funding remained. GNODRP is coming to a crossroads because most funding for unmet needs ends in 2008 or 2009. Most of the funding for case management, which was used by the member long- term recovery structures within GNODRP, came from UMCOR (Katrina Aid Today funds), and those funds are virtually exhausted. Funding for housing rebuilding typically came from the Salvation Army and Red Cross, and that is nearly exhausted as well. Leaders in the organization are aware that recovery from Katrina is likely to be a 10- to 20- year effort, and they are concerned about developing new resources to sustain the momentum. The challenge of maintaining the attention of national policymakers and funders is increasing as other events overtake the 2005 hurricanes and interest wanes in the general public.

Many long-term recovery structures, like VFCC, are sufficiently established that although they will become dormant, they can easily be reconstituted when needed. As one affiliate noted, he could be "neck deep…with VFCC tomorrow" working on a relief effort. VFCC's office, warehouse, and network connections survive. The office is donated by a board member, the director frequently donates his own time, and the churches and personal relationships remain, so the organization is able to weather periods with no financing and reorganize when the need arises. VFCC is also part of the Emergency Operations Center Disaster Plan, and the Office of Emergency Preparedness director sits on the VFCC board.

Common Ground Health Clinic and the Community Initiatives Foundation have continuing missions—the former to provide health care, and the latter to address the continuing needs of children and families whose precarious circumstances will require assistance with housing, mental health, employment, and a host of other issues that emerged as a result of the storm. The Clinic has undergone a maturation process in recognition of the need to professionalize and enhance the quality of care. Collaborations remain in place and current funding is expected until at least 2010. Community Initiatives Foundation maintained a clear understanding of mission but recognized that it and collaborators were working in uncharted territory and addressing a level of need that no one had experienced before. The work of the foundation has adapted as needs have changed, moving from facilitating various services for the children in the shelter and then in the trailer park to addressing the range of other services required to stabilize the families and resettle them in new housing.

The Larger Context: Connections to Traditional Disaster Relief and Human Services Systems

FBCOs are often resistant to connecting either to traditional response systems or other human service systems. Except for the two FBCOs that are part of the formal response system, connections were rare or precarious among the studied sites.

Emergency Response

Connections to the local offices of emergency preparedness were one way FBCOs connected to the traditional response system. VFCC had been previously part of emergency planning for Vermilion Parish as a result of Hurricane Lili in 2002. United Way was part of the plan in Lake Charles' disaster response system. GNOCDRP was created to coordinate long-term recovery structures in nine parishes. Other organizations studied had only occasional informal contact with the office of emergency preparedness or had no contact at all.

Problems exist with creating and maintaining connections between the traditional response systems and FBCOs. Some officials interviewed who were responsible for emergency planning were clearly focused on how to incorporate local FBCOs into their disaster response plans, though the specifics were not always clear. In one site, the FBCO director and another local leader had participated in regional or state disaster response planning, but had mixed views about the effectiveness of these efforts. These planning efforts could be a useful way to share information, but in this instance they were viewed as inappropriately detail-oriented or lacking in recommendations that resulted in action. Another intergovernmental task force that included nongovernmental organizations was also intended to be a venue for sharing information. However, according to at least one FBCO member who participated for over a year, the task force was ultimately unable to focus on larger, strategic issues that were critical to effective service response.

The magnitude of the 2005 hurricanes brought in numerous outside agencies that were often a dominant presence in relief and recovery activities on the ground. Among those groups and individuals that provided emergency assistance, cross-group communication was often minimal, especially concerning coordinating volunteers and distributing donations. The lack of coordination reportedly created duplication of services and oversupplies of certain types of donations. Some questioned whether office of emergency preparedness directors might exercise more power over registering and restricting incoming FBCOs. In one instance, the parish office of emergency preparedness aggressively restricted the number and type of FBCOs entering the area; the results, reportedly, were positive. Other OEPs were unable to get all, or even a majority, of incoming organizations to cooperate. Efforts that were successful used local leaders in traditional nonprofit organizations, such as the United Way and community faith-based organizations, to coordinate activities.

Traditional disaster relief agencies, such as the Red Cross and FEMA, received mixed reviews from many in the field. Some had positive views of the Red Cross, which provided shelter and human services in the immediate aftermath and funds for long-term recovery. Many of those interviewed had contact with both FEMA and the Red Cross and in some way used their resources; for one site, a FEMA voluntary agency liaison was a major player in the creation of the disaster response organization.

Case study organizations, however, were not typically willing to become official shelters under Red Cross regulations, and the general perception was that both the Red Cross and FEMA were overwhelmed by the magnitude of the storm, the duration of needed assistance, and the nature of need, including psychological trauma, enduring medical needs, domestic violence and civil disorder, family reunification, and the variety of human services, including children's services and schooling that became an issue as the emergency continued. FEMA was derided for its slow, rigid bureaucracy and the absence of a strategy to provide social services as a part of the provision of emergency housing. As described earlier, hundreds of families were housed in trailers for months or years, isolated from local communities or job opportunities, with no common areas for playing, eating, socializing or problem-solving among the residents. FEMA, in the eyes of some respondents, became an obstacle rather than a facilitator to bring services in or create community in these situations. Also noted earlier, both the Red Cross and FEMA used rotating teams consisting largely of outside volunteers, and the longer the emergency endured, unfamiliarity with the local area became a problem. On the other hand, the military was lauded by several respondents for its clear hierarchy, clear parameters for services, and respectful demeanor.

Long-Term Recovery Structures

Another venue for FBCOs to connect to the traditional response system was through local long-term recovery committees. Three sites were part of or connected to formalized long-term recovery structures to address unmet needs; the others deliberately worked outside the traditional long-term recovery process, using instead their own professional or informal networks. Those working within the structures saw them as a way to increase efficient use of funding, and to pool other resources and case managers to ensure that services were not duplicated and that unmet needs were addressed. Several interviewees who worked within those systems saw significant improvements in the process over the long term and believed they were able to provide more comprehensive assistance to those with documented need.

Two sites declined invitations to participate in long-term recovery structures or resigned after participating for a short time, viewing these structures as too slow and burdened by documentation requirements, red tape, and poorly managed funding streams. Others felt that the power to allot money was in the hands of too few people and personal connections often decided who would be funded and who would not. As noted earlier, one complaint was that the organizations were not accountable for the funds they used and the process was not transparent. In that site, the committee was challenged when funds were provided to a local construction company owned by a board member's family.

Accessing the Broader Human Service System

Connecting to the larger human service system to provide needed services that are outside the traditional disaster response model was less common. Large disasters reveal the underlying needs of vulnerable populations that make recovery more elusive. The massive loss of publicly subsidized housing, the pervasive occurrence of undocumented succession of privately owned homes that could impede access to assistance for repair or reclamation, the sluggish implementation of Louisiana's Road Home program, and the spike in rental costs as a result of the storms made resettlement for low-income populations a major challenge. Mental health issues for children and families traumatized by the storms made mental health services, limited under the best of circumstances, a critical need for storm victims. Health care for low-income populations was increasingly strained with the collapse of facilities and services for the uninsured. Family and legal problems, which may have followed individuals into the storms, were often exacerbated by the effects of the storm, requiring new levels of case management and the services to back it up.

For those FBCOs that do not typically provide social services or do not interact with the public human service system, it was difficult to understand the need to connect to the larger human service system. It was rare for most of the FBCOs studied to have formalized connections to public human services structures to enhance their efforts, for example to access mental health services or subsidized housing. These FBCOs' only contacts with the larger, public human service providers were either through long-term recovery structures or were informal, or relied on the doggedness of organization staff. Previous formal connections to the department of human services, the penal system, schools, and other public agencies were either unused or were so altered by the storms that they were unrecognizable and would have to be recrafted. Almost none of the study sites, moreover, had set up formal connections or agreements for future disasters. In most instances, public human service providers and the FBCOs viewed relief efforts with different lenses; each generally had little acknowledgment or understanding of what the other was doing or that each may have a role to play in the other's efforts. The problem also worked in the other direction: human service providers who are charged with serving vulnerable populations are unlikely to understand how to connect with the FBCO community involved in disaster relief in order to connect human services with the efforts of the FBCOs. Further, nongovernmental organizations do not represent a coherent whole themselves, and their own turf issues can create challenges to mutual support, particularly if competencies and responsibilities have not been sorted out before a disaster.

Within the public sector, working across agencies to coordinate services, or across governmental jurisdictions, may be especially challenging. In one instance a group was created to connect public agencies with nongovernmental organizations and to facilitate intergovernmental coordination. The group met intensively for over a year following the storms and reportedly had many successes in addressing issues, such as recognizing the formaldehyde problem in FEMA trailers. But getting necessary action from multiple levels of government proved more elusive. Decisions about housing replacement were caught in the debate between the city, public housing authority, HUD, and other interests about whether public housing would be replaced. FEMA had never dealt with a disaster of this magnitude, was more concerned with logistical issues than individual service needs, and reportedly could not make local decisions without national approval. Another issue cited was the interest in maintaining local discretion, although local capacity in a large-scale disaster may be inadequate.

Experts who worked with Katrina victims described the particular needs of traumatized populations for systematic screening and assessment, to establish a baseline of psychological status, and to respond to an inevitable spiral of challenges—high rates of school truancy, high rates of parental depression, and post-traumatic stress disorder (PTSD), which fuels children's difficulties, all of which must be followed by long-term treatment. One expert suggested that nearly everyone in the FEMA trailer park had some measure of PTSD. Art therapists reportedly found that 80 to 90 percent of teens in Renaissance Village would not go to school—they could not sit still, and were ostracized by local teens in the district school, reinforcing their need for some sort of alternative school. The attempt to develop a charter school, described earlier, might have helped.

Further, vulnerable populations often begin with an array of challenges, which are then exacerbated by the trauma of evacuation and dislocation. The low-income African American populations in New Orleans were supported by strong family and social networks. When those ties were broken, as they were by the evacuation and ad hoc resettlement in trailer parks, they were difficult, if not impossible, to reestablish. Another way of understanding this is the need to capitalize on these bonds in a disaster response whenever possible. Common Ground Health Clinic served constituents in its community and required training to heighten staff sensitivity to racial discrimination and enhance their ability to work with the local population, which may over the long term provide a model for other disaster responses.

Addressing the full dimensions of psychological trauma was, according to experts interviewed, not purely for humanitarian reasons. Without attention to the trauma, there was greater potential for persistent dysfunction and inability to resettle successfully—to reestablish housing, jobs, and functional families, to ensure school attendance, and to avoid substance abuse, domestic violence, and other forms of child and adult delinquency. As one respondent described the context, screening and assessment services were not planned for, and many people were trying to pump services into Renaissance Village that were not well coordinated and only exacerbated a "very broken system."

With no prior planning for services in response to a disaster, and relationships among human service providers, official disaster responders, and nongovernmental organizations not well developed, it is much more difficult to know who to talk to or how to coordinate responses after the fact. The problem is further complicated when local and state entities must interact with outside entities, both federal agencies and nongovernmental emergency responders. Similarly, it is difficult to convince public or private organizations to collaborate without roles that are understood and funding to support their efforts. One informant familiar with the efforts to get behavioral health services to children in Renaissance Village observed that as the magnitude of the disaster increases, the need for persistent relationships increases exponentially; it took over a decade for him to forge relationships with providers of behavioral health services in his city.

Summary of Key Case Study Findings

The case studies offer a number of findings that are key to anticipating the role and effective use of FBCOs in future disasters.

The magnitude of the disaster propelled most in the case studies into action. While some FBCOs may respond in future disasters as they have in past disasters, the magnitude of the disaster in 2005 was the primary reason that FBCOs studied responded, and it raises the question of who and how many would respond in future disasters. The unprecedented level of devastation from the hurricanes and subsequent flooding, the breadth of population affected, the depth and duration of need, and the extent of donations and volunteers that needed to be managed, however, explain why most of the FBCOs studied responded.

The depth and duration of need also exposed the limitations of traditional response models, which were overwhelmed and unprepared to provide the assistance needed, particularly as the crisis wore on. The magnitude created long-lasting need for a range of human services, including temporary housing that exceeded the capabilities of traditional shelter and emergency aid providers, health and mental health services for psychological trauma, and services to address enduring medical needs, domestic violence, family reunification, and special schooling arrangements as the emergency continued. FEMA was criticized by interviewees for its slow, rigid bureaucracy and the absence of a strategy to provide social services as a part of the provision of emergency housing. Long-term recovery structures were also criticized for their red tape and lack of transparency.

Chance explained the direction that the responses often took. Most FBCOs studied had no prior disaster experience and no preconceived plan for response. Rather, they responded to the needs as presented, relying on the skills and expertise of their leaders, their ability to give large amounts of time, often pro bono, and their ability to understand their own limitations and look to others for additional help. The case study organizations were also innovative in their uses of the Internet to overcome communications problems, to solicit and vet donations and volunteers, and to connect with social and professional networks for help.

Familiarity with local areas and perceived legitimacy were keys to overcoming distrust of severely traumatized individuals. Traditional responders, such as the Red Cross and FEMA, were typically unfamiliar with local conditions and local facilities and services, and any knowledge gained on the ground was lost as new teams were rotated in.

Few accountability mechanisms were in place to provide a clear picture of services provided and people served among the FBCOs studied. The lack of guidelines and specificity for use of funds and populations served, or standards regarding what constituted need or service units, makes it difficult to assess the content and appropriateness of services provided by the FBCOs studied. How FBCOs ensure equitable treatment among recipients, and how individuals sort themselves among, for example, religious and secular providers, deserves attention.

Connections between FBCOs studied and the larger human service or disaster response systems were often limited, with little recognition about what role each might play in the other's efforts. For FBCOs that did not typically provide social services or interact with the public human service system, there were neither formal nor informal connections to enhance their efforts, for example to access mental health services or subsidized housing. Vulnerable populations often have an array of preexisting challenges, which are exacerbated by the trauma of evacuation and dislocation, and the breaking of essential family and social networks that are difficult, if not impossible, to reestablish. Without attention to the full dimensions of psychological trauma, there was greater potential for persistent dysfunction and inability to resettle successfully.

Among the many organizations that provided emergency assistance, cross-group communication was often minimal, especially concerning coordination of volunteers and distribution of donations. This reportedly resulted in duplication of services and oversupplies of certain types of donations. While official emergency response planners may have new appreciation for the role that FBCOs can play in disaster response, the case studies suggest that it will be critical to understand their specific abilities, resources, and interest in participating in future disaster responses as part of official response planning.

PART III. CONCLUSIONS

Faith-based and community organizations played a prominent role in the relief and recovery efforts after hurricanes Katrina and Rita. The magnitude of their response in 2005 was directly related to the magnitude of the storms, but their experiences provide very important lessons about what FBCOs can be expected to do in future disasters.

The key findings of the telephone survey and case studies, summarized in Parts I and II, address the five research questions of this study: specifically, what are the characteristics of FBCOs that provided disaster-related human services; what services were provided, and to whom; what resources (monetary, material, and human) were used to deliver services; what networks facilitated the ability of FBCOs to deliver services; and what lessons can be learned from these relief efforts? Together, these findings create a detailed portrait of the breadth, depth, and complexity of activities undertaken by smaller and nontraditional responders in the days, weeks, and months after the storms.

The analysis raised three overarching questions about the potential role that FBCOs might play in future disasters:

1. At what points in the relief and recovery efforts and under what conditions are these types of FBCOs most likely to provide assistance;
2. Do FBCOs perform differently or provide different services than those provided by traditional responders and public agencies; and

3. Can or should FBCOs be expected to interact with traditional disaster responders or other human service providers during disasters to facilitate a broader or coordinated response?

Timing and Reasons for FBCO Involvement in Relief and Recovery Services

Although hurricanes are common in the Gulf Coast, hurricanes Katrina and Rita were so powerful and damage so extensive that the response to the storms was unprecedented. About two-thirds of the FBCOs in the survey said that this was the first time they had provided disaster relief services, and all but one case study organization were new to disaster work. Several factors affected FBCOs' responses to this disaster, including timing and distance from the storm's impact. The case studies suggest that the magnitude of the storms and its effect was the primary motivator.

Timing and Types of Services Given

Disaster response can generally be divided into two phases: immediate rescue and relief services and long-term recovery services, although the distinctions between the two can be sometimes blurred. According to the survey findings, FBCOs were more likely to engage in immediate relief services than long-term recovery services. Roughly 70 percent of survey respondents provided some type of immediate relief, such as food, water, clothing, and temporary shelter. In contrast, less than half provided longer-term services. Housing repairs were the most common long-term service (given by 42 percent of FBCO respondents), while only 20 to 30 percent of FBCOs provided other long-term services, such as mental health counseling or job training.[16] Volunteers were continuing to come to the Gulf Coast to assist with recovery efforts when our fieldwork was conducted in the spring and summer of 2008, though these efforts were considerably diminished, as was the local capacity to house and coordinate the efforts.

Distance from the Storms' Impact

Distance from the storms' impact may dictate how quickly FBCOs respond and how long they continue to give services. The survey found that FBCOs away from the storms' impact areas were both quick to respond and to leave—that is, more than half ended their assistance within three months after the storm. Understandably, fewer FBCOs in the primary impact area responded immediately—no doubt because of the devastation in these areas and the restrictions imposed on returning to areas under evacuation orders that lasted many weeks after the storms. But over time, more than half of FBCOs in the primary impact areas began to provide some type of long-term recovery service and continued to do so at the time of the survey.

Five of the case study organizations illustrate the types of FBCO assistance provided in the primary impact area. For example, one priest, whose church was severely damaged and whose congregation had evacuated, attached himself to a church outside the impact area and returned to New Orleans daily to help his congregation and neighborhood residents clean up and rebuild. Both Mississippi cases began almost immediately to rebuild their own or others' facilities. The two case study organizations in southwestern Louisiana were able to respond immediately to Hurricane Katrina and within days to Hurricane Rita.

The survey data underscore the point that many FBCOs, particularly religious congregations, are able to provide immediate, emergency relief services, but they are less likely to have the capacity or interest in sustaining their involvement over a long period. As noted earlier, housing rehabilitation may be the exception. Congregations in particular have engaged in sustained housing rehabilitation work in the Gulf Coast area. However, this work is undertaken by a smaller share of FBCOs than those that responded immediately after the crisis, and it is often assisted by running formalized programs that bring volunteers from outside to help.

Magnitude of the Storms' Impact

The magnitude of the 2005 storms appears to be both the catalyst that motivated many FBCOs to provide assistance and the determinant of specific responses. According to case study informants, the storms were like nothing they had experienced in the past. The hurricanes affected more people and the effects lasted longer than previous disasters in this country. Eighty percent of New Orleans, a city of 440,000, was flooded, and the timing and pace of the evacuation created major problems for those who did not leave early or had no means of transportation to leave.

The storms' magnitude also provoked attention to the personal and social dimensions of the event, including permanent loss of housing, widespread family dislocation and emotional trauma, and the particular vulnerabilities of low-income minority populations. These problems would be long-lasting and change over time as many evacuees were unable to resettle, some remaining in temporary trailer parks for nearly three years, and requiring new approaches to address the problems created by the hurricanes. However, specific disaster responses appear often to owe as much to chance as to deliberate planning.

While there is no reason to believe that the same humanitarian instinct that motivated FBCOs to respond in 2005 would not apply again in a disaster of similar magnitude, there is little evidence to suggest that they will be better prepared. According to the survey, less than a quarter of the respondents had created new emergency plans, new partnerships, or lists of local services, and more than a third had taken no steps to prepare for a future emergency. Officials charged with emergency preparedness who were interviewed in the case studies were aware of the importance of including FBCOs in their planning as a result of their presence in the 2005 hurricanes, but the details of how FBCOs are included were sometimes difficult to discern. The creation of the Greater New Orleans Disaster Recovery Partnership resulted from recognizing the need for coordination among multiple responders and interest in better regional preparedness for the next disaster. Yet, several case study organizations were not interested in formally committing themselves or their resources to a role in a future disaster, or being credentialed as an official Red Cross shelter, which would require conforming to Red Cross rules and regulations.

Capabilities of Nontraditional (FBCO) Responders

Nontraditional responders often bring knowledge of local communities, heightened sensitivity to the needs of disaster victims, and capabilities to collaborate and reach beyond bureaucratic rules and boundaries to provide the flexibility necessary to adjust to changing circumstances. But their efforts also raise questions about accountability for services provided and populations served, and about their ability to connect to traditional responders and professional human service providers, particularly in addressing the complex and long-term needs of victims of disaster. Several themes emerge from the study findings.

Knowledge of Local Area and Its Resources

The assistance FBCOs provided after the 2005 hurricanes was delivered in the context of perceived failure by governmental agencies and others officially charged with disaster relief. One of the complaints case study respondents lodged against Red Cross and FEMA was that their teams were generally not local and were unfamiliar with the local geography, facilities, social services, and other venues that might provide help. Because relief and recovery work wore on for months, staff was rotated in and out, and any gains that may have been made in understanding the local situation were lost in the rotation. Additionally, respondents said that rules seemed to change with each changing shift, creating confusion and frustration, and increasing a sense of insecurity when reassurance was critical. Even under the worst circumstances, when many human service agencies are damaged and inoperable, and therefore unavailable as referral sources, knowledge of the local topography and how to make one's way around is an advantage. Units in responder agencies that had regional or local ties were cited as more helpful to the recovery effort.

In contrast, the FBCOs studied were generally staffed by people who knew the local area, often by individuals who were in the business of helping people—such as clergy, clinicians, or other social service providers—and often by those who were victims themselves in the widespread disaster. As such, they were perhaps able to express a level of sensitivity, empathy, and responsiveness that staff from other kinds of organizations might not. As noted earlier, one observation repeated by several focus group participants was that the FBCO staff member helping them rebuild their houses always seemed to be able to anticipate what they needed and know how to get it. Some in the field also commented about the freedom from rules and protocol evident in local operations, such as small, locally run shelters that were not officially certified as shelters and therefore not subject to others' rules. Whether those rules would have added a measure of protection to the service recipient or provided other benefits is unknown.

Some local FBCOs may be able to provide the sustained commitment to hurricane victims necessary to achieve long-term recovery. One good example from the case studies was the omnipresence of the director of the Community Initiatives Foundation and others who returned repeatedly to help. The ability to connect with the sometimes confusing mix of actors in the FEMA trailer park and the sustained presence built trust among traumatized storm victims who were otherwise unreceptive to help. Other local FBCOs were less interested or able to make a sustained commitment.

Collaboration and Networking

The findings from both the telephone survey and the case studies illustrate that FBCOs often used informal networking and formal collaborations to expand their capabilities. It was hypothesized that vertical hierarchies, such as national affiliates or umbrella governing bodies (e.g., a regional diocese) would provide some measure of support to local FBCOs' efforts. The survey suggests that these affiliations did not facilitate collaboration, and the case studies suggest that individual social and professional connections more often provided the basis for collaboration and financial support.

Formal affiliations, however, can play a role in disaster responses. The Interfaith Disaster Task Force, for example, provided coordination and technical assistance to membership organizations in Mississippi. Collaboratives, such as GNODRP, expanded contacts, provided funds, and were a conduit to link volunteers from around the country with relief efforts on the ground. If familiarity and connections exist between local community-based organizations and professionals in disaster response or health and human service areas, those connections can be called upon in a disaster. The case studies suggest that much of the formal social service system in the heavily impacted areas was inoperable in the early days after the storms, and the FBCOs that provided assistance were operating in that breach. But the studies also suggest that prior familiarity can get needed services back on line, as in the case of Hope Haven, or facilitate access to services, as in the case of the collaboration between CIF and the Coalition for the Homeless to use CDBG funds for resettlement.

Networks and collaborations can also be important tools for expanding expertise. Several case study organizations brought a particular expertise to the relief effort, such as in management, housing operations, logistics training, or human service delivery. Others quickly sought the help of experts after recognizing the challenges they confronted, particularly in dealing with emotional and psychological trauma.

Long-term assistance may be difficult for FBCOs to provide if they are not professional human service providers or do not have strong links to the professional social services community. The case studies illustrated that the lack of connection to the larger professional provider system generally made it difficult for many FBCOs to access services needed to address complex recovery problems.

Accountability

The lack of accountability of many FBCOs that participated in the relief and recovery efforts makes it difficult to assess how services provided do or should fit into the larger plan for disaster response. Few FBCOs kept detailed records of the numbers or characteristics of those who received emergency services. Even among the organizations that kept records or felt that they had a good sense of the magnitude of services delivered, definitions of units of service are unclear, do not easily translate into individuals served, and are often not comparable from one organization to the next. Providers who offered highly professionalized services, such as Common Ground Health Clinic, or services that created liability issues, which would require service recipients or volunteers to sign waivers, are exceptions.

Determining who was eligible to receive services was often not well thought out. FBCOs frequently responded to the needs in front of them, giving little time or thought to establishing criteria for who should be (or was) served. Except for negotiations within a long-term recovery structure, the case study organizations often made no attempt to use income levels or prospects for insurance reimbursement or other types of assistance as a screen for assessing need for services. Long-term recovery structures typically used some type of eligibility threshold, but, in several instances, the process of determining these criteria and the advocacy of case managers was questioned for its lack of transparency. Some interviewees in the case studies questioned whether, in a disaster of this size and complexity, the huge sums FEMA contracted for case management rather than for a richer array of human services such as mental health services, job training, or child care represent an inherent imbalance in the approach to disaster services.

The general lack of accountability during the crisis and its aftermath can be seen in the conflicting stories of acts of generosity and potential underlying discrimination. Neither the survey findings nor the case studies provide a clear picture about how individuals were triaged for help—for example, directed to one emergency shelter rather than another. How much of this help was unconditional and untainted by racial or class distinctions is not known. Some interviewees tell of unlikely but fortuitous liaisons between hurricane victims and military units. Others tell of the chaos and heavy-handed response of some law enforcement units, both to the evacuation order and to the threat of civil disorder in New Orleans. The variations clearly speak to the need for better understanding of how assistance is distributed, and how maintenance of order can be achieved with equanimity in a crisis of this magnitude.

Connections to the Larger Whole

The FBCOs operated within the context of a massive humanitarian response, including official emergency responders (e.g., military, law enforcement, fire and rescue, and offices of emergency preparedness), religious and secular organizations with dedicated arms for disaster services, and a historic outpouring of volunteers, cash, and in-kind contributions from around the country and, in some cases, around the world. Where the FBCOs in this study fit in that larger whole is important to understand in planning for more effective response in the future.

Hurricanes Katrina and Rita resulted in massive loss of housing (much of which has still not been recovered), behavioral health issues for large swaths of the population that require sustained treatment, and a range of family dysfunctions created or worsened by the effects of dislocation. These effects require responses far beyond traditional disaster response models— and beyond the capabilities of most FBCOs that are not human service providers.

It is difficult to know from either the survey findings or the case studies how well the efforts of the FBCOs studied penetrated the universe of need and whether better connections with both traditional disaster responders and those that provide longer-term services would produce a more effective response. To be sure, thousands of units of assistance (e.g., water and cleanup supplies, food, clothing) were distributed, though it is difficult to make any judgment about the numbers of individuals served. For those that sheltered evacuees, the numbers range from less than a dozen to over a hundred. For the one case study organization that was well connected to the overall emergency response structure, the contribution of its FBCO shelters to the total is knowable; for others, it is unclear. Survey respondents indicated that a large share of people served were low income and families with children.

For many FBCOs, understanding the need to connect with public human service systems or other human service providers and how to do it was not part of their experience. Similarly, FBCOs are fairly isolated from the larger disaster response system. According to the survey respondents, only 15 percent worked with state and local governments, and less than 10 percent worked with federal government agencies. Survey respondents often cited poor communication as one barrier to working with government agencies. Most FBCO connections were with other FBCOs—that is, congregations were most likely to work with other congregations and nonprofits were most likely to work with other nonprofits. The result is a silo effect not only within the larger disaster response system but also among FBCOs. As noted above, some disaster response officials appreciate the FBCOs' contributions in the 2005 hurricanes. It will be important to see how FBCOs are integrated into future response efforts.

As the case studies showed, FBCOs rarely had formalized connections to public human services structures, especially for gaining access to mental health services or subsidized housing. Assistance for any long-term services other than housing recovery appeared circumscribed by which organizations participated in roundtables that addressed unmet needs, and by specific funding allocations. Other contact with human service providers was likely fortuitous.

As noted above, both the survey findings and the case studies suggest that small, community- based organizations, both religious and secular, have special capabilities to offer in disaster relief, including the ability to respond quickly with critical knowledge of local areas and local facilities, operate outside the constraints of formal rules and protocols, and possibly provide a level of comfort and assurance that was difficult to find in the cacophonous aftermath of the 2005 storms. In general, however, connections to the larger disaster response apparatus, which might have expanded or strengthened their response, were difficult to achieve and frequently not sought.

Lessons Learned

Many organizations that are not traditional disaster responders, including small community- based social service providers and local congregations, played important roles in the aftermath of hurricanes Katrina and Rita. The findings from the telephone survey and the case studies suggest several lessons about what roles they might play in future disasters.

- **Those preparing emergency preparedness plans need to better understand the availability and capabilities of FBCOs.** How well that knowledge has been incorporated in local area planning efforts is unclear in the cases studied. Simply being able to identify who is left after a disaster, what their needs are, and who might provide assistance is critical to a response effort. The survey findings tell us that most respondents provided assistance; how many other organizations were unavailable because they were wiped out by the storm is unknown.

  The study suggests that it would be helpful to incorporate into disaster plans an inventory of local FBCOs and their contact information. Ideally, the nature of their facilities, their capabilities, and prior experience would be incorporated into disaster planning. Some FBCOs have limited capabilities, but those capabilities can be used strategically to implement a community's overall disaster response effectively. Locally based organizations can operate outside the constraints of official disaster responders, maintain flexibility, and craft innovative solutions to new needs and as needs change over time. But with no guidelines or oversight and limited recordkeeping, it is unclear how services are distributed and whether they are distributed equitably. To better account for the services that FBCOs can provide, disaster response planners can also provide guidance on how to document services provided and recipients served, including how to count service units and measure outcomes, and how to determine eligibility and triage people to ensure that all who need help receive it.

- **Recovery services needed after a disaster of this magnitude extend far beyond the traditional boundaries of emergency relief.** Longer-term recovery activities in a traditional disaster response model are largely focused on physical rebuilding and dependent on a limited circle of organizations providing aid. These traditional models are not well equipped to deal with deep and sustained injuries of disaster victims, both physical and psychological, and they are not well connected to the broader universe of expertise and service delivery systems that might provide appropriate and sustained interventions.

  The case studies illustrate that neither the traditional disaster responders nor the FBCOs studied were well connected to those that might provide behavioral health services, transitional and permanent housing, or school structures and educational experts able to address the psychological and emotional challenges of traumatized children and adolescents. The need for such services may be especially critical for low-income and vulnerable populations who may have preexisting disabilities that can be exacerbated by a disaster, and who generally have limited options for successful readjustment and resettlement.

  Similar to incorporating an inventory of FBCOs into emergency preparedness planning, a map of current human service providers, including governmental and private providers as well as regional and national specialists in trauma and vulnerable populations and who might be called upon to assist, would be a valuable component of such a plan.

- **Many FBCOs involved in long-term recovery appreciate the need to coordinate activities, as evidenced by new attention to data-sharing mechanisms among traditional responders.** The experience of the FEMA trailer park in one case study demonstrates the critical need for coordination among a wider array of providers, from federal, state and local agencies; experts in various specialized interventions; and private donors whose contributions may be critical to success.

- **Major disasters generate major humanitarian responses, which sometimes include those with the best intentions but uneven capabilities.** The case studies suggest that successful interventions appear to recognize the importance of seeking out the best performers—those with proven track records, the ability to work with the populations affected and whatever challenges they present, and the ability to integrate their work with others. Those who are not sufficiently experienced, not culturally competent, or cannot recognize appropriate ways to coordinate their services with others are likely to be less successful in their relief efforts or can create problems for others trying to provide assistance.

- **Soliciting and managing cash and material donations as well as volunteers is a key to effective disaster responses.** Some FBCOs studied learned to use the Internet to disseminate real-time information, reach out for help, solicit and vet volunteers, share databases, and establish 211 directories to identify resources. Emergency preparedness planning could include consideration of how to control donations, including instruction on the best tools to solicit and manage donations. Government or FBCO entities can set up web sites that can be shared among responders, serve as clearinghouses, manage solicitations, and allocate resources, including donations, volunteers, and emergency services.

A model for working together was developed in the Washington, D.C., region after the 9/11 attacks. Nonprofit leaders and government representatives worked together to develop guidelines for sharing data, scaling up for volunteer efforts, and soliciting and handling monetary and in-kind donations.[17] New methods for maintaining access to 211 directories when local telephone service is disrupted have reportedly been developed since the 2005 storms and were used in the Gulf region after the 2008 storms.

- **How FBCOs will respond in the future will likely depend on the magnitude of the disaster and the extent of damage they sustain to their own operations.** But many that were new to disaster response in 2005 learned much about how to provide disaster- related services, and how not to repeat mistakes that hampered their response. An effort should be made to incorporate those experiences into disaster preparedness planning, including how to increase flexibility for traditional disaster responders, what rules can be relaxed and what rules cannot, and how to tap the expertise of those who participated in disaster response to teach others what they learned. The fact that social and professional connections were so important to case study organizations reinforces the need to nurture connections, perhaps through strategic conferencing and other methods, to create awareness of how to tap connections before disaster strikes.

The Gulf Coast hurricanes of 2005 have put a new lens on the limits of understanding among researchers and policymakers of the breadth and depth of a major disaster's effects. More work remains to understand the effects of the disaster and the most effective ways to provide immediate and long-term assistance. Collecting and reexamining data on the effects of the storms, particularly on the most vulnerable populations, and incorporating these lessons into planning for future disaster responses is clearly important. Data sharing among organizations, such as FEMA, that have detailed information on hurricane victims could be used to provide follow-up services for individuals who still need help. These data also could be used to support needed evidence-based research on the effects of the storms and outcomes of sustained treatment, particularly mental health services, for individuals who are the victims of major disasters. The data could also provide needed evidence for proposed changes in disaster response planning.

APPENDIX A. METHODOLOGY FOR THE TELEPHONE SURVEY

This appendix provides detailed information on the methods used to design and conduct a telephone survey of faith-based and community organizations in the Gulf Coast area that participated in relief and recovery efforts after hurricanes Katrina and Rita. It is organized into four main sections:

1. Sample design
2. Data collection procedures

3. Survey rates
4. Survey weights

Sample Design

The goal of the sampling strategy was to select enough organizations to complete 200 telephone interviews while maximizing the response rate. To assess the level and types of disaster relief and recovery work undertaken by faith-based and community organizations (FBCOs), we wanted approximately 100 interviews completed with faith-based organizations sampled from the American Church List (ACL)[18] and 100 interviews with community-based nonprofit human service organizations sampled from the database maintained by the National Center for Charitable Statistics (NCCS).[19] All organizations in the states of Louisiana and Mississippi were eligible for the study, as were all organizations within a 50-mile radius of the Houston Astrodome. The geographic area around the Houston Astrodome was selected because the Astrodome was a major receiving center for hurricane evacuees.

The sampling strategy was designed to oversample the areas either directly affected or partially affected by either hurricane Katrina or hurricane Rita. To accomplish this, the two lists (ACL and NCCS) were divided into seven geographic strata. There were three geographic strata in both Louisiana and Mississippi, which we describe as "primary" (i.e., counties or parishes directly impacted by the storm); "secondary" (counties or parishes that were partially impacted or adjacent to the areas of direct impact); and "tertiary" (all other counties or parishes in the state). The seventh and final stratum was Texas, which was defined as organizations within 50 miles of the Houston Astrodome.

To identify which counties (i.e., FIPS codes) in Mississippi were impacted by the hurricanes, we used FEMA's definitions for disaster areas found in "FEMA-1604-DR, Mississippi Disaster Declaration as of 10/27/2005" at http://www.gismaps.fema.gov/ 2005graphics/dr1604/dec_1604.pdf. FEMA's report helped us code the 82 counties in Mississippi as primary, secondary, or tertiary impacted areas. For Louisiana, the Congressional Research Service report "Hurricane Katrina: Social-Demographic Characteristics of Impacted Areas" at http://www.gnocdc.org/reports/crsrept.pdf (November 4, 2005) helped us code the 64 Louisiana parishes as primary, secondary, or tertiary.

Sample Sizes by Geographic Strata

Random samples of organizations were selected within each of the seven strata. These samples were further stratified by either type of nonprofit organization (direct service provider, community group, or facility provider) or by type of church (Baptist, Lutheran, Catholic, etc.). Table A1 shows how many interviews we aimed to complete in each of the seven sampling strata. The total number of organizations actually sampled in each stratum was two to three times greater depending on the expected response and eligibility rates.

The Sampling Process

The sample was released in three waves so sampling adjustments could be made based on actual response and eligibility rates, described below, and to avoid sampling too many organizations.

Sample release I (November 2007)

The first release consisted of 122 churches and 119 nonprofit human service organizations that were drawn randomly within seven strata (three impacted areas for each of the two states of Louisiana and Mississippi, as well as one impacted area in Texas). Each stratum of churches was sorted in ascending order, beginning with state, county code, impacted area code (1, 2, or 3), denomination type, membership size, and attendance size. The strata of nonprofits were sorted in ascending order, beginning with state, county code, impact area code, organization type (direct service provider, community group, or facility), total expenses, and NTEE (i.e., activity) code. Systematic sampling was then performed with random seed numbers assigned to the strata to randomly select the first observation. From there, between 10 and 20 observations were drawn per stratum.

Sample release II (December 2007)

The second sample release consisted of 140 churches and 106 nonprofit organizations. The number of churches was higher than the sampled nonprofit groups since early indications suggested that the response rate would be lower for churches and congregations, which were harder to reach than nonprofits. Therefore, the decision was made to sample more churches to increase the chance of attaining our original completion goals. The sampling procedures applied were the same as in the first round of sampling, namely seven presorted strata from which 10 to 27 organizations were randomly selected per stratum. New random seed numbers were assigned to each stratum.

Table A1. Initial Sample Size Goals by Geographic Strata

Location	Churches (n)	Nonprofits (n)
Primary Impact – Mississippi	15	15
Primary Impact – Louisiana	20	20
Secondary Impact – Mississippi	15	15
Secondary Impact – Louisiana	20	20
Tertiary – Mississippi	10	10
Tertiary – Louisiana	10	10
Tertiary – Texas	10	10
Total	**100**	**100**

Sampling release III (January 2008)

The third sample release consisted of 72 churches and 56 nonprofit organizations. Again, more churches than nonprofits were represented in the sample to increase the probability that despite the lower response rate among churches, their higher proportion in the sample would increase the probability that the number of interviews completed with churches would be close to our goal of 100. The third release applied the same stratified sampling method used for generating the first and second sample releases.

Based on all three sample releases, a total of 615 organizations were drawn for the survey: 334 churches and 281 nonprofits.

Data Collection Procedures

In November 2007, the Louisiana State University Public Policy Research Lab (PPRL) began the telephone survey of churches and nonprofit organizations throughout Gulf Coast areas affected by hurricanes Katrina and Rita. The survey was completed in February 2008. Data collection was suspended for about 10 days (total) during the Thanksgiving and Christmas holidays.

To maximize the response rate, the sample was released in waves. Overall, the three sample releases combined consisted of 615 organizations, which yielded a total of 574 organizations for which contact information could be found. Every effort was made to research each disconnected number on the Internet to locate that particular church or nonprofit. A group of interviewers was hand-selected and dedicated specifically to this project from beginning to end. A team leader was designated to coordinate the survey in the field. Each week, the team leader emailed a research report of disconnected numbers to the PPRL lab manager. No telephone number was labeled "permanently disconnected" until a thorough search was done to locate that entity. The lab manager sent the Urban Institute survey team a progress report at the beginning of each week. Each Wednesday, the lab manager and the Urban Institute survey team held a conference call to discuss that week's progress report and any other issues.

In general, it was fairly difficult to reach people on the first try. Most often, an interviewer would reach an answering machine. This was especially true when trying to reach churches, although if the call was answered by a secretary, the interviewer would inquire about the best time to try to reach the pastor. In general, it was noted that a good time to interview individuals at churches was Monday through Friday between 11:00am and 3:00pm. However, interviewers found no consistent pattern regarding the optimal days or times to reach potential respondents. Nonprofits were easier to contact than churches and more likely to respond to the survey. The interviewer most often spoke with the pastor of a church or the director of a nonprofit organization. Once the interviewer was able to reach a person knowledgeable about the organization's relief and recovery activities, reception toward participating in the 15–20-minute survey was mostly positive. A total of 271 organizations responded to the survey. Of these 271 organizations, 202 provided relief services and therefore were interviewed for this study.[20] The distribution of completed interviews by our seven geographic strata is shown in Table A2.

Table A2. Final Sample Size of Organizations That Provided Relief Services, by Geographic Strata

Location	Churches (n)	Nonprofits (n)
Primary impact – Mississippi	22	16
Primary impact – Louisiana	19	20
Secondary impact – Mississippi	13	13
Secondary impact – Louisiana	25	22
Tertiary – Mississippi	12	7
Tertiary – Louisiana	8	11
Tertiary – Texas	7	7
Total	**106**	**96**

Survey Rates

Two types of survey rates—response rates and eligibility rates—were calculated to provide a full assessment of the survey's quality.

Response Rates

The survey response rate is an important measure of the quality of a survey. Its importance depends upon whether the nonrespondents would have answered the survey questions differently. To calculate the response rate, we divide the number of organizations that responded to the survey by the number of organizations that were sampled for the survey, minus the organizations determined not to be operating at the time of the study. However, there were many organizations that we were never able to contact and thus potentially might not have been operating at the time of the survey. Therefore the response rate for this study is an estimated response rate using the final call disposition results shown in Table A3.

If we assume all the unable-to-contact organizations were not in operation, we would report a 67.1 percent response rate: (271/(615 - 211)) or 271/404 = 67.1.

If we assume all the unable-to-contact organizations were in operation at the time of the survey, we would report a 52.6 percent response rate: (271/(615 -100)) or 271/515 = 52.6.

We believe the best estimate would be to assume that the proportion of the unable-to-contact organizations that are not in operation would be the same as the proportion of organizations that were not in operation in the sample for which we were able to determine their operating status. More specifically, we were able to determine operating status for 504 organizations (that is, 615-111 = 504). Hence the overall estimated response rate for this study is 55 percent: (271/(615-100- (100/504) x 111)) = 271/493 = 55.0 .

Table A3. Final Call Disposition Results

Final Call Disposition	N	Percentage
Responding organizations	271	44.1
Nonresponding organizations	133	21.6
Unable to contact	111	18.0
Organizations not operating at the time of the study	100	16.3
Total	**615**	**100**

Table A4 shows the response rate for each sampling stratum. The calculation of this rate assumes that the proportion of the unable-to-contact organizations that were not in operation would be the same as the proportion of organizations not in operation from that sampling stratum.

Eligibility Rates

In addition to reporting the response rate, it is useful to know what percentage of the responding organizations provided relief services. We are calling this the eligibility rate, defined as the number of organizations who said that they provided services over the total number of organizations that responded to the survey (i.e., both those that did and did not provide services). Overall, 74.5 percent of organizations that we talked with said that they provided some relief services. Table A5 shows the eligibility rate for each sampling stratum.

Survey Weights

Survey weights are sometimes needed to analyze survey data. Most survey weights first adjust for unequal probability of selection that is often built into the sample design, and then adjust for key differences between the sample population and target population, which can help reduce the potential for nonresponse bias.

Table A4. Response Rates by Geographic Strata

Location	Churches (%)	Nonprofits (%)
Primary impact – Mississippi	54.9	78.7
Primary impact – Louisiana	50.9	72.9
Secondary impact – Mississippi	36.7	70.0
Secondary impact – Louisiana	44.3	74.1
Tertiary – Mississippi	45.0	66.7
Tertiary – Louisiana	24.3	83.3
Tertiary – Texas	33.6	52.6
Total	**42.7**	**71.8**

Table A5. Eligibility Rates by Geographic Strata

Location	Churches (%)	Nonprofits (%)
Primary impact – Mississippi	88.0	66.7
Primary impact – Louisiana	65.5	64.5
Secondary impact – Mississippi	81.3	61.9
Secondary impact – Louisiana	92.6	88.0
Tertiary – Mississippi	80.0	58.3
Tertiary – Louisiana	88.9	64.7
Tertiary – Texas	70.0	70.0
Total	**80.9**	**68.6**

For this study, finding organizations that were open and operating was actually a larger issue than nonresponse.

Given the dramatic changes that occurred in the sample region because of the hurricanes, it is unrealistic to assign probabilities of selection to the organizations we were sampling.

Likewise, creating target population control totals is also not realistic given how many organizations we were unable to contact, definitional issues, and relatively small sample size in some of our sampling strata.

Therefore, for this study the analysis was done without survey weights and the analytical results should not to be used to make population estimates.

APPENDIX B. TELEPHONE SURVEY QUESTIONNAIRE

Form Approved
OMB No. 0990-0318
Exp. Date 10/31/2010

Survey of the Services Provided by Faith-Based and Community Organizations after Hurricanes Katrina and Rita

Hello, my name is _____. I'm from the Public Policy Research Lab at Louisiana State University. We are conducting a survey regarding the help that faith-based and community groups provided to people during and after Hurricanes Katrina and Rita. I would like to talk with you about relief and recovery activities that your organization may have provided because of the storms.

OPTION: If individual asks about sponsorship –
The survey is part of a larger study that is being conducted by the Urban Institute, a nonprofit/nonpartisan research organization in Washington, DC. The study is funded by the U.S. Department of Health and Human Services.

ALTERNATIVE FIRST PARAGRAPH WHEN RETURNING CALL:
Hello, my name is _____ and I'm from the Public Policy Research Lab at Louisiana State University. I'm returning your call about the survey we are conducting about the help that faith-based and community groups provided during and after Hurricanes Katrina and Rita. Thank you for contacting us.

REMAINDER OF TEXT IS SAME FOR ALL PHONE RESPONDENTS

The purpose of the study is to learn about the ways that faith-based and community groups helped in the relief efforts during and after the hurricanes and to help government officials and community leaders learn how to work with these groups in future disasters.

Before we begin, I want to assure you that your answers will be treated in a private manner within the limits of the law. We will not report information that will identify any particular individual or organization. Your answers will be combined with those of other people in organizations that provided similar services.

We appreciate your willingness to participate in this survey. You do not have to answer any questions you don't want to answer, and you may stop at any time.

Initial Screener Questions

Before I begin the survey, please tell me:

S1.   Did your organization provide any relief services during or after either Hurricane Katrina or Rita?

            _____ yes _____ no

        [Interviewer: If respondent asks, a relief service might be food, water, clothing, temporary housing, family reunification, counseling, etc.]

S2.   Would you describe your organization as a:

            _____ Nonprofit organization or community-based group

            _____ Faith-based organization (such as a church, congregation, or affiliated with a faith program)

            _____ Government agency

            [Interviewer: Do not read this last probe. Check if respondent volunteers this information.]

            _____ Something else (describe) _____

        [Interviewer: Some groups may be both non-profit/community-based and faith-based. If so, check both.]

        [Interviewer: If government agency, end the survey.
        This survey is only for community and faith-based groups, so those are all the questions we have for you. I appreciate your willingness to participate. Good-bye.]

S3a.   Are you familiar with the hurricane relief efforts that your congregation/organization provided?

            _____ yes (if yes, continue to S4)

            _____ no (if no, ask S3b)

S3b.   If no, who should we speak to about your organization's hurricane relief efforts?

        Name: _____ Position: _____
        Phone: _____
        [Might be a pastor/leader, congregation administrator, head of the ministry, social services coordinator/manager, executive director, etc.]

        Is [name of individual] available now? Can you transfer me to him/her?
        Can you suggest a good time to reach [name of individual]? _____

        Thank you for your time. I will call back later to reach [name of individual].

S4.   What is your position at [name of congregation/organization]? _____

S5.   How long have you been with [congregation/organization name]? ___yrs. __mos.

S6.   How long have you been in this position? _____yrs. _____mos.

I. Profile of the Congregation/Organization:

I'd like to begin by getting some information that describes your congregation/organization.

Q1.   How many years has the congregation/organization been in existence? __yrs __mos
[Interviewer: Answer should refer to the local group (such as the local YMCA), not to a larger umbrella group (e.g., the national YMCA).]

For nonprofits, skip to Q4.

For congregations and faith-based organizations, ask Q2 and Q3:

Q2.   You indicated earlier that you were faith-based. What is your congregation/organization's religious affiliation or denomination? *[Interviewer: Do not read the list; check category that best fits R's answer.]*

Adventist	Latter Day Saints/Mormon
Baptist	Lutheran
Brethren	Mennonite
Catholic	Metaphysical
Christian/Churches of Christ	Methodist
Episcopal	Orthodox
Evangelical Misc.	Pentecostal
Holiness	Presbyterian
Independent Fundamentalist	Other _____
Jewish	

Q3.   Approximately how large is the congregation? (i.e., how many members?) ___ (#)

Q4.   Was this the first time that your organization/congregation provided disaster relief services after a hurricane? ____ yes ___ no

Q5.   Did you have any paid staff providing any type of social services *[for faith-based groups say: social ministries]* before hurricanes Katrina and Rita? _____ yes _____ no

Q6.   Currently, about how many paid staff members do you have working on hurricane relief efforts this month? ____

Q7.   Did you have any volunteers providing social services *[for faith-based groups say: social ministries]* before hurricanes Katrina and Rita? _____ yes _____ no

Q8.   (If yes) Approximately how many volunteers do you have working on hurricane relief efforts this month? ____

Q9.   How many hours will the typical volunteer work this month? _____

II. Services Provided after the Storm

Let's begin by talking about the types of relief and recovery services that your congregations/organization provided during or after the storm.

Q10.   Did your organization/congregation provide any of the following types of immediate services during or shortly after the storms? [check all that apply]
   a. Search and rescue activities   ____ yes   ____ no
   b. Drinking water/emergency supplies   ____ yes   ____ no
   c. Transportation out of the affected areas ____ yes   ____ no

d.	Temporary housing/shelter	___ yes	___ no
e.	Food/meals	___ yes	___ no
f.	Clothing/household goods	___ yes	___ no
g.	Money or in-kind donations for victims	___ yes	___ no
h.	First Aid/medical services	___ yes	___ no

Q11.   (If yes) Approximately when did you begin providing these services? Was it:
       _____ during the storm or immediately afterward (that is, the first week after the storm)
       _____ not in the first week but during the first month after the storm
       _____ sometime after the first month

Q12. Are you still providing any of these services? _____ yes _____ no

       If no, when did you stop providing these services?
       _____ After one month
       _____ After three months
       _____ After one year
       _____ Sometime later than one year

Q13.   Did your organization/congregation provide any of the following services? [check all tha
       apply]
       a. Family reunification/location of missing persons ___ yes   ___ no
       b. Housing repairs/rebuilding/cleanup   ___ yes   ___ no
       c. Job training/employment services   ___ yes   ___ no
       d. Child care or school services   ___ yes   ___ no
       e. Mental health, counseling, support groups or other trauma services   ___ yes ___ no
       f. Spiritual counseling   ___ yes ___ no

Q14.   (If yes) Approximately when did you begin providing these services? Was it:
       _____ during the storm or immediately afterward (that is, the first week after the storm)
       _____ not in the first week but during the first month after the storm
       _____ sometime after the first month

Q15. Are you still providing any of these services? _____ yes _____ no

       (If no) When did you stop providing these services?
       After one month

       _____ After three months
       _____ After one year
       _____ Sometime later than one year

Q16.   Did your organization/congregation assist people with the following types of paperwork?
       [check all that apply]
       a. Applying for welfare
       b. Applying for FEMA claims
       c. Applying for private insurance claims (i.e., homeowners or renters insurance)
       d. Applying for legal services

Q17.   (If yes) Approximately when did you begin providing these services? Was it:
_____ during the storm or immediately afterward (that is, the first week after the storm)
_____ not in the first week but during the first month after the storm
_____ sometime after the first month

Q18. Are you still providing any of these services? _____ yes _____ no

(If no) When did you stop providing these services?
_____ After one month
_____ After three months
_____ After one year
_____ Sometime later than one year

Interviewer: Skip Q 19-20, if respondent answered only one type of service in Q10, 13, or 16.
Q19.   Of all the services that you named, which one has been the primary focus of your congregation's/organization's efforts? _____

Q20.   Of all the services you named, which one needed the most staffing or volunteer assistance? _____

III. Who Received Services:
Next, I'd like to ask about the people you helped after the storm.

Q21.   In total, how many people you did you help? _____ *[Read options if necessary.]*
_____ <50
_____ 50-100
_____ 101-250
_____ 251-500
_____ 500 – 1,000
_____ > 1,000
Q22.   Of these people, approximately what percent of them were:
[Interviewer: These percentages do not have to add to 100%.]

Groups of People	**Percent**
Elderly or disabled	_____
Low-income	_____
Families with children	_____
Immigrants or non-English speakers	_____
Members of your congregation (for faith based)	_____
Your usual client/customer base (for non-faith based)	_____
People who lived outside of your community	_____
Any other specific groups of people	_____
If yes, (specify) _____	

IV. Staffing of Services:
Let's talk now about the staffing and volunteers that you used to provide your services.

Q23. Did you use <u>paid</u> staff to provide services to people in need during the first 3 months after the storm?

    ____ yes ____ no (if no, skip to Q26)

Q24. (If yes) Approximately how many people worked in this capacity? _____
[Interviewer: If R cannot provide a number, ask: Would you say it was]
    ____ 1-5
    ____ 6-10
    ____ 11-20
    ____ >20

Q25. Compared with before the storm, was this
    ____ a substantial increase in the number of paid staff (more than 10%)
    ____ a modest increase (up to 10%)
    ____ about the same number of paid staff as before the storm
    ____ a modest decrease in paid staff (less than 10%)
    ____ a substantial decrease (more than 10%)

Q26. Did you use volunteers to provide services to people in need during the first 3 months after the storm?

    ____ yes ____ no (if no, skip to Q33)

Q27. (If yes) Approximately how many people worked in this capacity in a typical week?
    ____(#)
[Interviewer: If R cannot provide a number, ask: Would you say it was]
    ____ 1-25 volunteers
    ____ 26-50
    ____ 51-100
    ____ >100

Q28. Compared with before the storm, was this
    ____ a substantial increase in the number of volunteers typically used (more than 10%)
    ____ a modest increase (up to 10%)
    ____ about the same number of volunteers as before the storm
    ____ a modest decrease in volunteers (less than 10%)
    ____ a substantial decrease (more than 10%)

Q29. How did you recruit volunteers after the storm (check all that apply)? *[Rotate list.]*
    ____ Word-of-mouth
    ____ Outreach efforts (e.g., posters, newsletters, flyers)
    ____ Media coverage
    ____ Existing roster of volunteers
    ____ Your congregation/membership
    ____ Other local organizations or congregations
    ____ National organizations or affiliates
    ____ Web sites
    ____ Other (specify) _____

Q30. Which of the recruiting activities was the most effective?

Q31.   Did you recruit too many, about the right amount, or not enough volunteers?
____ Too many volunteers
____ About the right amount of volunteers
____ Not enough volunteers

Q32.   In using volunteers, did you experience problems with any of the following? *(rotate lists)*
____ Providing housing or food for the volunteers
____ Transporting volunteers to the work area
____ Volunteers who lacked needed skills or training
____ Managing/supervising the volunteers
____ Having insurance to cover the volunteers
____ Any other problems (specify) _____
[Interviewer: Do not read this last probe. Check if R volunteers this information.]
____ None of the above; had no difficulties in using volunteers.

V. Networks and Partnerships
Now, I'd like to ask about other nonprofits, religious groups, businesses, or government agencies that you may have worked with in providing relief services.

Q33.   Are you part of a larger organization, or in any way formally affiliated with a religious or other type of organizational structure? [*e.g., the Archdiocese, the Southern Baptist Convention, PRC, YMCA*]?
____ yes ____ no (If no, skip to Q36)

Q34.   (If yes) What is the name and the location [*city, state*] of that affiliate? [*open, specify*]?
_____(name) _____(city/state)

Q35.   Did they help you in any way with disaster relief services?
____ yes ____ no

Q36.   Did you work with any other organizations to deliver disaster relief?
____ yes ____ no (If no, skip to Q42)

Q37.   (If yes) Can you tell me which of the following organizations you worked with [*Rotate list*]:
K-12 schools	___
Universities	___
Hospitals	___
Churches/faith-based orgs	___
Nonprofit groups	___
Businesses or employers	___
State or local government	___
Federal government	___

Q38.   Please give me the name and location [*city, state*] of the three most important group(s) with whom you worked? [*open, specify*]
1. _____(name)
_____(city/state)

2. _____(name)
_____(city/state)

3. _____(name)
   _____(city/state)

Q39.   Did any of the relief work that you conducted with these organizations involve: [check all that apply]
_____ Receiving financial support from these groups;
_____ Referring individuals or families that <u>you</u> were serving to these other organizations;

_____ Receiving referrals <u>from</u> these other organizations to <u>your</u> organization for services;
_____ Providing advice or instructions <u>to</u> these other organizations;
_____ Receiving advice or instructions <u>from</u> these organizations;
_____ Sharing resources such as space, equipment, supplies, cash contributions, etc
       What things did you share (specify: _____)

Q40.   Were any of these arrangements created because of the storm or were they a continuation of existing relationships that existed prior to the storm?
_____ new
_____ continuation of existing relationships
_____ both *(check if this response is volunteered)*

Q41.   Would you say that these arrangements worked
_____ very smoothly
_____ somewhat smoothly
_____ reasonably well
_____ not too well
_____ not at all well
_____ mixed experience *(check if this response is volunteered)*

Q42.   Were there any organizations that you tried to work with but were unable to?
_____ Yes
_____ No (skip to Q45)

Q43.   (If yes) Which types of organization were these?
_____Nonprofits
_____Faith-based
_____Businesses
_____Government
_____Other

Q44.   Why did you have difficulty working with these groups?
       _____

VI. Resources
Q45.   Please estimate approximately how much money you have spent to date to provide hurricane relief services?
_____ ($ amount)
_____ Don't know; didn't keep records

Interviewer: If respondent has difficulty giving an amount, prompt R as follows:
_____ Was it less than $500
_____ $500 - $2,500
_____ $2,500 to $5,000
_____ $5,000 to $10,000
_____ $10,000 to $50,000

_____ $50,000 to $100,000
_____ $100,000 to $500,000
_____ $500,000 to $1 million
_____ More than $1million

Q46. Did you charge a fee for any of the relief/recovery services that you provided?
_____ yes _____ no

Q47. Did you receive financial support for your relief services from any of the following sources? [check all that apply]
_____ Individuals (e.g. financial donations)
_____ Religious or faith-based organizations (e.g., the Southern Baptist Convention, United Methodist Committee on Relief, etc.)
_____ Nonprofit organizations (e.g., Red Cross; United Way)
_____ Private foundations
_____ Businesses
_____ Federal government
_____ State or local government
_____ Other (please specify) _____

Q48. Of the sources that you identified, which one provided the most financial support for your relief/recovery services? _____

Q49. **For nonprofits, ask:**
Excluding these relief services, approximately what is the size of your organization's annual operating budget this year?
$_____
_____ Don't know
_____ Refused

Interviewer: If respondent has difficulty giving an amount, prompt R as follows:
_____ Was it less than $500
_____ $500 - $2,500
_____ $2,500 to $5,000
_____ $5,000 to $10,000
_____ $10,000 to $50,000
_____ $50,000 to $100,000
_____ $100,000 to $500,000
_____ $500,000 to $1 million
_____ More than $1million

For congregations/faith-based organizations, ask:
Excluding these relief services, approximately how much will you spend this year on your social ministry programs?
$_____
_____ Don't know
_____ Refused

Interviewer: If respondent has difficulty giving an amount, prompt R as follows:
         _____ Was it less than $500
         _____ $500 - $2,500
         _____ $2,500 to $5,000
         _____ $5,000 to $10,000
         _____ $10,000 to $50,000
         _____ $50,000 to $100,000
         _____ $100,000 to $500,000
         _____ $500,000 to $1 million
         _____ More than $1million

Q50.   Did your congregation/organization apply for any reimbursement from the federal or
       state government?
         _____ yes
         _____ no (if no, skip to Q56)

Q51.   (If yes) Which agency was that? (Specify) _____

Q52.   How would you describe the process of seeking reimbursement? Would you say it was:
         _____ Very easy (skip to Q54)
         _____ Somewhat easy (skip to Q54)
         _____ Somewhat difficult
         _____ Very difficult

Q53.   Why do you say it was difficult? _____

Q54.   Have you received any reimbursement for the services you provided?
         _____ yes (If yes, skip to Q56)
         _____ no

Q55.   If no, how long has it been since you first applied for reimbursement? __yrs __mo

VII. Lessons Learned

I have three more questions regarding what you believe are the most important lessons learned
from your experiences providing relief services.

Q56.   What went well in your efforts to provide services after the storms?

Q57.   What did not go well or could have gone better in these efforts?

Q58.   What do you have in place now that you didn't have before to use in future hurricanes or
       other emergencies?
         _____ Partnerships/collaborations
         _____ Directories of services (e.g., 211 or 311)
         _____ Emergency action plans
         _____ List of volunteers for relief work
         _____ Other (specify) _____

THAT COMPLETES THE SURVEY. THANK YOU FOR PARTICIPATING.

End Notes

[1] The White House. "Fact Sheet: The Federal Response to Katrina: Lessons Learned." Accessed November 19, 2008, at http://www.whitehouse.gov/news/releases/2006/02/20060223.html.

[2] According to *the 2005 Louisiana Hurricane Impact Atlas,* 108,456 square miles of land were affected by hurricane Katrina. The land area of Great Britain is approximately 95,500 square miles. See http://lagic.lsu.edu/lgisc/publications/2005/LIGISC-PUB-20051116-00_2005_HURRICANE_ATLAS.pdf.

[3] U.S. Department of Homeland Security. 2006. *Current Housing Unit Damage Estimates: Hurricanes Katrina, Rita, and Wilma.*

[4] Louisiana Recovery Authority. 2005. "Addressing the Challenges of Recovery and Rebuilding from Hurricanes Katrina and Rita: Overview of Comparative Damage." Accessed March 8, 2008, at http://www.lra.louisiana.gov/assets/12212005.ppt.

[5] See, for example, Tony Pipa, 2006, *Weathering the Storm: The Role of Local Nonprofits in the Hurricane Katrina Relief Effort,* Washington, DC: The Aspen Institute Nonprofit Sector Research Fund; James J. Carafano and Richard Weitz., 2006, *Learning from Disaster: The Role of Federalism and the Importance of Grassroots Responses,* Washington, DC: The Heritage Foundation; and the 2005 Louisiana Survey Post- Hurricane Community Audit, conducted by the Public Policy Research Lab, Louisiana State University, Accessed March 8, 2008, at www.survey.lsu.edu/projects.html#2005fla.

[6] See, for example, Tobi Jennifer Printz, 1998, "Faith-Based Service Providers in the Nation's Capital: Can They Do More?" Charting Civil Society Brief 2, Washington, DC: The Urban Institute; Mark Chaves and William Tsitsos, 2001, "Congregations and Social Services: What They Do, How They Do It, and With Whom," *Nonprofit and Voluntary Sector Quarterly* 30/4: 660–83; and Fredrica D. Kramer, Demetra Smith Nightingale, John Trutko, Shayne Spaulding, and Burt S. Barnow, 2002, "Faith-Based Organizations Providing Employment and Training Services: A Preliminary Exploration," Washington, DC: The Urban Institute.

[7] Traditional responders include government emergency response agencies, such as FEMA, and national and international nongovernmental organizations dedicated to disaster relief.

[8] A larger sample would have increased our ability to analyze the data by smaller subgroups or simultaneously by multiple subgroups. However, budget constraints and a lack of information at the outset of the study regarding how many organizations were recipients or providers of assistance, particularly in the heavily impacted areas, made the benefits of drawing a larger sample unclear.

[9] The sampling frame for this study is congregations and nonprofits that were listed in these two data sources. We were unable to identify a source that contained information on organizations that operated before the storms but closed as a consequence of the storms.

[10] Two sources were used to identify impacted areas: for Louisiana, the Congressional Research Service report "Hurricane Katrina: Social-Demographic Characteristics of Impacted Areas" and for Mississippi, "FEMA-1604-DR, Mississippi Disaster Declaration as of 10/27/2005." See Appendix A for further detail.

[11] To estimate this number, we assumed that the proportion of the unable-to-contact organizations (111) that were not operating was the same as the proportion of not operating organizations (100) in the sample for which operating status was known (that is, 100 divided by 504 organizations).

[12] Additional data runs, not shown in this analysis, generally indicated that the age of an FBCO was not correlated with the size of the organization, the number of staff, or the number of volunteers. The only exception was that secular nonprofits tended to be larger as the age of the organization increased, but this association between age and size did not apply to faith-based organizations.

[13] These categories are not mutually exclusive, so a particular individual may fall into more than one category.

[14] Long-term recovery structures are known variously as long-term recovery committees, long-term recovery organizations, long-term recovery groups, or unmet needs committees. Throughout this document, we refer to them generically, as long-term recovery or unmet needs structures.

[15] The organization currently supports only seven parish long-term recovery committees. There are no formal arrangements as of this writing with two parishes, St. Charles and St. John.

[16] Spiritual counseling was mentioned by 75 percent of the faith-based respondents and 20 percent of the secular nonprofits. It is unclear, however, if spiritual counseling was provided on an individual basis or as part of worship services, Sunday sermons, or general social ministries.

[17] The Nonprofit Roundtable of Greater Washington. 2005. *Working Together When the Worst Happens: Nonprofit Emergency Preparedness in the National Capital Region.* Washington, DC: The Nonprofit Roundtable of Greater Washington.

[18] The American Church List contained 14,213 organizations in the combined Louisiana, Mississippi, and Houston, Texas (Astrodome) region. The American Church List is widely considered the most comprehensive source of information on churches and religious congregations in the United States and Canada.

[19] There were a total of 2,957 nonprofit human service organizations in the combined Louisiana, Mississippi, and Houston, Texas (Astrodome) region in the 2005 NCCS public charities database. The NCCS database is a repository of all U.S. nonprofits that file annual Forms 990 with the Internal Revenue Service. Because

nonprofits with less than $25,000 in gross receipts and religious groups are not required to file Forms 990, they are underrepresented in the database. However, the database captures the majority of revenues, expenditures, and assets of the nonprofit sector.

[20] Compared with the final sample, organizations that did not provide services after the hurricanes and were therefore ineligible to complete the survey were more likely to be nonprofit organizations and in the primary impact area.

INDEX

D

Index

Q

R